BLOOD ON THE WATER

THE GREAT LAKES DURING THE CIVIL WAR

FREDERICK STONEHOUSE

D0167929

Avery Color Studios, Inc.
Gwinn, Michigan

© 2011 Avery Color Studios, Inc.

ISBN: 978-1-892384-61-4

Library of Congress Control Number: 2011901143

First Edition 2011

10   9   8   7   6   5   4   3   2   1

Published by Avery Color Studios, Inc.
Gwinn, Michigan 49841

BLOOD ON THE WATER

THE GREAT LAKES DURING THE CIVIL WAR

TABLE OF CONTENTS

[1] Parts of this story are taken from my book *Wood on the Bottom*, Avery Color Studios, 2008.

INTRODUCTION

When we think of the Civil War we inevitably recall the great and bloody battles like Shiloh, Fredericksburg, Gettysburg among many others. Perhaps we remember the story of the ironclad slugfest between the Confederate *Virginia* and Union *Monitor*. But the term "Great Lakes" never comes into play regarding the Civil War.

Putting things into perspective, the greatest number of Civil War battles were fought in what can be characterized as the South. Of 2,261 "battles" only one percent occurred in what could charitably be called the north; Pennsylvania, Ohio, Indiana, Illinois and Minnesota. Given the southern edges of Ohio, Indiana and Illinois, this is stretching things a bit.

Roughly three percent of the battles were in the "west;" California, Oregon, Nevada, Utah, Idaho, New Mexico, Colorado, Indian Territory, Dakota and Arizona. That leaves 96 percent in the South.

My point is that Civil War "battle action" was nearly all in the Southern theater. There was very little actual **combat** in the North. But there was plenty of action, though of a different sort!

A few years ago I was teaching a college class in U.S. History at and covering the chapter on the Civil War when I realized the disconnect between the Great Lakes and the war in general, at least in the way it is generally taught. As a retired military officer and a student of military and maritime history I realized there was a story here not well told.

A quick map reconnaissance shows the front line of the war was the border between the Northern and Southern states. Generally speaking, the North attacked the Southern perimeter, slowly squeezing the Confederate states inward. Having "interior lines," the South was able to shift forces relatively quickly to counter Union blows. Southern deep rear areas were largely safe from direct Northern attack, at least until Sherman sliced through from Atlanta to Savannah and then north to Virginia late in the war.[1] But the North was different. The rear area of the northern Union states butted up against either the Great Lakes or St. Lawrence River, across which was Canada.[2] And Canada (aka British North America) was considered pro-Southern although technically neutral. In effect the North had a hostile force to the south and a potentially hostile (or perhaps semi-hostile) one to the north.

The actual frontline (the border of the Confederacy) was well guarded and patrolled. Major Union Armies kept in contact with Confederate Armies and far ranging cavalry troops reported any sudden movement of the enemy in time to counter them although

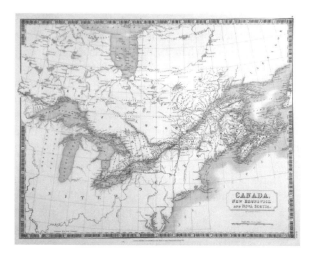

The long and generally unguarded border with Canada (aka British North America) offered an excellent area for Confederates to stage operations into the rear of the Union.

on occasion intentions were misread leading to unplanned combat. An ever-tightening Union Navy blockade slowly cut off vital imports along the Atlantic and Gulf coasts. When the South lost the Mississippi River after Grant captured Vicksburg in July 1863, the river in effect became the western border of the Confederacy. Understand however there were many variations within the frontline trace as situations and strategy dictated.

The border with Canada was largely unguarded, either by the Union Army or Navy. While a few scattered forts provided a modicum of local protection, they added little to overall defense. While the *USS Michigan* was the most powerful warship on the Lakes, it certainly couldn't patrol all five Great Lakes in an adequate fashion. The lack of a defended U.S. border was a golden opportunity for the South to use Canada as a jumping off point to attack not Northern Armies, but the "soft" targets of the Union industrial, transportation and logistical base "safe" in the rear. Said somewhat differently, the Great Lakes were both a target in that they contained unprotected shipping and ports and a highway to fat targets inland!

All this given, the Great Lakes and surrounding areas were a hotbed of potentially war-changing activity. The action was far different than the clash of armies but perhaps potentially just as important.

Late in the war, the Confederates would establish a Canadian Mission in Canada and try to strike the North from across the border. Like the tentacles of an octopus, the Confederate Canadian operation reached far into the Great Lakes rear setting up various plots and schemes but it was a case of too little, too late and too ineptly done. But what **could have been** is staggering! For every plot, scheme and plan in this book, just think of the potential damage that could have been done had they been successful.

Writing about various intelligence activities and plots emanating from Canada during the war is difficult for a variety of reasons including a lack of general records and the questionable accuracy of others. When the South collapsed, Confederate Secretary of State Benjamin Judah reputedly burned many of the Richmond documents thus hiding Southern plans and actions for all time. Individuals also destroyed private records, too. Everyone was concerned about not leaving a paper trail that could incriminate themselves or others, leaving the opportunity for charges of violations of the laws of war. Some people later published their memoirs, but likely inflated their own importance, ignored activities or could have created actions that never happened.

In some measure the Civil War was a "gentlemen's" war, which doubtless affected developing an operational imperative to attack rear areas with full force and power inflicting the maximum damage. During subsequent wars, WW I, WW II, Korea, etc. there was no such hesitation. Rear areas with industrial activities and large civilian populations were specifically targeted for destruction.

I wrestled with the organization of this book for some time. While the premise is simple, the Great Lakes area was the soft underbelly of the Union and, as the Civil War dragged on, became an increasingly important target for the Confederacy; the details supporting it are complicated. It is difficult to advocate this hypothesis without providing an understanding of background, thus the need for the early chapters.

An ancillary premise is that the Confederacy missed golden opportunities by not pursuing the "target rich environment" of the Great Lakes, destroying vital transportation infrastructure that would have materially affected Northern war-making potential and siphoned critical troops from the battlefield to protect assets.

I tried to steer a middle ground on the story of the Northwest Conspiracy, breakout of prisoners from Camp Douglas in Chicago, Sons of Liberty, Order of American Knights, Knights of the Golden Circle and Copperheads. Many historians disagree with the seriousness of the threat ranging from a full-blown insurrection to nothing but a hoax. What is not in dispute, however, is **if it all worked as advertised**, it would have been a game changer for the South.

Lastly, I have a bias against the Confederacy. I hope it does not detract too strongly from the book. The Civil War wasn't about "states rights" as Confederate apologists claim. Rather it was a war **fought to make men free**, that no people had the right to hold others in slavery. To somehow claim otherwise is so much claptrap.

Often this drivel about states rights is wrapped up in the "myth of the Lost Cause," a term given to a literary and intellectual movement seeking to reconcile traditional southern white society to the defeat of the Confederacy. Supporters of the myth try to portray the Confederacy's cause as noble and leaders as exemplars of old-fashioned chivalry defeated by the overwhelming force of Union armies and not through better military skill. Such claims do not stand investigation. Time and again the drumbeat of Union victories, Petersburg, Gettysburg, Vicksburg, Shiloh, Lookout Mountain, Atlanta, etc. all give lie to the Lost Cause myth. Personally I think the Lost Cause supporters have better press agents than the Marine Corps! Lost Causers also argue secession was constitutional and a fair response to Northern economic and cultural assault against the South. Most important, slavery was a good institution and slaves were loyal and faithful to their masters. To see just how inane the whole Lost Cause argument is, I encourage readers to do their own research.

Lastly, reputedly over 5,000 books have been written about the Civil War so there certainly is a plethora of viewpoints.

Footnotes:

[1] The term "rear area" has very specific meaning depending on the military organization involved. For the purposes of this book it simply means the area far to the rear of the forward trace of the battlefield where manufacturing, transportation and logistic activities were located.

[2] With the exception, of course, of Lake Michigan which is wholly within the U.S.

Note: All photos NARA

CHAPTER ONE
WAR OBJECTIVES-
NORTH AND SOUTH

Military

As the American Civil War dragged on, the Union strategy of squeezing the Confederacy everywhere (aka the "Anaconda Plan") was paying clear dividends. Gradually the Atlantic coast ports used by the blockade runners to bring vital supplies to the South were choked off by the Union Navy. Northern field armies continued to press inward to the heart of the South inexorably bringing rebel territory back under the stars and stripes.

Although the South had the advantage of defending interior lines, (it is easier to shift armies and concentrate forces within a circle than having to attack and move armies around the exterior) by the beginning of 1864 the Confederate States of America (CSA) was generally losing everywhere. Each loss took resources of equipment and most important - men, off the Confederate board.

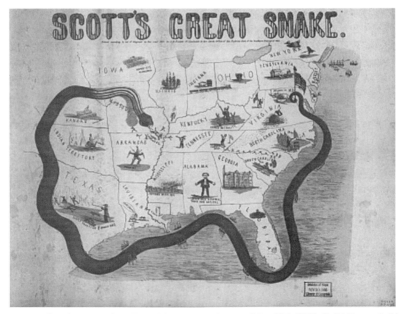

The Anaconda plan was developed by Union General-in-Chief Winfield Scott. Initially greatly derided, it proved the eventual blueprint to U.S. victory.

Lee's great northern invasion was turned back at Gettysburg in July 1863 and, simultaneously Vicksburg fell with a thump that echoed across the length and breadth of the South. The tremendous soldier losses of Lee at Gettysburg estimated at upwards of 25,000 men (roughly 34 percent of his command) could never be made up, at least not in quality.[1] Critical, too, Lee's vaunted aura of invulnerability as a commander was shattered. He would fight again and again, but each time being bled of soldiers more and more. With the loss of Vicksburg, the Gibraltar of the Confederacy and another 31,000 troops, the South was cut in two.

Following his crushing defeat at Gettysburg Lee's and the Confederacy's fortunes went into precipitous decline.

Vital supplies and troops from the west were prevented from reaching the east.[2] The Confederate states of Missouri, Arkansas, Louisiana and Texas were nearly completely chopped off from the rest of the nation. Heavily armored Union ironclads patrolled the Mississippi from St. Louis to the Gulf with impunity. The ability of the South to shift armies from west to east (or reverse), as needed, was gone.

Just as bad, the deteriorating Southern railroad system, never robust to begin with, was rapidly disintegrating under wartime pressure. Moving men or supplies anywhere was difficult, further impeding military operations. Under the best of circumstances, rails and rolling stock needed periodic replacement and rebuilding but the South had only a very limited quantity of resources to do the job.

Southern conscription was proving ineffective in meeting the critical need for soldiers, infantry especially. There were too many loopholes, ways men could evade the draft. The desertion rate was climbing, too, with men taking "French leave" to go home and take care of their starving families. Leaders may want to die for a lost cause but rarely their followers.

The most ready source of soldiers seemed to be the men held in Northern prison camps. "If we could only find a way to free them, they would flock back to the bonnie blue flag and our armies would again have the soldiers needed to destroy the Union" was the pipe dream of many Southern leaders. But the critical question was how to tap into this resource?

Political

British diplomatic recognition was critical to the South. From the very beginning of the war it was a vital national goal but one doomed to failure.

Southern diplomats thought it almost a given that British recognition would happen soon after the guns forced the surrender of Union troops at Fort Sumter on April 14, 1861. After all, the South was the major supplier of cotton to the great British textile mills. In fact the South supplied nearly 90 percent of all the cotton in the world, including Northern mills. The war would surely disrupt the supply and cause the British mills severe economic hardship since they were using over four times the cotton Yankee mills did. An increasingly effective Union blockade of the Southern ports would only make the shortage of cotton worse adding to pressure for British intervention. In fact, in 1862 the cotton shortage in Britain directly forced two million people out of work and indirectly three million more including women and children. A sixth of the entire British population was affected. Over 90 percent of the cotton used by French mills also came from the South adding to hope for their assistance. From a Northern perspective, cotton represented 60 percent of the value of all U.S. exports. Northern bankers, underwriters and shipping companies were closely linked with the cotton trade and the war directly struck at their pocketbooks.

When and if the British government recognized the CSA as a new nation, the Union could be faced with the potential of having to fight the British too, assuming of course the British would come to the aid of their new "cotton" ally. France joining the fray was also not beyond the realm of dreaming. While this all may have seemed very logical to the South, the British looked at it much differently and, in measure, far more realistically.[3]

Cotton was a vital raw material for the great British mills.

When the war started, Great Britain officially announced her neutrality but granted the Confederacy "belligerent power" status to allow British merchants trade with the South. This was a very cautionary action for Her Majesty's government. While it was certainly a prelude to formal recognition, which doubtless could have happened if the war turned heavily toward the South, it was only a half step at best. The South needed full diplomatic recognition and ultimately military support.

For Great Britain to maintain her economic dominance, it was vital British merchants have unrestricted access to worldwide markets including American. Regardless of how the conflict finally played out, she didn't want to lose American markets North or South. To achieve this critical objective, she needed to walk the diplomatic tightrope between the two; placate the CSA without overly angering the Union. The half measure of "belligerent power" status accomplished that goal but it pleased neither side. Critical for the South, however, it also allowed the purchase of absolutely vital war supplies, including arms and ammunition from Britain and the construction and arming of warships in British dockyards. To comply with the Queen's Proclamation of Neutrality of May 15, 1861, however, completed ships were met off-shore by merchant vessels carrying their arms and ammunition, the actual transfer occurring at sea. Belligerent status also gave the Confederate warships the same rights as U.S. Navy warships in foreign ports. Considering the South would be fighting a commerce war, using cruising raiders to attack U.S. merchant shipping anywhere in the world, access to foreign ports to arm and refit was critical.

As it became clear the South was unable to withstand Northern pressure on land or sea, the economic benefit to Britain of trading with the CSA became increasingly negligible, especially given the strangling blockade. For example, in 1862 one of eight blockade runners were captured by the Union Navy. By 1863 it was one in four; 1864 one in three and 1865 one in two. The interception rate even at a one-in-four rate was too great to maintain Southern imports.

Considering the Northern industrial and economic boom brought on by the war, Britain naturally gravitated towards supporting the North as a trading partner. Her heart may have been with the brave Southern cavaliers but business is business!

As the war dragged on, it became more apparent the British would never formally recognize the CSA or send their Navy to break the increasingly effective Northern blockade. Stymied by the lack of official help from Britain, the South was doomed unless it could change the equation, literally dramatically alter the battlefield.

The South clearly couldn't win the land battle. Regardless of the mythic bravery of the Southern soldier, the North had many more troops. The Southern population stood at roughly 9 million, forty percent of which were slaves. Blacks could obviously not be used as soldiers, at least according to the Confederate point of view. It is sometimes forgotten, however, that while the Southern slaves were not formed into combat regiments, they did provide critical home front labor thus releasing white workers for the Army. Thus the disparity of population between North and South is somewhat negated.

John Bell Hood was considered one of the South's rising stars before he destroyed his army against the rock of Sherman.

The South was also largely rural and agrarian with an overwhelming Anglo-Saxon Protestant population (less slaves). By contrast, the North had about 23 million people with immigrant ships arriving daily from Europe adding to the salad of religious and ethnic diversity. In addition, Lincoln had no problem with forming regiments of African-Americans.[4] By war's end 200,000 served. Roughly 20 percent of all black males and suffered a casualty rate 40 percent higher than white regiments. Twenty-one black soldiers were awarded the Medal of Honor.

When the war started, many "experts" believed the South had the better military leaders. Men like Robert E. Lee, Braxton Bragg, P.T.G. Beauregard, Albert Sidney Johnston, Joseph E. Johnston, Edmond Kirby Smith and John Bell Hood were thought far superior generals to anyone the North had. With the exception of Lee, all proved "generally" inadequate to the challenges they faced.[5] Although the North suffered through generals like George McClellan, Ambrose Burnside and Joe Hooker, in the end leaders like U.S. Grant, William T. Sherman, Phil Sheridan, George Thomas and George Meade among others emerged leading the North to final victory.

On the plus side, the South did have seven of the nation's eight military colleges, thus providing a flood of theoretically trained leaders.

The North also had overwhelming industrial and economic power, processing fully 80% of total U.S. industry. For example, at the start of the war:

-97% of the firearms manufacturing base (forcing the importation of most of the CSA weapons from Europe). There wasn't a single rifle factory in the South.

- 93 % of the pig iron manufacturing capacity (a single ironworks was in Richmond).

-71% railroad track, a terrific advantage in moving armies and supplies. As the war went on, the disparity grew larger in terms of new lines and

Joseph Hooker wasn't equal to the task as commander of the Army of the Potomac dueling with Lee but he was an effective corps commander.

repair of old, including rolling stock.

- 93% of the manufacturers, think uniforms and other critical gear such as tents and field packs.

-90% footwear (armies march and this means boots).

- A powerful merchant marine allowing not only coastal transport but intercontinental trade.

- A relatively powerful navy as compared to the South's virtually none and the capacity for rapid expansion.

- Vast iron and copper resources including those in the Michigan's Upper Peninsula.

The longer the war went on, the greater the disparity grew. The North became stronger and South weaker.

General William Tecumseh Sherman's March to the Sea made the Confederacy howl!

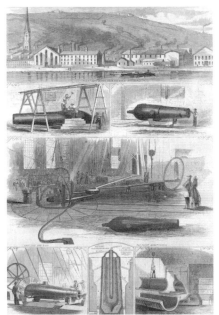

Manufacturing cannon, especially the large variety, was not only technologically difficult but resource intensive, challenges for the industrial poor South.

Canada

At the start of the War, British North America consisted of five provinces running east from Lake Superior to the Atlantic and two more to the west. Upper and Lower Canada, considered a single province for administrative purposes, was culturally cut into Canada West (aka Ontario) and Canada East. The Maritimes' New Brunswick, Nova Scotia, Prince Edward Island with Newfoundland hanging around the administrative edge, occupied the far east. Vancouver and British Columbia took care of the far west, both under a single governor. The massive hunk of terrain called Hudson's Bay Territory had a law unto its own, administered by a governor in Fort Garry. Many of the residents of Canada West were Loyalists who fled America following the Revolution and still had deep feelings of enmity to her.

Defending Canada was always a problem. Britain traditionally maintained a small but professional army. Where and how it was stationed was of vital national interest. In measure, it was deployed around the world in small penny packets supporting the Empire the sun never set on.

Within weeks of the Confederate assault on Fort Sumter, the British government put the wheels in motion to reinforce Canada with land forces. There were a mere 4,000 British Army troops in country and the provinces had only 10,000 poorly trained reservists available. The British were operating on the theory the best way to prevent a potential attack was to be ready to defend against it. While there was no imminent threat of a Federal attack in the midst of a bloody Civil War, it couldn't be ruled out.

The first reinforcements sailed from Britain in July amid great celebration. There was nothing secret about the troop movement. The British wanted the world to know they were taking firm action to defend Canada. Putting 2,144 officers and men aboard the *Great Eastern*, the largest ship in the world, was a way of emphasizing the political importance of the action. Among the troops was a battalion equipped with the new Armstrong breech loading cannon, a technological marvel of great promise. The troops, ship and artillery were all part of a strong political message to the U.S. that British North America would be defended against any attack.

Following the *Trent* affair and the escalating tensions between the U.S. and Britain, the Governor General of Canada, Lord Charles Stanley Monck, appointed a royal commission to report on a system of fortification and defense.[6]

After due study, the commission recommended a fleet of 72 gunboats on Lake Ontario and the St Lawrence River and a new naval base to replace the old one at Kingston on Lake Ontario, a force of 18,000 soldiers in Canada East and 47,000 in Canada West, enlargement of canals and a inter-colonial railway plus so many fortifications on the border that one official was moved to comment: "What is the good of all these little forts? They can detain an enemy for a very short time but must eventually fall. Why waste troops to defend them and money to build them?" It should be noted that by the start of the Civil War, Britain had essentially abandoned virtually all of her Great Lakes forts. For example, Penetangusihene on Georgian Bay, St. Joseph Island on the St. Marys River, Fort Malden opposite Detroit. Fort York (at today's Toronto) was still maintained, however.

The Inspector-General of Fortifications took the view, that should the Americans attack, the loss of Canada was certain. In effect, Canada was surrendering the initiative to the U.S. and would therefore fail.

After completing an evaluation ordered by the Governor General, a Royal Engineer captain took a different tack. Rather than committing large numbers of troops to defending Canada, he suggested attacking U.S. territory at the first moment possible and seizing Fort Montgomery at Rousie's Point near Plattsburg and Fort Niagara just below Buffalo. Holding both would forestall attacks on Montreal and Toronto.

Key Canadian targets like the Welland Canal were virtually indefensible to American attack being open to waterborne assault from each end (at Lakes Erie and Ontario) and landward from Niagara Falls.

Perhaps of most concern was the tremendous advantage the far greater amount of U.S. flag shipping on the lakes gave the Union. Much of it could potentially be quickly converted to ad hoc warships with the addition of guns and perhaps iron plate as needed. Other ships were fully capable of transporting Union troops, artillery and associated logistic train to wherever needed. The much smaller British flag commercial fleet would be quickly overwhelmed.

Most important, the British had not maintained warships on the lakes up to the limits of the Rush-Bagot Treaty.[7] While small vessels used for general government work could be equipped with light guns they were of no real use as warships. The *USS Michigan* ruled the lakes and there was nothing Britain could do to change it, at least on a ship to ship basis. That the *Michigan* was in excess of the treaty requirements was immaterial. Since her beam was too large to fit through the Welland Canal, she was captive to the Great Lakes.

Complicating British action were the harsh winters, which closed down all navigation on the St. Lawrence River. Traditionally civil winter communication was through Portland, Maine, and west via rail. Sending military equipment through the U.S. was forbidden, so this route was unavailable, shutting off winter reinforcement.

In the end, Britain was in no real position to defend Canada with anything but near token forces. As the preeminent world power, the super power of the day, she needed to balance her resources out over a number of areas of potential danger, not over weighing one at unacceptable risk of another. With the real fear of a European conflict, she had to keep major force structure close to home. Mistrust of France's Napoleon III played deeply into British defense planning. The French were always a potential enemy to be guarded against. Japan was making menacing sounds in the Far East and New Zealand needed to be stiffened with Imperial troops. Canada was only half a world away. New Zealand was ALL the way away! In the event of emergency, forces could be sent to Canada quicker than to New Zealand.

The politicians concluded defending Britain was far more important than worrying about far flung Canadian provinces in anything more than a token commitment. This obviously did not please her loyal Canadian subjects.

In the end, Britain provided modest forces to defend Canada but on the condition Canada would take the lead herself. Britain would provide additional rifles and other equipment but the bulk of the men to use them would need to come from Canada.

The size of the eventual British reinforcement was minimal; 14,436 men, 11,175 of which arrived after the *Trent* crisis. Included were 16 batteries of artillery for fire support. Given the Canada posted troops in country, Britain had roughly 18,000 regular soldiers, mostly in the east. This is about the size of a single typical Union Army corps. Seven infantry corps were deployed by the Union Army of the Potomac at Gettysburg plus a cavalry corps! The British troops were better than nothing, but hardly a formidable force. It is reasonable to say a determined Union attack would have brushed them aside. Remember, the British troops were present more as a political tripwire than a powerful defending force.

At the height of the Canadian war scare, local towns demanded protection. Simcoe wanted new Armstrong guns, Port Dover fortifications and Dundas 50 heavy batteries of guns. Of course all of this military protection would be instantly (and magically) provided! Concern was high enough merchants in some cities closed their shops during the afternoons to allow employees who were members of newly formed militia units time to drill. Even students at the University of Toronto formed a rifle corps.

There was a stiff price for Canadian military readiness, however. For instance even after another commission considered the situation and recommended building a gunboat flotilla on the Great Lakes to the limits of the Rush-Bagot Treaty, raising a 50,000 man active army and 50,000 man reserve, the cost was considered unbearable. For example, a 28-day training period alone cost a tenth of the entire Provincial revenue. In the end, little of value would be done.

Britain's "big stick" was the Royal Navy, long recognized as the largest and best in the world and fully capable of what today is called "power projection." There were few areas of the world the Royal Navy could not reach and influence. For various reasons, the British did not attempt to "protect" the Great Lakes with naval might or significant seacoast defenses. Given the annual closing of the St. Lawrence River during winter ice and the lack of "big boat" access via canals around rapids etc., British options for major naval reinforcement were limited.

The Rush-Bagot Treaty didn't require both countries to dismantle their warships so they were simply placed into storage. Storage doesn't mean forgotten about, but that was largely what the British did. When the British examined their "stored" fleet at Kingston, it was found to be rotten beyond use. The same was true for a warship the U.S. stored at Sackett's Harbor in Lake Ontario.

Had the U.S. and British come to blows, it is likely the war would have been fought on three fronts. The first on the U.S. - Canada border, would have been strictly a British

The USS Michigan, *shown here after the war, was the most powerful naval vessel on the Great Lakes.*

holding action at best; British ground forces likely slowly retreating under U.S. pressure. The Great Lakes would have only been a navigational obstacle. Given the greatly larger U.S. merchant fleet, as well as the powerful *USS Michigan*, the Union could attack wherever she desired. Minor fortifications would have been bypassed or overwhelmed.

The second front would have been the High Seas. If the North thought the deprecations of a few Confederate commerce raiders like the infamous *Shenandoah* were noteworthy, the massive British Navy would have swept the oceans of shipping in relatively short order. The economic impact to the U.S. would have been significant.

The third front would have been the U.S. Atlantic coast. In spite of the size and power of the British Navy, given the number of Union seacoast fortifications and growing coastal ironclad fleet, British success in the littoral was questionable.

The logistic support for a battle fleet so far from home waters would have been staggering in expense and difficulty. The opportunity for U.S. interdiction would have compounded the challenge.

Throughout the war the problem of submarines plagued both sides. The Confederate *H.L. Hunley* is credited with being the first submarine to sink a warship doing so in February 1864 in Charleston Harbor. The Union *Alligator* launched in May 1862 was lost in a gale off Cape Hatteras in April 1863 after a spotty record. What is often forgotten is the role Michigan City, Indiana inventor Lodner Phillips played in submarine development. In the 1850s he built operational two man submarines he tested in Lake Michigan. Apparently he offered to construct submarines for the Navy but was rebuffed. It wasn't until later in the war his proposals were accepted but then seem to have been swallowed by oblivion or less obvious features incorporated into later designs.[8]

USS Michigan

The only significant U.S. Navy presence on the lakes was the 163-foot *USS Michigan*, the first iron-hulled warship in the Navy. The iron parts were fabricated in Pittsburgh, hauled to Erie, Pennsylvania, where she was assembled and commissioned in September 1844. This was 15 years prior to Britain's first iron hulled warship *HMS Warrior* and 16 years prior to the French *Glorie*. The U.S. was clearly leading the technological wave of iron shipbuilding. The impetus for the *Michigan* on the Great Lakes was to deter any hostile moves by British armed steamers during a Canadian rebellion. She proved an excellent deterrent.

Reputedly, the choice of iron for the hull instead of wood was that of the Secretary of the Navy who determined, "to use the immense resource of our country in that most valuable metal" and, "to ascertain the practicability and utility of building vessels, at least for harbor defense, of so cheap and indestructible a material."

In today's parlance, the *Michigan* was the big guerrilla, easily the most powerful vessel on the Great Lakes. Wherever she was, she was mistress of all her guns could hit. She was very well armed with one 30-pounder Parrott rifle, five 20-pounder Parrott

The British launched the iron hull warship HMS Warrior *in 1859.*

rifles, six 24-pounder smoothbores and two 12-pounder boat howitzers. She effectively gave the U.S. unchallenged mastery of the water.

The *Michigan* was normally based out of Erie, Pennsylvania, an ideal position to counter anticipated British threats from Canada. In 1851, she assisted in the arrest of "King" James Jesse Strange, who headed a Mormon colony on Beaver Island in Lake Michigan. Strang was eventually acquitted of all charges but later assassinated by his own followers. During the same decade, she was deliberately rammed by a steamer operated by the infamous Michigan timber pirates, but her iron hull suffered no damage.

During the Civil War, she was a key target for Confederate raiders intending to capture her, turning her guns against key Great Lakes cities and infrastructure. Those stories are told in Chapter 6.

The *Michigan's* Civil War duty began easily enough. Starting on May 9, 1861 (less than a month after the Confederated bombarded Fort Sumter) she began touring the Great Lakes ports enlisting men into the Navy. Certainly most enlistees saw the Navy (three hots and a hammock plus a ration of grog) as a far better option than joining one of the many state volunteer regiments and becoming part of the "poor bloody infantry."[9]

Her recruiting work was very successful, convincing over 4,000 men to sign up. Most of the initial recruits went to the Atlantic with the bulk of those following going to the Mississippi and the gunboat navy.

In late July, 1863, she was in Detroit to deter potential draft riots. Similar duty was performed at Milwaukee and Buffalo. The latter city port was especially volatile as a "mob" of 4,000 men was threatening to burn down all the grain elevators. As Buffalo was the key port for the trade and grain was a critical wartime commodity, the elevators

The French La Glorie *came off the stocks in 1860.*

were vital. The gunboat's presence apparently awed the mob and the elevators remained standing. With the intelligence of the threat to Johnson Island, she relocated to Sandusky Bay in late October and took up a commanding position just off the prison assuring the prisoners of a dose of shell in the event of riot or escape attempts.[10, 11]

Like all Great Lakes vessels, when the ice came in the winter, she went into winter lay-up until navigation opened in the spring. Although her iron hull was safe against the ice, her large sidewheels were vulnerable.

Following the war she continued in service being renamed *U.S.S. Wolverine* in June 1905 to free up *Michigan* for a new seagoing battleship.[12] Decommissioned in May 1912, she was turned over to the Pennsylvania Naval Militia serving for 11 years as a training vessel. After suffering a major mechanical breakdown in 1923 and deemed not economically repairable, she was given to the city of Erie as a historic relic. When a foundation was unable to raise the funds to preserve her, she was cut up and sold for scrap in 1949. All that remains of this once proud warship is her bow and cutwater on display in the Erie Maritime Museum.

The Revenue Cutters

The U.S. Revenue Marine Service, Alexander Hamilton's old tax collecting "navy," had a presence on the Great Lakes well before the Civil War. The first evidence of a Revenue cutter was the *Alexander J. Dallas* home-ported in Detroit as early as 1819. In the intervening years, the Revenue Marine expanded its mission to include law enforcement and assistance to ships in distress.

As Secretary of the Treasury Hamilton knew it was critical to collect taxes on imported goods to keep the new nation financially solvent, he also realized that based on long colonial tradition, shippers would try to circumvent any normal collection effort. Along these lines, he proposed to build ten manned and armed cutters to ensure collecting the tax revenue. Congress accepted his argument establishing the Revenue Marine in 1790. Because the U.S. Navy was disbanded following the Revolutionary War between that date and 1798 when the Navy was finally established for good, the Revenue Marine was the nation's only armed sea going force!

In 1857 six small 50-ton cutters, 57-foot, 6-inches in length, 17-foot, 6-inches in beam and 5-feet, 10-inches in depth were built by the Merry and Gay shipyard in Milan, Ohio, for a contracted price of $4,050 each. They were constructed of white oak, yellow pine and locust with copper fastenings. Each also had a centerboard for shallow water cruising. All were named for the members of Presidents James Buchanan's cabinet. A single six-pounder cannon was their sole armament. It was scant firepower to defend a potentially contentious border.[13]

All the new cutters were stationed on the Great Lakes at the beginning of the Civil War and all save one were sent to saltwater once hostilities began. The *Black* (Jeremiah) was homeported at Erie and sent to Boston; *Brown* (Aaron V.) homeported at Milwaukee and sent to Salem, Massachusetts; *Cobb* (Howell) homeported at Oswego, New York, and sent to the East Coast and destroyed by a gale at Cape Ann, Massachusetts, in December 1861; *Thompson* (Jacob) homeported at Detroit, sent to Boston;[14] *Toncey* (Issac) homeported at Michilimackinac and sent to Castine, Maine. Only the *Floyd* (Jacob) remained on the Great Lakes, stationed at Marquette to protect

The six small Revenue Cutters on the Great Lakes were similar to, but smaller than the Cutter Gallatin. *Credit Coast Guard Historian's Office*

the iron ore shipping and docks. She was also occasionally sent to Bayfield, Wisconsin, but as mining had not yet started there it was strictly for general customs duty.[15]

Immediately bringing the small cutters to saltwater reflected two things. First, the critical need for navy assets in what was seen as the primary theater of operations. Lincoln had declared a blockade of the Southern ports and since the U.S. Navy had far too few ships and men to even begin to enforce it, whatever small aid the Revenue Cutters could provide was important. The small cutters could also patrol the small rivers and inlets larger ships could not approach. The second reason was the relative lack of importance the North attached at least initially to the Great Lakes. Had the cutters been left at their original homeports, they could have provided a level of deterrence against Confederate mischief, especially if up gunned with a few more six pounders. That the *Floyd* was assigned to duty in Marquette reflects the recognition of importance given to the iron ore trade both in protecting it against Confederate action but also southern inspired labor strife. Virtually all the miners were immigrants from a plethora of countries and considered ripe for "organization" and potential disruption of work. If additional naval force was necessary, the *Michigan* could always provide it but the gunboat couldn't be everywhere.

There was also some thought of renaming the *Floyd* since the honoree was now a Confederate general. His career was a bit checkered, however. Appointed Secretary of War under President Buchanan in 1857, when the president decided to hold Charleston Harbor and not withdraw the garrison at Fort Sumter, Floyd resigned in protest in December of 1860. Even worse, he was later accused of surreptitiously helping the Confederacy by falsely sending arms and other war material to Southern arsenals prior to the war so it would be allegedly stockpiled for the rebels. He was relieved of his command in March 1862 by the Confederate supreme command for desertion. But despite the disgrace, he later was commissioned a Major General in the Virginia militia and raised a band of guerillas operating against Union forces. He died in August 1863 of failing health apparently caused by the strain of campaigning.

U.S. Great Lakes Fortifications

Numerous fortifications were on the shore of the Great Lakes. Some of them played a role in the war. Others didn't. None of the forts saw active combat.

Youngstown, New York - Fort Niagara

It was vital during the colonial wars in North America to control the mouth of the Niagara River, the gateway to the Great Lakes. Over time French, British and American forces maintained fortifications at or near the present fort trading ownership as military fortunes rose and fell. When the Erie Canal opened in 1825, the strategic value of Fort Niagara decreased as trade now bypassed the area it guarded.

Like many of the old fortifications along the northern border, Fort Niagara was unoccupied when the Civil War began but increasing tension between Britain and the U.S. caused the fort to be garrisoned again in 1861. When the British reinforced Canada with more troops, the opportunity for invasion across the ill-protected northern border was considered very real.

U.S. Army Engineers took a good look at the old fort and decided modernization was needed to increase its capability as a force multiplier and construction of concrete and brick revetments and gun casements began in 1863. However, the pressing need for more troops at the battlefields caused the garrison to be shipped south the same year. Regardless, the improvements continued. In the event it was necessary to quickly garrison the fort again, it would be in an improved state of readiness.

Sault St. Marie, Michigan - Fort Brady

With the end of the War of 1812, the Falls of the Saint Marys River (commonly called the Soo today) were unoccupied by any military force although the British exercised de facto control from their base on Drummond Island at the southern end of the river. To bring the Soo under American control in 1822, General Hugh Brady moved a battalion from Sackett's Harbor, New York, to the village and constructed a stockade and barracks on the land overlooking the rapids. The traditional wooden stockade included blockhouses at the southwest and northeast corners.

Prior to the Civil War the fort was occupied by only a small caretaker detachment, the bulk of the soldiers being transferred to Fort Mackinac. At least one field piece was left in position allowing the caretaker sergeant in charge to render a salute to the first boat in the spring.

Following the Civil War, a second fort was built in the same location with guns facing Canada to better protect the locks. The fort remained until 1892 when it was relocated to Ashmun Hill, the present campus of Lake Superior State University.

Old Fort Brady was a quiet backwater of Army life.

Fort Wilkins at the tip of Michigan's Keweenaw Peninsula, never saw action in the Civil War, or any armed conflict of any kind.

Copper Harbor, Michigan - Fort Wilkins

The fort, just east of Copper Harbor, Michigan, at the north end of the Keweenaw Peninsula, was built in 1844 with the mission of maintaining the peace between newly arrived copper miners and the local Ojibwe. The Treaty of La Pointe recently ceded the area to the U.S. and trouble was expected. In fact there was no difficulty and the troops had no real purpose. Most of the force was sent to Mexico for the Mexican-American War and in 1846 the fort was abandoned less a single sergeant left as a caretaker. When he died in 1855, the post was leased to a physician intending to establish a health camp. Following the Civil War, it was garrisoned with soldiers waiting to serve out their enlistments prior to discharge and was permanently abandoned in 1870. Fort Wilkins was an utter non-factor in the Civil War.

Mackinac Island, Michigan - Fort Mackinac

The fort on Mackinac Island was established in 1781 when the old one on the mainland south of the straits was abandoned and various components moved across the ice to the bluff above the harbor. During the American Revolution, the British realized the old fort on the beach was essentially indefensible and rather than risk losing it to the Americans, abandoning it and establishing one on the island was a military necessity. What remained of the old fort was burned.

Following the American Revolution, Mackinac Island including the new fort became American territory however it took the new nation 13 years to finally assume effective control. The British garrison reluctantly retreated to St. Joseph's Island, at the mouth of the St. Marys River and established Fort St. Joseph.

During the War of 1812, a British force from St. Joseph's Island assaulted Fort Mackinac from the rear and after a brief skirmish, the outnumbered and out gunned

Fort Mackinac's only duty during the Civil War was to briefly house three Confederate political prisoners.

American garrison surrendered. Following the War, the fort was returned to the U.S. as part of the settlement treaty.

Fort Mackinac became increasingly obsolete as the old frontier became civilized. Like Fort Wilkins and other northern posts, it was largely abandoned as garrison troops were shipped south for duty in the Mexican War. At the start of the Civil War, the garrison again "shipped" out for duty on the far-flung battlefields, leaving a single sergeant behind as caretaker. Its only role during the Civil War was during the summer of 1862 when the fort served as a prison for three wealthy and influential Southern political prisoners: General William G. Harding, Washington Barrow and Judge Joseph C. Guid, all of Tennessee and deemed dangerous enough to warrant seclusion. The men were brought to the island on May 10, which likely provided a breath of fresh northern air to the Southerners. The guard force was made up of a small volunteer militia contingent from Detroit called the Stanton Guard, the regulars long sent off to the battlefields. The prisoners were not closely held, but generally allowed the freedom of the post. All in all, it was not an unpleasant confinement for the Tennesseans or difficult duty for the guards. When the enjoyable summer breezes began to pick up a hint of the winter cold coming, two of the three prisoners immediately decided to sign loyalty oaths and were released. The third held to his principals and was transferred to another prison. Mackinac did nothing more during the war.

Following the War it was garrisoned again but for no good purpose beyond operating the National Park established on the island in 1875. The fort was finally abandoned for good in 1895 and today is part of the Mackinac Island State Park operations.

Detroit, Michigan - Fort Wayne

Fort Wayne is the third fort built to protect Detroit. The first was erected by the French in 1701 and surrendered to the British during the French and Indian War in 1760. The second known as Fort Lermoult was built by the British and turned over to the Americans as part of the treaty ending the Revolution. General Hull notoriously surrendered it to the British in the War of 1812 without a modicum of resistance. Returned to the Americans following the War it was allowed to fall into disrepair, sold to the City of Detroit and demolished.

As the result of various rebellions in Canada in the 1830s and the need to preserve American neutrality and the belated recognition that the northern border was essentially undefended, in 1841 Congress authorized money to construct a chain of protecting forts. There was special concern about countering British Fort Malden at Amherstburg just across the Detroit River. Fort Malden would not be abandoned until 1851.

The new American fort, named Fort Wayne in honor of Revolutionary War General "Mad" Anthony Wayne, was built along the riverfront three miles south of the city. The design was rather standard for the time, star-patterned, walls of earthen ramparts faced with cedar, covering vaulted brick tunnels containing gun ports. Additional emplacements for 10-inch guns were on top of the walls. A dry moat surrounded the fort and a small lunette fronted the river.[16]

Before the fort was completed in 1853, the U.S. and Canada largely settled the political tensions that led to its construction so it was left without a garrison. Nor were guns apparently ever mounted. Whether the guns were mounted or not is a minor point

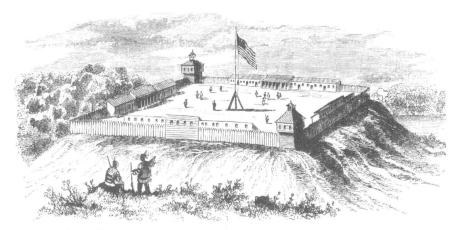

Fort Wayne at Detroit was considerably upgraded during the Civil War to help deter British aggression from Canada just across the river.

as, with some warning, guns can be installed and prepared for action as can the fort be garrisoned. The time consuming part was actually building the fort.

The Civil War suddenly made Fort Wayne very relevant. Given the known British bias for the Confederacy, the U.S. feared a quick cross river strike by the British at Detroit. Seizing the fort would also effectively close the Detroit River to U.S. shipping, thus disrupting the Union war effort. In 1863 the fort was strengthened with new walls faced with more substantial brick and concrete than the original cedar.

The fort also served as a muster point for various Michigan State Militia units mobilizing for the war. It was also a good place for wounded soldiers to recover. There was very little room inside the walls to house troops not directly concerned with the defense of the fort, normally heavy artillery units, so mustering units remained outside the fort. As the fort grew busier as a muster and logistic center, quarters, warehouses, mess halls, etc. were soon occupying the surrounding grounds. Sidewheel steamers were also moored along the river to provide additional temporary quarters for newly arriving troops.

The use of the fort didn't end with the Civil War. Additional changes were made as the nation faced other conflicts, each time Fort Wayne adapted to meet the new missions. In 1949 it was turned over to the City of Detroit.

Oswego, New York - Fort Ontario

Fort Ontario, at the present day city of Oswego, New York, dates from the French and Indian War. Originally called the, "Fort of Six Nations" it was destroyed by the French but rebuilt in 1759. A detail from a New York regiment destroyed the fort again in 1778 after the British abandoned it during the Revolution only to have the redcoats return and rebuild it four years later. With the signing of Jay's Treaty in 1796 it was turned back to the Americans.

Fort Ontario commanded Oswego Harbor.

During the War of 1812 the British attacked and destroyed the fort yet again. When tensions with Britain increased, the present five-walled fort was built in 1839-1844 in part to guard against smuggling between Canada and the U.S. Like Fort Wayne it is essentially a classic Vauben design.[17] A dry moat surrounded the fort with earthen bastions beyond. It was rebuilt during the Civil War as a defense against potential British attack in support of the Confederacy, however, most of the guns were removed and sent south for use in field operations.

The installation saw additional use during, up to and through World War II, finally being transferred to the State of New York in 1949.

Green Bay, Wisconsin - Fort Howard

Fort Howard as it existed in the Civil War dated from the 1816 stockade built to help protect early settlers from hostile natives and later formed the basis of law enforcement during the early days of the Wisconsin frontier. The garrison was withdrawn in 1841 to participate in the Seminole War, returned in 1849 and the fort given caretaker status in 1852. During the Civil War it served as a muster post for newly recruited troops until 1863 when it was turned over to the Department of the Interior Land Office for surplus sale. It served no other purpose during the war.

Fort Howard on Green Bay briefly served as a muster point for Wisconsin troops prior to deployment.

Canadian Forts

Toronto, Ontario - Fort York

The original fort at York was built in reaction to American attacks on the city during the War of 1812. A new fort was operational in 1841 but the old one was still

Fort Henry was considered the strongest fort on the Great Lakes, Canadian or American.

maintained including a seven-gun battery installed during the Civil War. The battery commanded the Lake Ontario approach to the city.

Kingston, Ontario - Fort Henry

Fort Henry is considered to be the strongest fort on the Great Lakes, British or American. The first fort was built following the War of 1812 to protect the critical border between Lower Canada (Quebec) and Upper Canada (Ontario). Under the press of tension along the U.S. - Canadian border, the old fort was replaced with a new one between 1837 - 1848.

The fort also protected the Lake Ontario end of the Rideau Canal, which ran between Kingston and Montreal bypassing the St. Lawrence River, which was dangerously close to the U.S. and possible interdiction. More elaborate defensive works were planned but funding ran out due to cost overruns.

The new fort was six-sided with a dry moat and numerous wall-mounted guns. The walls were straight sided without bastions but casemates provided sufficient space for all normal military functional support. With border tensions essentially eliminated following the Civil War, the fort was abandoned to caretaker status in 1870 but saw use during both World Wars as a P.O.W. and internment camp.

References

James P. Barry, *Old Forts of the Great Lakes, Sentinels in the Wilderness*, (Lansing: Thunder Bay Press, 1994), 110-111, 118-119, 120, 134-135, 140-141.

William Gilmore Beymer, *On Hazardous Service, Scouts and Spies of the North and South*, (Harper and Brothers: New York, 1922), 209-211, 232.

Thomas Boaz, *Guns For Cotton: England Arms the Confederacy* (Shippensburg, Pennsylvania: Burd Street Press, 1996), 2-3.

Donald L. Canney, *U.S. Coast Guard and Revenue Cutters, 1790-1935* (Annapolis: U.S. Naval Institute Press, 1995), 26.

Civil War Artillery Definitions - http://www.civilwarartillery.com/.

Confederate Casualties - Vicksburg - http://americancivilwar.com/statepic/ms/ms011.html

Dictionary of American Fighting Ships, *USS Michigan* - http://www.history.navy.mil/danfs/m10/michigan-i.htm.

Dictionary of Canadian Biography - http://www.biographi.ca/009004-119.01-e.php?&id_nbr=5077

Eighteenth, Nineteenth & Early Twentieth Century Revenue Cutters - http://www.uscg.mil/history/webcutters/USRC_Photo_Index.asp.

Edward Everett, *The Rebellion record: a diary of American events, with documents...*, Volume 1 (New York; D. Van Norstrand, 1866), 10.

Fort Henry, Ontario - http://en.wikipedia.org/wiki/Fort_Henry,_Ontario.

Fort Howard - http://en.wikipedia.org/wiki/Fort_Howard_%28Wisconsin%29.

A Brief History of Fort Mackinac - http://www.mackinacparks.com/history/index.aspx?l=0,1,4,32,39,44.

Fort Ontario - http://en.wikipedia.org/wiki/Fort_Ontario.

Fort Wilkins, Historic State Park - http://en.wikipedia.org/wiki/Fort_Wilkins_Historic_State_Park

Gettysburg Casualties - http://www.militaryhistoryonline.com/gettysburg/getty4.aspx

Great Ships *Michigan* - http://www.historycentral.com/navy/Steamer/michigan.html.

Historic Fort Wayne - http://www.michigan.org/Property/Detail.aspx?p=G21079.

Edward McPherson, *The political history of the United States of America, during the Great Rebellion* (Washington, DC: James B. Chapman, 1882), 28.

I Remember When - 1923 - http://genealogytrails.com/mich/chippewa/remember.html.

Major General John B. Floyd - http://www.mycivilwar.com/leaders/floyd_john.htm.

Navsource Online, Gunboat *Michigan* (IX-31) - http://www.navsource.org/archives/12/09905d.htm.

T. Michael O'Brien, *Guardians of the Eighth Sea: A History of the U.S. Coast Guard on the Great Lakes* (U.S. Coast Guard, 1976), 5-7.

Old Fort Brady - http://www.lssu.edu/brady/first.html.

Old Fort Niagara - http://oldfortniagara.org/history/history.php?period=8.

Palmerston's Follies: a reply to the French 'threat - http://www.napoleon.org/en/reading_room/articles/files/hicks_portsdown_forts.asp#ancre5.

Bradley A. Rodgers, *Guardian of the Great Lakes: The U.S. Paddle Frigate* Michigan (Ann

Arbor: University of Michigan Press, 1996), 82-84.

Herbert Reynolds Spencer, *USS Michigan - USS Wolverine*, 22-26.

U.S. Coast Guard History, *John B. Floyd*-
http://www.uscg.mil/history/webcutters/Floyd_1857.pdf.

USS Michigan - http://en.wikipedia.org/wiki/USS_Michigan_%281843%29.

USS Michigan BB-27 - http://www.cityofart.net/bship/michigan.html.

Footnotes

[1] Gettysburg Casualties - http://www.militaryhistoryonline.com/gettysburg/getty4.aspx.

[2] Confederate Casualties - Vicksburg - http://americancivilwar.com/statepic/ms/ms011.html.

[3] Thomas Boaz, Guns For Cotton: England Arms the Confederacy (Shippensburg, Pennsylvania: Burd Street Press, 1996), 2-3.

[4] The formation of African-American Army units didn't happen until the fall of 1862 when losses of white troops made it imperative.

[5] Lost Cause True Believers will doubtless dispute this evaluation but history speaks for itself.

[6] The *Trent* affair was an international diplomatic incident occurring when on November 1, 1861 a U.S. warship stopped the British mail packet *Trent* and removed two Confederate ministers enroute to London. The action was a major violation of British neutrality and potentially could have led to war had not Lincoln (after a judicious cooling off period) quietly released the diplomats and disavowed the Navy captain's unlawful action.

[7] The treaty limited each nation to not more than four ships of 100 tons burden. The *Michigan* was 582 tons. When the War started she was being used for recruiting duty in Buffalo and armed with a single 18-pounder gun. She was quickly "up-gunned."

[8] William Gilmore Beymer, *On Hazardous Service, Scouts and Spies of the North and South*, (Harper and Brothers: New York, 1922), 209-211, 232.

[9] "Let us be clear about three facts: First, all battles and all wars are won in the end by the infantryman. Secondly, the infantryman always bears the brunt. His casualties are heavier, he suffers greater extremes of discomfort and fatigue than the other arms. Thirdly, the art of the infantryman is less stereotyped and far harder to acquire in modern war than that of any other arm." Field Marshal Earl Wavell.

[10] A hollow cast iron projectile containing a bursting charge ignited by means of a fuze. A shell fired at troops was set to go off in the air above the target or, if ricochet was desired, to plunge into the column before detonation.

[11] Bradley A. Rodgers, *Guardian of the Great Lakes: The U.S. Paddle Frigate* Michigan, (Ann Arbor: University of Michigan Press, 1996), 82-84.

[12] The new *USS Michigan* and her sistership *USS South Carolina* were the first dreadnaught battleships built by the U.S. Navy and were actually laid down before the famous *HMS Dreadnaught*. Had the U.S. Navy contractors build quicker, the U.S. Navy would have had the first all big gun battlewagons rather than the British.

[13] A "six" pounder fired a six pound cannon ball.

[14] The *Thompson* was named for Jacob Thompson the ex-Secretary of the Interior and "Resident Director of Operations" in Canada against the Union. See Chapter 6.

[15] The government sent the vessel to Detroit in 1864 where she was decommissioned and sold at a public auction. Eventually renamed the *Alice Craig*, she worked in the commercial fishing and cargo industry for a time from Two Rivers, Wisconsin, and later Bayfield. On November 18, 1887 she wrecked near Bayfield during a Superior gale.

[16] A lunette is an outwork shaped like a half-moon. It is intended to engage an enemy prior to his reaching the main fort. Since "star" forts were based on the work of Sebastian Vauban, a 17th century French military engineer, French terms were used by military engineers to name the various components.

[17] Sébastien Le Prestre de Vauban (1633-1707) was one of the greatest military engineers in history. During his lifetime he fortified over 160 locations in France. His designs were widely copied throughout Europe and North America.

CHAPTER TWO
POLITICAL ENVIRONMENT

The Civil War represented a far different age than present. Dealing waves of violent and bloody death on an enemy was thoroughly honorable if you stood in tight ranks on a battlefield while pouring volley after volley of deadly Minie balls into his closely packed formations.

Killing enemies by secret assassination was never recognized as legitimate action, especially during the Civil War although it is far more accepted today. It is fair to ask the question, is "servicing" a group of terrorists with a Hellfire missile fired from a drone "flown" by a pilot in a bunker thousands of miles away an acceptable act of war, just an example of technology reaching deeper into a battlefield or is it really murder? How would a Civil War soldier have viewed such death?

During the Civil War, honorable combat meant face to face and death by stealth was generally viewed as dishonorable.

Niagara Falls Peace Conference

Given the desperate Southern military situation in 1864, Jefferson Davis authorized George N. Sanders of Kentucky and Commissioner Clement Clay to conduct a peace conference with the North in July 1864 at Niagara Falls, New York. The actual location of the conference was the Clifton House Hotel, a popular hotel situated on the edge of the Niagara gorge.

Sanders was one of the really strange figures involved with the Confederate Canadian "legation." In a way, he was like a Civil War version of James Bond without the secret part, suave and sophisticated, always in the company of beautiful women and a pocket filled with ready cash. He seemed to know everyone worth knowing, including presidents and kings. Prior to the war, he was the U.S. Consul in London. It was said it didn't take him long to bring Clay completely under his power with lavish soirees and fawning flattery. His skill was being himself, a hopeless meddler without the ability to "bring home" a project or task. His role in the "peace" conference doomed it to failure.

Considering the North held all the cards, the conference was certainly a doomed effort from the start. The conference was not helped by *New York Tribune* editor Horace Greeley, a notorious "peace at any price" Democrat endorsing the talks. He sent a letter to Lincoln extolling, "our bleeding, bankrupt, almost dying country longs for peace, shudders at the prospect of fresh conscription, of future wholesale devastation and new rivers of blood." Greeley could always turn a phrase! To assure a proper showing of

George Sanders played a critical role in the Confederate Canadian operation.

his seriousness, Lincoln sent his Chief of Staff John Hay to represent him. The conference, however, wrecked on the shoals of reality as Hay pounded home to Sanders and Clay that the North would not accept political independence for the South and that slavery must be abandoned. In turn, the two Confederates reiterated Davis's equally rock fast position that he would only agree to complete independence.

The real agenda for Davis wasn't to secure a negotiated peace but rather to embarrass Lincoln before the upcoming November 1864 election to show the South was ready for peace but the president was bent to continue the bloodletting. It was nothing more than political theater and a drama Lincoln clearly won.

Fugitive Slaves

Canada had long been a haven for runaway slaves from the U.S. but mostly from the South.[1] They entered Canada in a variety of ways. Once the slaves made their way to a Great Lakes border state via the Underground Railroad, it was comparatively simple to

This pro "peace at any price" poster shows a powerful South and defeated North. It played well to Democrats willing to sell out the North.

take a boat across the water to freedom and the smaller the water the better. For example, crossing the Detroit River from Detroit to Windsor was popular as was the bridge at Niagara Falls. A number of steamers also hauled escapees across the lakes to Canada during the course of normal business. Nothing about the trip from bondage to freedom was easy or guaranteed, even with the full assistance of the Underground Railroad, but it was a journey many thousands of slaves risked and successfully completed.

A Nest of Rumors and Spies

During the Civil War, Toronto as well as the Canadian eastern cities were similar to Lisbon during the early days of World War II. Confederate diplomats, couriers, spies and agents regularly passed through going and coming from Europe as well as the South. Union agents intermixed among them, often "tailing" them as they came and went. Escaped Southern prisoners were also in the mix as well as a host of newspaper reporters, foreign diplomats, military observers and businessmen added to the boiling cauldron of intrigue.

As a neutral country, Canada offered protection of a sort to the Southern agents from Northern interference. Confederate agents could travel easily (generally speaking) through the Northern states gathering all manner of information from industrial data to movements of the Union Army. After slipping across the Canadian border, the agents could make their way quickly across Canada to Halifax and thence to Europe or Bermuda and a blockade-runner home.

A group of fugitive slaves at a Northern Underground Railroad "terminal." It took tremendous courage to hazard such a dangerous journey.

Even at major crossing sites like Detroit and Niagara, the border was extremely porous. A rowboat was all that was needed to slip across the Detroit or St. Clair Rivers and even the mighty St. Lawrence was little barrier. During the winter it was just a short walk across the frozen rivers. Even when passports were required toward the end of the war, no photographs were included so true identification of the bearer was marginal.

Complicating things was the methodology of espionage. Today spies can carry information in reduced format such as photographic microdots, electronic chips or not carry it at all, sending it by radio burst transmission via satellite. During the Civil War, agents and couriers had to carry the material on their person in the form of paper messages. If stopped and searched whether they were caught or not often depended on how cleverly the material was hidden. Papers could be sealed into book covers, sewed into dresses or men's clothing or written in invisible ink on innocuous correspondence. They could even be pressed into button like shapes and sewn onto clothing.

To combat the actions of the many Southern agents as well as the various plots hatching against the Union, both the U.S. State Department and Army sent counter spies into Canada. A number were successful in infiltrating into Confederate operations and keeping the North well appraised as each intrigue matured. As the war progressed and Confederate use of Canada as safe haven stressing the declared neutrality increased, the Governor General also used agents to keep the Southerners in check, feeding the results of his efforts to various U.S. consuls as appropriate.

Canada's Fears

Canada of course was still known as British North America, a colony of Great Britain but none the less Canadians had a very apprehensive view of the U.S. Paranoid Canadian political leaders saw the U.S. as an aggressive neighbor who could likely attack them once they finished off the South.

Canada saw the United States in the mid-1800s as a dangerously aggressive country which would eventually attack Canada when strong enough. After the outbreak of war in 1861 Colonel Garnet Wolseley, on assignment to the British Army in Canada, recommended to his superiors that the Confederates be officially given diplomatic status. Such meddling in nonmilitary affairs didn't help the political climate between the two nations. Woolsey, however, thought such status could help balance U.S. potential aggression.[2]

Complicating relations was the knowledge that it was clearly in Britain's political interests to have the South succeed, thus dividing the U.S. into two relatively weak countries rather than a single powerful one. Britain was the lone world "super power." The U.S. was on the path to becoming one, so cutting her down was a good outcome.

General Canadian opinion held the South merely wanted to make its own way in the world with a clear contrast in political and cultural differences than the North. This was not much different than what the original colonies did in 1776. In reinforcement of this idea, some Canadian newspapers called the war the "American Revolution."

Worried about potential Northern aggression, the Canadian Minister of Colonial Defense considered increasing the active militia to 100,000 men. In addition, Britain formulated a response to a possible U.S. invasion force striking north through the traditional Hudson Valley-Lake Champlain route. At the first warning of such a move, the British planned to capture the forts on the U.S. side of the international border. This counterstrike would slow any Northern advance. To stiffen the Canadian militia, a 50,000 man British expeditionary force would reinforce the 25,000 men already garrisoning Montreal to delay an American advance. This was of course only a plan and tempered by military and economic reality.

Britain also planned to use her maritime might. As the most powerful naval force in the world she would be foolish not to employ it to her greatest benefit. The Royal Navy would employ a two-pronged plan; attack U.S. warships and merchant vessels on the high seas and blockade northern ports. In theory it was a naval slam dunk! But theory is one thing and reality quite another. The reality was the U.S. was building ironclads and iron warships in copious numbers since the success of the "cheese box on a raft," the *USS Monitor* in her fight with the bigger *CSS Virginia* in Hampton Roads in March 1862. Remember, too, the first iron-hulled warship in the world was built in the U.S. The *U.S.S. Michigan*, launched in 1844, predated the French *Glorie*, the first ocean going ironclad commissioned in 1860 and British *HMS Warrior*, Britain's first iron hulled warship commissioned in August 1861. Given the success of the unique *Monitor* design, the U.S. Navy began producing many of the unusual craft. While the first ones were not especially seaworthy, later ones were. In fact, following the war, a

The USS Monitor, *called by detractors nothing more than a "cheesebox on a raft" proved a powerful naval craft.*

small flotilla crossed the Atlantic on a "show the flag" mission to Britain. In point of fact, the Royal Navy had nothing comparable to the U.S. ironclads although they were embarking on a major iron shipbuilding program. While the British sailing navy could rule the high seas and wreak havoc on merchant shipping, if the fleet as existed during the Civil War closed with the coast in tight blockade or attempted to land troops, U.S. ironclads would chew up the wooden ships and spit 'em out! This bit of jingoism aside, the U.S. ironclad ships gave major pause to any British plans for armed intervention.

Hysteria was further inflamed when firebrand U.S. newspapers demanded the annexation of Canada in December 1864. Doubtless they were goaded into such demands by the continued Canadian support for the South.

Rumors played a role in U.S. - Canada relations. In 1861, when General Scott was in Europe, it was reported (gossiped) he was negotiating a deal with France that would return French Canada to them if they would support the U.S. in the event of a British war. Another rumor claimed the North would seize all British assets in the U.S. A third had the U.S. realize it couldn't conquer the South so instead it would grab Canada in compensation. While such rumors were common during war, they none the less raised the stress level of all sides.

Recruiting and Deserting

Both the U.S. and Canadian citizens and authorities were unhappy with the dual issues of recruiting soldiers for both Union and Confederacy from Canada and the large number of deserters seeking refuge in Canada.

Once the Monitor *design proved itself in combat the U.S. Navy quickly built a fleet of 50 of the powerful warships.*

Union recruiters from the border states, especially Michigan and the Buffalo area of New York, saw Canada as a fertile ground for finding new soldiers. Confederate recruiters saw the same opportunities and were also adept at exploiting them. That such activity was a violation of Canadian neutrality as proclaimed by Queen Victoria on May 13, 1861 and the Foreign Enlistment Act of 1819 was of no mind, efforts by the Canadian Governor General to prevent Canadians from being recruited were also largely ineffective.

How many Canadian citizens joined the Union Army is debatable; figures range from 38,000 to 100,000. The most common number is around 40,000. While this can be taken as prima fascia evidence of Canadian support for the Northern cause, like most things, it can be complicated. Support for the North was higher in the beginning of the war when it was seen more as a crusade for slave freedom and also as a short war. Canadians enlisted in the North for the same reasons other men did; a sense of right and wrong and, in many instances, a desire to escape the drudgery of mind-numbing and soul sapping farming for a chance to see a bit of the world. Enthusiasm was so great at the start of the war, a Canadian Militia Colonel attempted to raise an entire 1,000 man regiment of lancers to be armed with sabers, carbines, pistols and lances for the Union. When the colonel applied for leave from his duties as a Militia officer, he was refused and later arrested for accepting a commission in a foreign army. Eventually all charges were dropped for lack of jurisdiction and he was in effect "cashiered" from the Militia.[3]

As the war dragged on and the Southern propaganda became more effective, support for the North faltered, as did enlistments.

When the U.S. began offering bounties for enlistment, the money was attractive enough to entice British soldiers stationed in Canada to desert for Union blue. Some payments ran as high as $250 after passing the surgeon's perfunctory check, $1,250 on enlisting and 1,160 acres at the end of the war. Considering Imperial soldiers could receive as little as six cents a day, the bounties were heady stuff. The desertion problem was significant enough that a special squad of British soldiers was stationed at the Windsor - Detroit ferry crossing to apprehend soldiers attempting to desert.

Efforts to attract the well trained British Regulars were often effective. In one instance 27 men deserted from one company of the 30th Regiment en masse. If the authorities caught a runner, the penalty was harsh. As prescribed in the Queen's Regulations the letter "D" for deserter was tattooed on his chest among other penalties.[4]

American Army justice for deserters was even harsher. During the Mexican - American War members of the infamous St. Patrick Battalion, a Mexican Army unit made up of Irish deserters from the American Army were especially punished. Those who were later caught were hung outright as traitors or given 50 lashes, had a two inch letter "D" branded into their skin with a red hot iron and wore heavy iron collars for the rest of the war. Neither the British or Americans took desertion lightly.

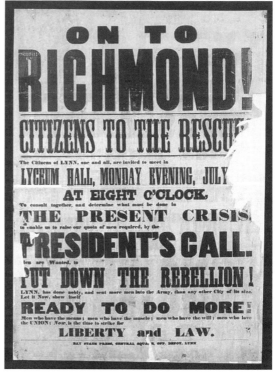

Recruiting was a constant and critical activity for both North and South.

Canadian men also took advantage of the bounties to cross the border, enlist and collect the bounty, then run back to Canada. It wasn't uncommon for some to do it again and again. Northern men also took the bounty and deserted, an act known as "bounty jumping."

Crimping or "Shanghaiing" men into the army was commonplace although both the North and Canadians tried to stop it.[5] As long as the North offered a bounty, it was a practice bound to continue. The Canadians countered with bounties of their own for apprehending Yankee enlistment officers or anyone trying to shanghai anyone.

The Canadian border areas also became a haven for Union Army deserters especially after the Conscription Act in March 1863. Reputedly there were so many "skedaddlers" in Canada they flooded the job market with cheap labor, in some instances willing to work without pay, just for room and board. Of course the U.S. wanted the deserters caught and returned to Federal custody. Canadians claimed they hadn't broken any Canadian laws so there was no basis for action. The issue would be an open wound between the two nations with the U.S. taking it as clear Canadian support of the Confederacy. In at least one instance, U.S. detectives went to Windsor and seized men involved in enticing men to desert. In another instance, Union soldiers entered a private home on Wolfe Island (in Canada) and hauled a deserter back to the U.S. Both actions engendered strong diplomatic protests.

Canadian authorities also crossed the border to drag back deserters too. A squad from a Canadian gunboat on the St. Clair River apprehended a deserter from the U.S. side of the river and Canadian police nabbed a couple of thieves back to their jurisdiction from Port Huron, Michigan. However, neither violation of sovereignty provoked a response from the U.S.

References

Confederate Military History - http://en.wikisource.org/wiki/Page:Confederate_Military_-History_-_1899_-Volume_1.djvu/557.

Michigan Historical Center, *Michigan and the Civil War, An Anthology,* (Lansing, Michigan: Michigan Historical Center, 1999), 115 - 118.

New York Times, July 31, 1872.

William F. Raney, "Recruiting and Crimping in Canada for the Northern Forces, 1861-1865," *The Mississippi Valley Historical Review*, Vol. 10, No. 1 (June 1923), 21-33.

Frank Howard Serverance, *Peace Conference at Niagara Falls 1864,* (Cornell University Press, 1914), 80-84.

Clark C. Spence, Robin W. Winks *William "Colorado" Jewett of the Niagara Falls Conference" *The Historian*, Volume 23, Issue 1, pp. 21-53.

William A. Tidwell, *Confederate Covert Action in the American Civil War - April '65,* (Kent, Ohio: Kent State University Press, 1995), 30-32, 35, 135, 155-159, 243.

Robin W. Winks, *Canada and the United States - The Civil War Years,* (Baltimore: Johns Hopkins Press, 1960), 179,193-195, 201.

Footnotes

[1] Slavery also existed in the North as evidenced by the infamous Dred Scott in 1857 although it gradually disappeared during the war and was eliminated by the 13th Amendment in 1865.

[2] Field Marshall Garnet Joseph Wolseley, 1st Viscount (4 June 1833-25 March 1913) was a highly decorated British army officer. His foreign service included Burma, the Crimean War, the Indian Mutiny, China, Canada, and widely throughout Africa and the Nile Expedition against Mahdist Sudan in 1884-85. His stellar reputation for efficiency led to the late 19th-century English phrase "everything's all Sir Garnet", meaning "all is in order." In short, his evaluation of the Canadian defense situation was highly regarded.

[3] William F. Raney, "Recruiting and Crimping in Canada for the Northern Forces, 1861-1865," *The Mississippi Valley Historical Review*, Vol. 10, No. 1 (June 1923), 22-23.

[4] Raney, 25.

[5] Shanghaiing is the old practice of conscripting men as sailors by methods such as trickery, intimidation, or violence. The men who did it were called crimps.

CHAPTER THREE

NAVIGATION

There were five major navigation assets vital to the Great Lakes at the beginning of the Civil War. All were vulnerable to Confederate interdiction and potential targets for direct attack or sabotage. Remember this was a "civil" war while opposing soldiers wore easily identifiable uniforms, civilians traveled about usually unchallenged. A wagon loaded with gunpowder could move undetected through areas that today would be guarded securely.

Erie Canal

The Erie Canal runs about 363 miles from Albany, New York, on the Hudson River to Buffalo, New York, at Lake Erie. Construction started in 1817 and the canal opened in 1825. It marked the first reliable transportation system between the eastern seaboard, namely New York, and the eastern Great Lakes. Most important, no portaging was required anywhere along the system. Canal boats were loaded at one end and not unloaded until the other end. Transportation cost was cut by 95% as compared to overland. It also provided easy transportation west for an expanding population,

The locks on the Erie were lucrative targets for sabotage.

opening the Great Lakes to a flood of immigrants. New York soon became the primary port of entry for European new citizens, many of whom would travel up the Hudson and use the canal to settle in the Old Northwest. For example, over 300,000 immigrants landed in New York between 1840 and 1845, but the population of the city increased by only 80,000. Many of the immigrants simply passed through New York bound west on the Erie.

The original canal was a mere four feet deep and 40 feet wide, included 83 locks and 18 aqueducts to enable boats to cross various ravines and rivers. The rise from the Hudson River to Lake Erie was 568 feet and each canal boat could carry 30 tons of freight.

It wasn't long before the canal made New York City the premier port in the U.S., serving as the gateway for the produce of the Great Lakes to reach the world and the products of the world to market in the Great Lakes. To handle the increasing demands of traffic, the canal was enlarged between 1836 and 1862. The new canal was 70 feet wide and 7 feet deep, and could handle boats carrying 240 tons. The use of bigger locks reduced the number to 72.

The canal also allowed New York to stay ahead of traditional rivals New Orleans and Montreal for international commerce and indirectly worked to preserve the Union. Prior to the canal, the bulk of the agricultural products from the Great Lakes (Old Northwest) and the Ohio Valley were shipped south via the Mississippi River to New Orleans. By the 1830s, the canal was the cheapest transportation system from the interior to the world and drained much of the traditional Mississippi traffic. When the railroads finally arrived, the canal was firmly established as the preferred highway to New York, the nation's most dominant and productive commercial center.

The success of the Erie Canal spawned a canal building boom in New York. Between 1823 and 1828, several lateral canals opened including the Champlain, the Oswego and the Cayuga-Seneca. All fed commerce to New York and reverse.

The canal also played two important roles during the Civil War. Politically it was critical in keeping the political and economic support of the Old Northwest and its loyalty to the Union. The canal provided a vital outlet for the agricultural products of the west. If it didn't exist, or was destroyed or damaged, the most obvious path to export was down the Mississippi to New Orleans. This would have created a strong commercial association with the South. Since the South was primarily an agricultural region as were large portions of the Old Northwest, the political implications for North and South loyalty is obvious. As long as it operated, the canal was a powerful bond between the industrial east and agricultural west. Without the canal, the only way Great Lakes commodities could reach market was through New Orleans and a threat of a Southern blockade would have massive economic impact. Had the Northwest "gone south" it is fair to argue the Union was doomed. If the canal was destroyed during the war by Confederate sabotage, the South would have had a stranglehold on the Old Northwest states. Perhaps worse, the lack of exports from the region reaching New York would have knocked the port from its number one ranking being replaced by New

The Erie canal moved an ever increasing amount of critical freight during the Civil War.

Orleans. The farms along the eastern seaboard didn't produce enough export to replace the missing Great Lakes trade. Said another way, for the Union to keep the economic, political and military support of the Great Lakes states, the Erie Canal needed to exist and continue to operate.

From a pure tonnage perspective the value of the canal during the war was staggering. By 1860, freight totals had increased to 1,896,975 tons eastbound and 379,000 tons westbound. In 1862, only a year into the war, canal freight grew to 3,000,000 tons and in 1863 over 5,500,000 tons.

Given the number of locks and aqueducts and the inherent fragility of a narrow industrial artery 363 miles long, it was a high value target. Had the Confederates interdicted it at any point, it would have caused the immediate diversion of Federal forces to guard against future attacks. The Confederates didn't have to "destroy" the canal but just a lock or aqueduct or two. One way or another, the Federal redirection of forces to protect the canal would have impacted those available for the battlefield. The Buffalo terminus was targeted in Lieutenant Minor's original Great Lakes plan as discussed in Chapter 6.

Welland Canal

The Welland Canal is a 27-mile long waterway through Canada connecting Lakes Ontario and Erie. It cuts through the Welland Peninsula allowing shipping to navigate around the 297-foot high Niagara Escarpment. It literally allows ships to go around Niagara Falls.

There were four Welland Canals, each an improvement on the previous. The current canal carries roughly 40 million tons of cargo annually. All versions were vital to the importance of Montreal, Detroit, Chicago, Windsor and Cleveland as it allowed eventual transit to the ocean (transshipping at Montreal).

The first canal opened in 1829 running from Port Dalhousie on Lake Ontario via circuitous route using existing rivers and lakes to Lake Erie. The 40 locks certainly complicated the voyage. The second canal with 27 locks became operational in 1854, concurrent with the opening of the Erie and Ontario Railway, running along the old portage road. Five years later, the Welland Railway opened parallel to the canal. Rather than compete with the canal, the Welland Railway was part of the system and provided transfer services to ships too large to fit into the canal locks.

The canal was an important concentration point for Confederate agents and sympathizers. Anyone traveling by water between Montreal, Quebec, Toronto, et. al., to points west such as Detroit or Windsor, had to use the canal. It was a perfect place to pass information, load equipment or personnel or transfer other material.

The second canal with its associated railway were both vital navigation assets to the Great Lakes and the industrial base on the U.S. side. Loss or disruption of the canal by accident or sabotage would negatively impact the Federal war machine.

Sabotage to the Welland wasn't unknown and is indicative of how relatively easy it was to damage. Although there have been a number of plots against the canal, only two have actually been carried out. The first was in September 1841 when a gate at lock 37 was destroyed by an explosive charge. Damage was mitigated when an upstream gate held, preventing a flood of water from rolling down the canal causing further destruction and perhaps death. Although never proved, it was believed an Irish-Catholic terrorist was responsible for the blast.

A second attack was in April 1900 at lock 24 when a charge of dynamite was set off against the hinges. The amount of explosive used was too small to cause more than minor damage.

Following the war, Port Colborne at the south entrance of the canal became a gathering place for many ex-Confederates hoping not only to escape the stifling southern heat but to them the equally stifling political atmosphere of Reconstruction. By the 1880's the town was an important summer tourist resort with passenger steamers and trains delivering hundreds of "summer folk" daily. A popular destination for many of the Southerners was the Humberstone Club. Included in the annual migration was Mrs. Jefferson Davis, wife of the former president of the Confederacy.

Ohio & Erie Canal

The success of the Erie Canal led directly to the construction of the 308-mile-long Ohio and Erie Canal completed in 1834 between Cleveland and Portsmouth, Ohio. It was considered the final link in an extensive waterway linking the Great Lakes with the Mississippi River System. Commodities loaded at Cleveland and intermediate points could travel from Ohio via the Mississippi to New Orleans and from Cleveland

A typical scene on the Ohio and Erie.

east to the Erie Canal and New York. For a time it was a vital part of the growing national transportation system. The 40-foot wide canal consisted of 146 locks with a change in elevation of 1,266-feet between the Ohio River and Lake Erie.

It also played a major role in establishing Ohio's economic development including industrial, commercial and political sectors. Not only did it provide cheap transportation but also waterpower to power manufacturing along the canal. From a population perspective this also opened new areas for settlement and development. The cities of Cleveland, Akron and Massillon also thrived transforming into leaders in shipping and production of grain, iron and steel.

Although the canal lost its major shipping role just prior to the Civil War when competition from railroads superseded it, it still provided waterpower to industry along its banks. Like the Erie Canal, its many locks were all vulnerable to sabotage with resulting industrial disturbance.

Miami & Erie Canal

The Miami and Erie Canal built between 1825 to 1845 ran 249 miles from Toledo to Cincinnati and the Ohio River. Its 19 aqueducts and 105 lift locks raised canal boats 395 feet above Lake Erie, and 513 above the river at Cincinnati. Soon after completion the canal was in stiff competition from railroads, which were expanding rapidly throughout Ohio. By the Civil War, the canal's importance had dropped significantly but it still provided a viable transportation link. Prior to the war, however, it was an important contributor to the state's economic success.

Illinois and Michigan Canal

Completed in 1848, the Illinois & Michigan Canal linked the Chicago River with the Illinois River at LaSalle. The 96-mile long waterway consisted of 15 lift locks, five aqueducts, and four hydraulic power basins. Economically and politically it helped change the center of Midwest trade from St. Louis to Chicago. This was especially true during the Civil War when the Union blockaded Southern ports greatly hindering trade from St. Louis, via the Mississippi River to New Orleans. While passenger travel initially was heavy on the canal, once the railroads began, the trade shifted to the much faster trains. However, the canal was extremely important for bulk commodities especially grain, lumber and stone. In 1864, 288 canal boats were so engaged.

The canal also was a significant potential military asset. The Rush - Bagot treaty limited the number, size and armament of warships, the U.S. and British Great Lakes warships. With diplomatic relations with Britain coming under severe stress for a number of reasons including *Trent* Affair and British "belligerent nation" recognition of the Confederacy, war was increasingly likely. From a naval aspect, the need to move Union ironclad and monitor warships through protected waters as well as quickly through internal canals was vital. In this case it was to allow the protected gunboats in the Mississippi to make their way up the Ohio to Lake Michigan. Considering British warships could enter the Great Lakes through the St. Lawrence River to Lake Ontario and the Welland Canal to Lake Erie and the western lakes, lake-borne trade and ports would be at the mercy of a British fleet. To counter the threat, American engineers worked to develop methods to decrease the draft of such ironclad warships as well as quickly increase the size of canals and locks to permit quick passage. The House of Representatives added emphasis to the need, instructing the Committee on Roads and

The Illinois and Michigan Canal in the spring with boats waiting for freight.

Before the Soo Locks Sault Ste. Marie was a backwater village existing on portaging small amounts of freight and the occasional ship around the rapids.

Canals to investigate the potential of increasing the waterway to allow steam navigation between the Mississippi and Great Lakes. When it became clear the British were not going to militarily support the South, canal planning ceased.

Saint Marys Falls Canal (aka Soo Locks)

The locks at Sault Ste. Marie, Michigan, allowing quick and economical passage between Lakes Huron and Superior were critical to the Lake Superior iron and copper trade. Both were key to developing the Union industrial might that eventually overcame the Confederacy.

Prior to the locks, all cargo had to be unloaded and portaged around the rapids on the St. Marys River, then reloaded on another vessel. It was a difference in elevation of roughly 21-feet, a not inconsequential amount for shipping. The portage was over a mile in length and involved a rickety plank railroad, wagons and oxen or mules. The only way for ships to go up or down was the same way, portage. Each vessel had to be hauled out of the water onto large rollers and slowly pulled around the rapids by oxen teams, then laboriously launched in the river above or below the rapids. Whether ship or just cargo, it was a long, slow and very expensive process that was strangling the development of Lake Superior commerce and national industrialization.

Michigan Governor Stevens T. Mason proposed a canal as early as 1837 but his recommendation didn't gain traction until 1852 when Congress officially authorized the construction by providing a land grant to the state to pay for it.

Work began June 4, 1853 and the canal was completed in April of 1855, finally removing the major deterrent to efficient iron and copper mining in the Lake Superior region. Lock dimensions were 350 feet long by 70 feet wide, with a depth over the sills of 11 feet six inches.

When the locks opened in 1855 the entire mineral bounty of Lake Superior was open for full exploitation by a hungry nation.

The first year the locks opened, 1,447 tons went through on various brigs and schooners. Coincidently, the first cargo of iron ore through the locks, 132- tons consigned to the Cleveland Iron Mining Company of Cleveland was carried by the brig *Columbia*. This was the same vessel that carried the first deck load of six barrels of ore from Marquette in 1852.

The Soo Locks were also indirectly tied to railroad development. In 1864 a new rail line was completed between the Marquette Range mines and the port of Escanaba on northern Lake Michigan. The rail line assured a longer year of shipping as Michigan froze later than Superior and opened earlier in the spring but also was a vital alternative if the Soo Locks were destroyed thus blocking all Superior shipping. Remember the Soo Locks were targeted for destruction in the original plan developed by Lieutenant Robert Murdaugh, Confederate Navy. See Chapter 6.

Lighthouses

Safe navigation was critical to the movement of people and cargo and effective lighthouses were part of the equation. While major lights were more important than minor ones, the loss of any light would impact the system. Therefore each lighthouse was a potential target for Confederate sabotage and destruction. The tower didn't need to be blown up, just take a hammer and smash up the lens or rotating mechanism. No clockworks or lens equaled no light and maritime mishaps would surely result!

Such destruction wasn't alien to the Confederates. The rebels were careful to destroy many Southern lights to prevent their use by blockading Union warships. Why provide friendly beacon for patrolling Yankee warships?

Whitefish Point Lighthouse, a critical navigation beacon for iron ore freighters.

References

Chicago and the Civil War - http://picturingchicago.nl.edu/explor5.pdf

Clinton's Big Ditch - http://www.eriecanal.org/.

Digging Clinton's Ditch - http://xroads.virginia.edu/~MA02/volpe/canal/impact.html.

Engineering the Erie Canal - http://www.americanheritage.com/articles/magazine/it/1986/1/1986_1_50.shtml.

Erie Canal Time Machine - http://www.archives.nysed.gov/projects/eriecanal/essays/ec_larkin4.shtml.

The Erie Canal, a Brief History - http://www.canals.ny.gov/cculture/history/.

Experience Port Colborne - http://www.portcolborne.com/page/history.

Rita L. Frese and David M. Young, Editors, *From Lumber Hookers to the Hooligan Fleet, A Treasury of Chicago Maritime History*, (Lake Claremont Press: Chicago, 2007), 79.

Sarah V.E. Harvey, comp. *Jubilee Annals of the Lake Superior Ship Canal - The World's Greatest Mechanical Waterway*, (Cleveland: Press of the J.B. Savage Company, 1906), 26-27.

Charles Moore, ed. *The Saint Marys Falls Canal - Exercises at the Semi-Centennial Celebration at Sault Ste. Marie, Michigan, August 2 and 3, 1905; Together With a History of the Canal by John H. Goff and Papers Relating to the Great Lakes*, (Detroit: Semi-Centennial Commission, 1907).

History of Port Dalhousie - http://www.portmemories.com/.

Illinois and Michigan Canal - http://encyclopedia.chicagohistory.org/pages/626.html.

Benjamin Lett - http://en.wikipedia.org/wiki/Benjamin_Lett..

Miami and Ohio Canal History - http://www.hiking.ohiotrail.com/trails/canal-history.htm.

New York Times, September 5, 1890.

Ohio and Erie Canal - http://wapedia.mobi/en/Ohio_and_Erie_Canal

Ohio and Erie Canal National Heritage Corridor - http://www.nps.gov/nr/travel/ohio-eriecanal/oec.htm.

The Ohio and Erie Canal - http://www.hmdb.org/marker.asp?marker=15190.

Welland Canal - http://en.wikipedia.org/wiki/Welland_Canal.

Chapter Four
An Industrial War

This chapter isn't an effort to exhaustively analyze the Great Lakes economy as it relates to the Civil War but instead to make the reader aware of some of the key components of it and potential for Southern attack. If the Confederacy had been more adept at striking out at Union industrial targets on the Great Lakes, it could have significantly impacted the Northern war effort.

At the start of the Civil War, the U.S. was harvesting a number of mineral resources including gold, coal, salt, petroleum, silver, iron and copper. Most of the gold and silver was coming from California, Nevada, Idaho and Montana. Pennsylvania was producing the bulk of the coal and petroleum and in 1860, half of the iron ore. By 1864, 80 percent of the anthracite pig iron was from the keystone state. Pennsylvania has a long history of iron production dating from Colonial times. The area around the Appalachian Mountains west of Philadelphia had deposits of iron ore, hardwoods, and limestone deposits, which led to many small iron furnaces rather than large consolidated industry. Other iron deposits were found nearby in Southern Ohio and northern Kentucky but overall the production was small and very localized to the point, that at one period over 500 iron furnaces were running at the same time. While the many small operators were sufficient for a pre-industrial America, when spurred by the great need of the industrial war, Pennsylvania operations were hopelessly inefficient but critically needed, regardless, because of the massive increase in demand. Wherever it came from, iron was needed.

Iron (and steel) was indispensable for all manner of war equipment: iron for cladding warships, cannon, rifles, bayonets, steam engines, locomotives, rails and shells are just a few. Copper was needed for sheathing the bottom of wooden ships for protection against marine worms, to make bronze field pieces, brass buttons, cartridges and telegraph wires as well as a host of other applications.

Overshadowing the tremendous surge in Northern industrial growth needed to meet military demands at the outbreak of the war was the incredible damage done to the national banking system by the nearly $300 million of uncollectible Southern debt to Northern banks. Prior to the war the North and South were thoroughly economically bound together regardless of the huge cultural divide of the coming conflict. Rebellion literally ripped the financial system of the nation apart. Thousands of banks collapsed or failed with the result that credit needed for rapid industrial expansion was in very short supply.

Steel manufacturing expanded little during the war with most of the needs imported from Britain. Although the Bessemer process was first used in the U.S. in 1862 at the

Eureka Iron Works in Wyandotte, Michigan, on the Detroit River south of Detroit, it was not completely developed until 1864. Bessemer steel was not made in the U.S. on large scale until after the war, leaving the nation virtually dependent on British imports for this vital commodity.

Most of the Union's salt was provided by New York until the war shifted into high gear at which point the old sources could not meet the new demands. The salt shortage from traditional sources was exacerbated when mines in Virginia and Ohio were destroyed. This basic mineral was vital for the preservation of meat and since armies move on their stomachs and salted meat was a vital commodity for keeping stomachs "mobile," it was a product of some importance. It was also used in the manufacture of glass, soap and medicine. When large and easily recoverable deposits of salt were discovered under Michigan's Saginaw Valley, it too became a major supplier. By 1862, 23 salt companies were operating in the area.

All of these minerals were critical for waging an industrial war. Fortunately for the Union, adequate supplies of all were located in Northern states.

At the start of the war, Philadelphia was the largest manufacturing center in the nation and spurred by wartime demands, continued to grow. In 1862, 58 new factories were built, 57 in 1863 and 65 more in 1864. Philly was a monster hungry for raw materials.

Iron

Although a dozen different iron "ranges" would eventually operate in the Lake Superior region, including Michigan, Wisconsin and Minnesota, only the Marquette Range was producing ore during the Civil War.

The Marquette Range was the first discovered in the early 1840s. Michigan State geologist Douglas Houghton found traces of iron during his early jaunts through the Upper Peninsula but it was William A. Burt, a U.S. Deputy Surveyor, who discovered the first major deposits in the hills west of Marquette when his magnetic compass began to swing wildly. Uncertain of what was causing the dancing needle Burt reputedly told his crew, "Boys, look around and see what you can find." What they found was a key foundation of national growth. Later and more detailed surveys revealed an ore body, "whose purity and magnitude are unrivaled." The area was utter wilderness with the nearest human habitation at the small mission community of Sault Ste. Marie, Michigan, 160 miles to the east.

In the early days, iron mining was comparatively easy. The prospectors who discovered the deposit later named the Jackson Mine reported, "a mountain of iron ore, 150 feet high." The nearby Cleveland "mine" deposit was said to be a ridge of ore a mile long, 180-feet high and 1,000-feet wide at the base.

The mines were all relatively shallow, open pit affairs with the first miners breaking it up with picks, sledgehammers and crowbars and shoveling hunks into wagons for transport to the forge. It was still very labor intensive, hammering drills by hand to set explosive charges in the right place to blast the ore or overburden into moveable pieces.

The first ore was mined by the open methods. Only after the easy to reach surface deposits were exhausted did miners go underground.

Eventually companies followed the ore body underground as the shafts went deeper and deeper.

Following the initial exploration, the Jackson Mining Company was formed and mining Michigan ore began in 1849. During the earliest phase of the range, ore was smelted at the mine site using charcoal made from local hardwood. Manhandling iron pigs to the ship was far easier than the raw ore.

Transporting the ore from the mines to Marquette for shipment was one of the first challenges to be overcome. Initially mule drawn sleighs were used but that limited it to winter only and was very slow and expensive. A plank road was better as it was year around, but it was still very slow and hard on the mules which were expensive to replace when worn out or injured, both frequent occurrences. When a railroad was finally built September, 1857, it provided an efficient means of transportation.

It is worth considering the vulnerability of the single railroad from mines to dock. A single charge of gunpowder exploding under one of the many trestles could immobilize it for weeks. The destruction of locomotives could have longer reaching impact. There weren't many of them and replacements would have to come from manufacturers as distant as the east coast. Adding to the potential for disaster the single rail line from mine to harbor couldn't keep up with demand. At the height of the war in 1863, 50 ships were waiting in Marquette for ore! Had the line been interdicted by the South shipping would have stopped entirely.

Marquette was the only port on Lake Superior shipping iron ore until 1876. Clearly it was a potentially fat target for Confederate agents.

The brig Columbia *carried the first cargo of Marquette Range iron through the Soo Locks in 1855.*

Rather than the bulk cargoes we see today the ore was carried in barrels, which were difficult to transport effectively. Moving the first load of ore to market in September 1853 was difficult in the extreme. Although only 152 tons, it took four small schooners to carry the barreled ore to the Soo where it was laboriously unloaded, portaged around the rapids, reloaded on other craft and taken down lakes to Erie, Pennsylvania, reloaded to canal boats and pulled by mule to the Sharon Iron Company in Sharon, Pennsylvania. All in all, it was a cost prohibitive process that nearly strangled the early mining industry.

The need for Lake Superior iron increased dramatically as the intensity of the Civil War escalated with a commensurate increase in shipping. For example, in 1860 the total output for the Marquette Iron Range was 114,401 gross tons; by 1865, it was 243,127 and arced skyward in the following years as the nation sped into the Industrial Age. During the war Marquette ore was used by 52 different furnaces and 34 rolling mills in areas widely scattered as Pittsburgh, Buffalo, Shenango Valley, New Castle, Sharon, Middlesex, Mahoning Valley, Youngstown, Niles, Mineral Ridge, Black River, Cleveland, Toledo, Massillon, Dover, Detroit, Wheeling, Zanesville, Ironton, Cincinnati, Kittanning and many local Upper Peninsula locations.[1] Production facilities were certainly not concentrated but much of the ore, at least that coming from the Marquette Range, was single source.

Once the Soo Locks opened in 1855 it was "Katy, bar the door." The cheap water highway to the mills and foundries of the lower lakes was open for business. The volume of ore shipped increased dramatically. The first year, 1,447 tons on various brigs and schooners took advantage of the locks. By 1860, 114,401 tons were moving through the Soo but briefly fell in 1861 to 49,909 tons with the outbreak of the Civil War. Business was confused with the implications of the war and it took some months before it was clear it would be a long struggle and iron was a vital component of it. That much more iron wasn't shipped is usually credited to a general lack of labor on the range. Men were either off at war or working at city jobs paying more than the difficult and dangerous ones on the desolate range paid. The same labor shortage affected the Michigan copper range.

Critical to shipping the ore was the development of dedicated "ore" docks later called "pocket" docks. The first dock specifically designed and built for loading ore was erected in Marquette in 1857. By later designs it was very crude, essentially nothing more than an elevated flat surface allowing ore in wheelbarrows to more easily be trundled down it and dumped into the vessel. By 1862 the next evolution in the ore dock appeared featuring an elevated railway trestle for ore railcars to dump directly into pockets or holding bins in the dock. When the vessel moored to the dock, a chute from the bottom of the bin was lowered to the vessel, a door opened and a "shot" of ore slid into the vessel. These early docks were the forerunners of those still used today. Schooners too adapted to the important new trade coming out of the yards with regularly spaced hatches to ease loading. Early steamers took a while longer to change and for a time ore had to be loaded through side hatches rather than through ones on deck. During the Civil War there were three operating pocket docks in Marquette.

While loading once the new docks were in place was comparatively easy, unloading was not. An average cargo ran about 300 tons and it took almost four long days to discharge it by hand. A rough staging had to be built into the cargo hold and a team of shovelers dug it out of the hold by hand, level by level, until finally reaching the deck where more men hand loaded it into wheel barrows and pushed it ashore over a narrow and rickety gangway. A later system used a block, tackle and large bucket lowered directly into the hold. A horse provided the lifting power. It was still backbreaking labor to dig it out of the hold by hand. One of the ore docks in Cleveland usually employed about forty horses in the work of unloading a schooner. The greater the efficiency of loading and unloading ore increased the amount shipped and every load was critical to the Union war effort.

It is important to realize these early docks were wood construction and often coated with tar to help prevent deterioration. As a result, they were highly flammable. The loss of a dock by fire or other cause would have literally shut down the bulk of the ore shipments from the Lake Superior mines. The pocket docks were potentially key targets for Confederate sabotage.

Over time prospectors spread out over the entire district looking for new ore bodies and more mines were soon in production. The common denominator being the ore (or cast iron pigs) was all shipped by water, down Lake Superior, through the Soo Locks

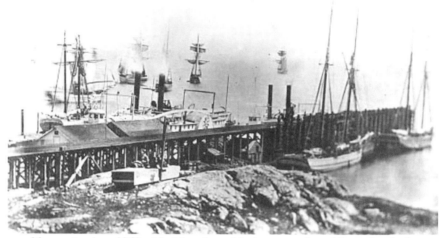

Marquette circa 1863 with ships alongside the very vulnerable pocket dock.

and south to the mills. If this production of iron could be stopped or interrupted, the consequences for the North could be far reaching. Destroy the railroad from mine to ore dock in Marquette, destroy the dock, sink the ship, destroy the lock at the Soo, create labor unrest ashore or afloat, or scare shipping off the lakes with ersatz "privateers", the result was all the same - far less iron for Union forces on the battlefield.

Industrial Transformation

Considering the plentiful iron ore deposits around Lake Superior, the rich coal fields of Pennsylvania and generally easy access to economical water transportation on the Great Lakes, the Midwest soon became a center of U.S. heavy industry.

Chicago is a good example of that transformation. By the early 1850s the city had several iron foundries using iron pigs (ingots) and producing products as diverse as stoves and boilers. In 1857 the first rolling mill started manufacturing iron rails for the quickly growing railroads. Other rolling mills soon followed the original 1857 start-up. In 1865, a Chicago mill was experimenting making rails made out of Bessemer steel, the first such rails produced in the United States. Considering the vast difference in railroads between North and South before and during the war and the vital part railroads played in moving entire armies and their constant supply, Chicago's role in providing the critical rails for new lines and repair of old, was nothing short of critical to Union success. If the South could stop the manufacture of rails, either at the factory or at the source of the iron, battlefield impact could be significant. Wars were not just fought by armies slugging it out on the battlefield, but by factories in the rear areas, too! By 1861 Chicago was the major railroad center in the U.S. linking Great Lakes states with the east coast.[2]

The popular Napoleon 12 pound cannon was made in both iron and brass.

Detroit also felt the sharp growth in iron-based manufacturing companies increasing by 174 percent between 1860-1870. The Michigan Car Company, the Detroit Bridge and Iron Works, the Detroit Safe Company, and the E. T. Barnum Wire and Iron Works were among plants started during the war and greatly expanded as the conflict grew. As in Chicago, stop the iron flow and the factories grind to a halt.

Besides handling an ocean of grain, Buffalo was also part of the iron trade. The Navy's first ironclad warship, the *USS Monitor*, the "cheese box on a raft" that emerged from the early morning mist at Hampton Roads, Virginia, in March 1862 to battle the much larger *CSS Virginia* to a standstill and save the Union fleet from destruction, had critical parts manufactured in the city. The Niagara Steam Forge Works produced the turret's port stoppers, heavy iron closures in the turret, which opened when the cannon was to be fired.

As in Chicago, labor unrest and racial tension were common. In late July and early August 1863, roughly one hundred Irish dockworkers and longshoremen walked off the job, striking to protest low wages. The question of whether the agitators were Confederate agents is fascinating. Anything to disrupt the Union rear was an advantage to the South. Employers responded by hiring black workers in place of the Irish. Since the Emancipation Proclamation was only months old, strikebreaking by blacks hit hard with the Irish. Are the Irish supposed to fight on the battlefields for a people who only steal their jobs at home? It took four regiments of infantry to restore order, soldiers who could better be used at the front. Tension along the docks increased.

Copper

Although Michigan copper was mined by prehistoric Indians and sought by early explorers, it was Michigan State Geologist Douglas Houghton who really publicized its remarkable availability and richness. After his survey report became public in 1841, it started a great rush of prospectors eager to find their fortune in the wild Upper Peninsula. The great copper deposits were located in a belt running roughly 100 miles southwestward through Ontonagon, Houghton and Keweenaw Counties.

Copper mining in the Upper Peninsula boomed and from 1845 until 1887 (when it was exceeded by Butte, Montana) the area was the leading producer of copper. In most years from 1850 through 1881, Michigan produced more than three-quarters of the nation's copper, and in 1869 produced more than 95% of the country's copper.

Copper from the Upper Peninsula mines was critical to the North during the Civil war, never dipping below 60% of the total consumed. Much of the shortfall had to be shipped in from California at great expense. The excellent transportation system of the Great Lakes was vital in moving the copper to the manufacturer. Once the Tariff Act of 1861 took effect, diminishing imports of copper from Chile, Michigan was the major supplier. As with iron, disrupt the mines, smelters, close off the shipping and the lack of copper impacts the Union war effort.

During the war there was a change in how copper was used. Previous to the war copper was important to sheath the bottom of wooden ships to prevent marine worm infestation. With the advent of iron hulled ships the use of copper for sheathing disappeared. Greater use of iron and steel for products such as pots and pans also decreased the need for copper. However, copper was needed for bronze cannons, military brass buttons, copper canteens, and various army and navy equipment. Bronze field artillery was highly desirable by cannon cockers for its durability and strength although iron and steel were far cheaper.

While the threat of Confederate sabotage of the Michigan copper and iron mines was always present, the greater wartime danger came from civil and labor unrest. The bulk of the population was young males as would be expected in a mining areas. The

The pre-Civil War Cliffs Mine was in full production when the Civil War erupted.

Unlike early iron mining, copper miners had to follow the veins underground from the start.

cloak of civilization was still a thin one. Bars and brawling were common outlets for excess energy. Although there was no real effort at this early period to organize miners, men often took a personal view of company labor practices. The situation was serious enough the Cliff Mine briefly organized a company militia to protect their interests in the event of "trouble."

The Grain Trade

While iron and copper were the "pointy end of the stick" in terms of military might, armies move on their stomachs and the grain trade was critical.

Buffalo was an especially important grain port. By 1846 more flour and wheat were shipping through Buffalo than New Orleans. The United States Bureau of Statistics stated that in 1860 the "bulk of produce of the Ohio Valley had been diverted to the lakes and Atlantic seaboard; but probably one fifth of it found its way to New Orleans." Buffalo's location at the western terminus of the Erie Canal was a perfect location to capitalize on the trade. A network of smaller canals stemming from the Erie Canal also benefited the city.

In 1855 the Buffalo Board of Trade proclaimed, "Buffalo is now universally acknowledged to be the greatest grain market on the Continent, not even excepting the City of New York." It continued to hold the lead until well into the 20th Century. Much of the grain to Buffalo was from Chicago. By 1861 Chicago's grain trade had increased to 50 million bushels a year, an increase of over 48 million bushels from ten years prior. It was said Chicago "fed the world."

As Marquette was the location of the first iron ore pocket dock, Buffalo was the site of the first grain elevator. By 1860, eleven elevators where on the waterfront and providing a storage capacity of over one-and-a-half-million bushels. Sixteen more were added during the war pushing Buffalo past London, Odessa, and Rotterdam to become the world's largest grain port. As with other period infrastructure, elevators were made of wood and extremely flammable. A dedicated Confederate saboteur with "Greek Fire" could wreak havoc.[3] Elevators were targeted by Confederate arsonists as well as competing elevator operators and anti-American terrorists from Canada. They were huge "soft" targets.

Feeding the Army

Chicago's role as a meat packer also boomed during the war. For example, in 1860, 270,000 hogs were slaughtered. With the stimulus of the war, it was soon more than 900,000. Disrupt the meat packing business and it impacts the battlefield. It is worth realizing that a considerable amount of meat packed in Chicago ended up in the South. Often the packed meat was shipped to Nye, New York, then "exported" on foreign flag ships to Canada before being reloaded (or direct shipping dependent on circumstance)

Providing canned (packed) meat for rations was important to the Army.

for Bermuda and a blockade runner in the South. Alternatively, it could go direct from New York City to Britain then to Bermuda and the South. Profit was excellent as should be expected.[4] Business rarely knows loyalty when in search of profit.

Both grain and meat were vital war winning commodities. The Union Army had to be fed and at the end of the war it numbered roughly a million men. Add in a growing civilian population and the importance of food as a war-critical material is evident. The ability to provide grain was tied not just to transportation but also to mechanization of farming. Devices such as the McCormick reaper, gang plow, thresher and mower were critical to producing more grain with less manpower, the latter being diverted into the Union Army. All of these devices were contingent on manufacturing and, in turn, on iron.

Labor Shortages

Labor was a war-winning commodity, too. Whatever the industrial job, it took men to do it and men were often in short supply. As immigrants poured off ships from Europe, Army recruiters were at the dock to welcome them, as were recruiters for industry. Both iron and copper mines suffered shortages of labor. Attracting men to work in the remote Lake Superior mining districts was difficult and expensive. Several of the companies went to the extreme of sending recruiters to Europe but when the new miners reached the U.S. they took jobs elsewhere or even enlisted in the Army. For some men, trading volleys of .58 caliber minie balls with Johnny Reb was preferable to working on the "range" or at least that was what Army recruiters convinced them of.

Labor shortages plagued both iron and copper mining companies and affected the flow of product to Northern factories.

References

American Colossus, the Grain Elevator - http://american-colossus.blogspot.com/2009/05/birds-eye-view-of-city-of-buffalo-ny.html.

Lewis Beeson, Dr. and Victor F. Lemmer, *The Effects of the Civil War on Mining In Michigan*, (Lansing, Michigan: Michigan Civil War Centennial Observance Commission, Republished Fort Wilkins Natural History Association) 2004, pp. 15-29.

Thomas Boaz, *Guns For Cotton: England Arms the Confederacy*, (Shippensburg, Pennsylvania: White Mane Publishing, 1996), 65.

Encyclopedia of Chicago, Iron and Steel - http://encyclopedia.chicagohistory.org/pages/653.html.

Rita L. Frese and David M. Young, Editors, *From Lumber Hookers to the Hooligan Fleet, A Treasury of Chicago Maritime History*, (Lake Claremont Press: Chicago, 2007), 11.

A History of Buffalo's Grain Elevators - http://www.buffaloah.com/h/elev/hist/1/index.html.

History of the Iron Ore Trade - http://www.clevelandmemory.org/glihc/oretrade.html.

A History of Buffalo - http://www.buffaloah.com/h/1865.html

James A. Huston, *Army Historical Series, the Sinews of War: Army Logistics 1775-1953*, (Washington, D.C.: Office of Military History, 1970), 176-177.

Iron and Steel Industry - http://www.answers.com/topic/iron-and-steel-industry.

Life and the Civil War, Northern Industry: Hopewell Furnace - http://www.brotherswar.com/Perspective-16.htm.

Michael Martin and Leonard Gelber, *A Dictionary of American History*, (Rowman and Littlefield Publishers, 1978), 600.

Pennsylvania Iron Works - http://www.oldindustry.org/PA_HTML/PaIron.html.

Michigan and the Civil War - http://www.thefreelibrary.com/Chapter+16%3A+Michigan+and+the+Civil+War.-a0155750776.

Michigan Historical Center, *Michigan and the Civil War, An Anthology*, (Lansing, Michigan: Michigan Historical Center, 1999), 68-70.

Michigan Iron Mines - http://www.geo.msu.edu/geogmich/iron-2.html.

Michigan Iron Mines - http://www.miningartifacts.org/Michigan-Iron-Mines.html.

Michigan State History - http://www.shgresources.com/mi/history/.

Angus Murdock, *Boom Copper, the Story of the First U.S. Mining Boom*, (Calumet, Michigan: Roy W. Drier and Louis G. Koepel, 1944), pp. 118-125, 161.

Ore Dock - http://en.wikipedia.org/wiki/Ore_dock.

Footnotes

[1] Michigan Iron Industry Museum, Negaunee, Michigan.

[2] Rita L. Frese and David M. Young, Editors, *From Lumber Hookers to the Hooligan Fleet, A Treasury of Chicago Maritime History*, (Lake Claremont Press: Chicago, 2007), xii.

[3] As defined in Chapter 6.

[4] Thomas Boaz, *Guns For Cotton: England Arms the Confederacy*, (Shippensburg, Pennsylvania: White Mane Publishing, 1996), 65.

CHAPTER FIVE
CONFEDERATE CANADIAN TEAM & MISSION

Casting about for a "game changer," something that could prevent their seemingly inevitable defeat, Southern leaders discovered the Great Lakes, the "soft underbelly" of the Union.

Other than Lake Michigan, all five lakes share a border with Canada (aka a colony of Great Britain known as British North America). Since Britain was a nominal ally of the South, Confederate agents could use Canada as a staging area for covert action through the Union's "back door." Just as important, the border was essentially unguarded, providing easy travel back and forth between the two nations.

In February 1864, the Confederate Congress passed a bill authorizing a campaign of sabotage against "the enemy's property, by land or sea" and appropriated Secret Service funding to pay for it. $1 million was earmarked for operations in Canada. Instead of providing gold, the government provided warrants drawn against supplies of cotton, often referred to at the time as "white gold." The actual money came from the sale from Confederate government cotton stocks. To provide a proper incentive for saboteurs, it was stipulated they could get cash rewards proportional to the destruction they caused.[1]

The money for the Canadian mission was provided by warrants drawn against Confederate government cotton. In this print, cotton is being transferred from train to boat.

To make the plan work, the South dispatched a special commission of three senior "diplomats" with loosely defined public roles as their cover as well as supporting operators. Among them were military officers dressed in civilian clothing and politicians. The leader was Jacob Thompson, ex-Secretary of the Interior under President James Buchanan and past Governor of Mississippi. He also had some military experience serving as a volunteer aide de camp to General John Pemberton in the Western theater and was at the Battle of Shiloh and Vicksburg in 1863, but his Army role was that of a non-combatant staff officer. It was later claimed Thompson tended to think all Canadians favored the South and often placed too much trust in friends from before the war. His suitability as an espionage chief is questionable. Before the war was over the North put a bounty of $25,000 for his capture which might help explain why he used several alias' including Captain Carson.[2]

Jacob Thompson

Also part of the "team" was Clement C. Clay, former U.S. Senator from Alabama. One of the Confederate agents described Clay as "a bad-tempered and sick old man unfit for service." He was also criticized for not being able to keep his mouth shut, telling old acquaintances everything he shouldn't regarding present and future operations. Like Thompson, he wasn't well suited for espionage. Clay also used alias' including Hope, Tracy and Lacey.[3]

The third man was J. P. Holcombe, a University of Virginia law professor. Holcombe's job was to secretly set up an organization to aid in the return of rebel soldiers to the South. To this purpose he located Southern sympathizers in Toronto, Niagara, Windsor, St. Chaterines and other border communities who provided clothing, food and money to help rebel soldiers reach Montreal, Quebec and Halifax where ships could carry them back to the South after running the Union blockade. Montreal also had very good rail connections to Boston and New York making the city an ideal transit point for agents and couriers. Although originally intended to only aid soldiers, Holcomb's organization soon became a conduit for recruiting refugees from the North to join the Dixie cause. When Holcombe eventually returned to the South, the job was taken over by Clement C. Clay.

Clement Clay was described as "a sick old man unfit for service."

The simple Confederate goal was to raise as much hell as they could in the Great Lakes states and the commissioners would oversee the various schemes. Although sometimes operating in the shadows, Thompson was clearly in charge of the mission. In today's parlance, he was the "station chief."

A postwar Federal report on Thompson's activities divided the men his group recruited to assist them into four categories.

1. Pure rebels - men connected with the Southern Army who went to Canada as a way of escaping to the south or pure deserters from either army.

2. Skedaddlers - men who "skedaddled" (ran) from the North before being conscripted. Invariably they were "fast young men having their own or parents pockets well lined and accustomed to live without labor of any kind, were not disposed to take a part on either side which would subject them to the inconveniences, hardships or privations of a soldier's life." There also were those who while they professed Southern principals, were of no mind to actually place their precious posteriors at risk of shot or shell.

3. Refugees - people who fled to Canada to express their opinions and beliefs without fear of retribution. As long as they were in Canada they were protected by British law.

4. Bounty jumpers and escaped criminals. Since there was no appropriate extradition treaty between the U.S. and Canada this lowest of all classes fled north to avoid apprehension. This was by far the biggest group of potential rebel manpower. One Federal agent derisively commented they were most frequently found in bar-rooms, pool halls and gambling dens.

It can be considered Thompson's team had five major objectives:

1. To attempt to arrange for peace via unofficial contacts with Northern businessmen and politicians. The infamous Peace Conference at Niagara Falls is an example.

2. If a "just" peace couldn't be arranged, undermine the Yankee war effort by whatever means possible including breaking the prisoners loose from Johnson Island and Camp Douglas among other camps. Knowing that literally thousands of their soldiers were within a dozen hours of Canada, it was a very appealing hope. It was also a very tall order, especially considering the lack of professional operators and

overall organization. However, the Southern leaders thought there were literally thousands of Confederate supporters not only in Canada but also in Illinois, Michigan, Iowa, Pennsylvania, Maryland, Delaware, Ohio, Indiana, Kentucky, Tennessee, New York and Missouri all of whom would rally to the cause and by force of arms release the prisoners in their states.[4] If the prisoners could be freed, they would form a de facto army around which all of the "disaffected" folks in the states would rally, increasing the effect and power of the new Southern "army." Given the huge threat formed by such a force, the only thing the Union could do was shift combat force from the battlefields to deal with it, which of course decreased their strength at the front leading to opportunity for Confederate attack. The series of resulting Confederate victories could be war altering! Some Southern operators even proposed putting field artillery on tugs and attacking Chicago or other Great Lakes ports from the water. Such assaults surely would have created panic and disrupted lake-borne trade.

3. Sabotage, etc. that would impact the Northern war effort directly or indirectly.

4. To promulgate the "breaking away" of various Great Lakes and surrounding states from the Union and organize them into what was called the "Northwest Confederacy" which would in turn align itself with the "Southern Confederacy." Even if the breaking away states did not align with the Confederacy militarily, their loss to the North would have immense military, political and logistic impacts. It could be war altering.

5. Considering the major Confederate war goal of bringing Britain and/or France in to the war on the Southern side, it was a Confederate ancillary goal of goading a war between the North and Canada (aka Britain). For example an extreme Union reaction to the St. Albans raid could unleash a Canadian counter attack resulting in a new war for the North and subsequent lessening of military pressure in the South. See Chapter 6.

It was remarkable it took the Confederates over three years before establishing a fully functional mission in Canada. Clearly the South realized the importance of securing aid and recognition from Britain and/or France but Confederate diplomats apparently didn't realize there were other opportunities. Remember, the South didn't have to subjugate the North to win, only to secure a peace allowing it to exist as a nation. By contrast, the North had to defeat and occupy the South to achieve victory. This was considerable difference.

Confederate Secret Service

The Confederate "Secret Service" was a generally disjointed compilation of ten different organizations without a central directing authority either for executing missions or analyzing intelligence. In spite of this handicap some successes were achieved but far fewer than what could have been given better organization and security. See Chapter 9 for a more complete discussion of the various groups and agencies.

Some operations were eminently successful and many others less so. Certainly most, at least in the early days of the war, suffered from a lack of professionalism and clandestine expertise. In this regard, the North was no different. It some respects it was like learning to ride a bicycle. It is easy to understand the theory of the balance thing but there is a steep learning curve before achieving success.

A key point to remember is while Thompson brought an operations group to Canada to launch clandestine strikes against the Union, there were a variety of other clandestine activities being made of which he likely had no knowledge.

Thompson established his headquarters at the Queens Hotel in Toronto. It was a popular place for Southern expatriates as reputedly nearly 100 were typically in residence.

From a pure information gathering perspective, Toronto was a good choice. Local papers as well as most of the population were supportive of the "cause" and visitors were well received. The hotel as headquarters was no secret lair and it made surveillance by both British (Canadian) and U.S. agents relatively easy. For example it was claimed the floor below Thompson's suite was completely occupied by Union detectives. Whether true or false is immaterial; that the claim was made at all speaks volumes of the lack of secrecy. Since the railway station was just opposite the hotel, it was very simple for Federal agents to keep track of various known couriers and other visitors coming and goings. Thompson later complained about detectives, "on every street corner." Although it is easy to surmise the hotel was only a front and a "secret" headquarters was really elsewhere, there is no evidence to suggest this was true.

A sub-headquarters was also established in the Niagara region of New York. It was convenient since the suspension bridge at Niagara Falls was a vital gateway into the U.S. for launching reconnaissance missions. Confederate agents and sympathizers in Fredonia, and Dunkirk, New York and Port Colborne, Ontario, were also handy to support various operations. The Genesee Hotel in Buffalo, just across the river, was also a known Confederate location for planning clandestine operations.

Money for mission planning was handled relatively openly. On arrival in Montreal enroute to Toronto, Thompson established an account with a branch of the Bank of Ontario. Although given the secret nature of their business the temptation is to assume there was a large strongbox filled with gold, the truth was more pedestrian with checks (drafts) issued as needed.

Dependent on mission planning needs, Thompson and other members of his team also held meetings in London, midway between Toronto and Windsor and St. Catherine's at the north end of the Welland Canal.

Regardless of the relative ease of operating in Canada, traveling to Canada was complicated. For example, Thompson and Clay left Richmond on May 3, 1864, boarded a blockade-runner in Wilmington, North Carolina, reaching Bermuda a week later. From there it was steamer to Halifax and then another up the St. Lawrence River to Montreal finally stepping ashore on the 29th.

The Commissioners communicated with Richmond via secret couriers. It could be a long journey for a courier, perhaps several weeks if by land and over a month if by blockade runner. The trip was fraught with danger at every step. Agents moving overland could be intercepted by Northern agents virtually anytime and documents seized. U.S. detectives cut open clothing, and pulled the backs off buttons to find hidden messages. One common route was to take the Grand Trunk Railway west from Montreal (or Toronto) then cross the Detroit/St. Clair River by ferry to the St. Clair Station in Michigan, and another train southwest from Detroit. Whether bound for Richmond or back to Toronto, it was a major artery for Southern agents and couriers. It some respects the route was an Underground Railroad for proponents of slavery.

The heavy reliance on couriers worked to the Union's advantage since one, Richard Montgomery, was a double agent! As needed, he carried critical dispatches from Confederate President Jefferson Davis to the Canadian station and reverse. He also made a stop both ways in Washington to allow the various dispatches, invariably in cipher, to be copied and decrypted. His principal contact in Washington was Assistant Secretary of War Charles Dana. Not wanting to arouse any Southern suspicion over their prize agent, Dana once arranged to have him "captured" and tossed into prison followed by a properly dramatic escape. Not content with the staged reality, Montgomery carefully shot himself in the arm to provide convincing proof of his desperate flight for the "cause". See Chapter 9 for details of this most remarkable man.

In one February 1865 instance, three Confederate agents were in the same railcar bound from Detroit south. When two Federal agents drew their revolvers to arrest them, the third agent took advantage of a moment of inattention to escape by jumping out a train window into the snowdrift. He managed to evade pursuing Federal searchers, finally making his way to safety in Richmond.

At sea, ships could be intercepted by the Union Navy and agents apprehended. As the war went on, the interception rate increased making it more and more difficult for blockade runners to reach a Southern port. Of course, since the ideal weather for running the blockade was during the worst weather, the threat of shipwreck was always present.

In addition to couriers, the Canadian commissioners used various ciphers and codes in both hand delivered messages and special inserts in newspapers. For example the *New York News*, *Herald Tribune* and others were widely distributed and commonly available in the south. It was an easy thing for a Southern sympathizer or spy to insert a coded message in a newspaper and be assured of eventual delivery.

One of the key "operatives" reporting to Commissioner Thompson was Captain Thomas H. Hines of Kentucky. Although only in his twenties during the carly part of the war he was an important aide to Confederate guerrilla raider General John

Captain Thomas Hines was Thompson's chief operating agent in Canada.

General John Hunt Morgan was a fearless Confederate cavalry officer.

Hunt Morgan while operating in Indiana and Ohio. Hines often did the reconnaissance prior to Morgan's raids. Such scouting was usually in civilian attire, making him a spy and subject to the death penalty if captured. During one of the deep strikes into the Union he and Morgan were captured, both ending up in the Ohio Penitentiary. They weren't there long.

On the night of November 27, 1863, Hines engineered the dramatic escape of Morgan and five of his officers. The group including Hines escaped from their cells in the "pen" by tunneling from his cell to the courtyard. The intrepid prisoners used a stolen shovel, two table knives, a couple of candlesticks (for tunnel illumination), a small wooden box and two wooden dishes.[5] After assuring the "coast was clear," they climbed the high stone wall with a rope made out of bunk coverlets and a grapple from a bent iron fireplace poker. Once over the top they were nearly home free. Making their way to a rail station in nearby Columbus they calmly boarded the train to Cincinnati arriving early in the morning. A few dollars to a boatman and they were quickly across the river to Kentucky where rebel sympathizers safely conducted them back home to the South.

When Hines reported for duty with Thompson he came highly recommended, his capabilities well proved by his duty with Morgan and the Ohio escape. His expertise as an escape artist came in handy several times during his espionage career. Once he hid inside a mattress that was in use to avoid being caught! At the end of the war in April, 1865, he was in Detroit and mistaken for infamous actor John Wilkes Booth then being hunted for the Lincoln murder. He only escaped by forcing a Detroit ferryboat captain to take him across the river to safety in Windsor at the point of revolver. He was never caught.

After the war Hines claimed he was made a "pro tempore" Major General when he was sent to Thompson and the Canadian mission. There is no record to support this assertion, many if not most of the Confederate records relating to secret operations were destroyed or lost. There are two aspects of the issue that are worth consideration. First, sending a mere Army captain to act as the military leader of the Canadian mission

Reputedly Hines led the escape of Morgan and several of his officers from the Ohio Penitentiary.

shows remarkable faith in such a junior officer. It also degrades the role by not assigning a more senior officer to the job. A brigadier general would seem more appropriate with Hines as an aide. When meeting and coordinating actions with officials of the Canadian government or various clandestine groups, rank means importance and implies respect and confidence. Second, promoting an officer from captain to Major General, a jump of four grades, is virtually unheard of, even in wartime as a "pro tempore."

Hines was clearly under the "command" of Thompson who warned him about the critical need to keep Canadian neutrality as a prime operational consideration. There is some thought, since Hines apparently had access to Confederate Signal Corps ciphers, that he may also have been "dual hated."

The Richmond government also provided Colonel St. Leger Grenfell, an English officer of reputed great experience and daring. His supporters claimed he had a, "romantic connection with nearly every important war in America, Europe, Asia and Africa for the past thirty years" and served as Morgan's adjutant and later on the staff of General Bragg. It wasn't uncommon to find such foreign adventurers in both armies.[6]

Another Confederate agent with Thompson was George N. Sanders. He had earlier been the U.S. Consul in London under President Franklin Pierce. He was also a strong advocate of ignoring Canadian neutrality and launching attacks against the U.S. from it with little regard for the ramifications.

Long associated with European radicals in the 1850's, Sanders was also an advocate of assassination as a way to deal with tyrants. From his perspective, Lincoln fit that category. Although the evidence is somewhat murky, it is likely Sanders was deeply involved in an initial plot to kidnap Lincoln as well as the later assassination by John Wilkes Booth. The desperate Confederate leadership believed the captured President

Lt. Colonel St. Ledger Grenfell was a British soldier of fortune who fell in with the Confederate cause.

could be a bargaining chip to force the Union to negotiate the end of the war. In spite of detailed planning, the kidnap plot fell apart at the last minute, which may have led to the frantic decision to assassinate Lincoln and other high-ranking government officials. Southern leaders thought their deaths would spread confusion in the Union leadership and in theory at least provide Confederate forces a chance to reorganize. Remember at this point in the war Southern field armies were in near hopeless condition suffering shortages in arms, ammunition, rations, medical supplies, virtually all the logistics of war plus being bled by constant Union attacks and a flood of desertions.

Much of the kidnap planning was done in Montreal at the St. Lawrence Hall hotel, the unofficial headquarters of rebel activity. Booth visited the hotel at least once, meeting with Thompson's men to build an operational mission team.

The Confederate "secret" organization in Canada was extensive and fully capable of supporting a wide range of underground activities. They had money, manpower and imagination as well as key supervising agents along the border. Robert E. Lee's uncle held down the post at Hamilton on Lake Ontario and other agents were at St. Catherine's on the important Welland Canal between Lakes Ontario and Erie.

The Southern hope was with luck the Canadian based agents could set local sympathizers and infiltrators to wage guerrilla warfare. Considering the large number of Confederate sympathizers in Canada as well as escaped prisoners, in theory a ready source of recruits was close at hand. Every activity they undertook had the potential to cause the Union to redirect resources to guard the lakes, which meant fewer soldiers on the battlefront. They hoped their activities would lead to a vast Northwest Conspiracy that could perhaps even knock the Great Lakes states out of the war with devastating effects on the Union.

Leaders in Richmond believed there was a vast "fifth column" of Confederate sympathizers, just waiting for direction in Indiana, Illinois, Ohio, and Michigan. An estimated 40 percent of the areas population was Southern-born and surely that is where their allegiance still lay, certainly not to Mr. Lincoln's evil North! Often called "Copperheads," they weren't necessarily pro slavery but did believe blacks were inferior to whites and didn't support the "holier than thou" attitude of the New England abolitionists. They could be of immeasurable help to the South.

To show their allegiance, members wore the head of Liberty, cut from copper pennies, on their lapels. As a result, their enemies called them Copperheads for the poisonous snake known for striking without warning. It was an apt moniker.

The evidence of anti-war feeling in the North to the extent of armed action in opposition was evidenced by the comments of a Michigan state senator who stated, "Here in Michigan, here in Detroit, and in every Northern State. . . there are some sixty-five thousand able-bodied men. . . who will interpose themselves between any troops that may be raised in Michigan and the people of the South."[7]

This was also a time when quasi secret societies were popular. In 1859 one "Dr." George Washington Lamb Bickley, a medical "professor" at the Cincinnati "Electric Medical Institute," had a fit of inspiration and created the Knights of the Golden Circle (KGC).[8] The new group was very pro-Southern and very pro-Manifest Destiny, especially as it applied to expanding slavery by appropriating Mexican territory for the cotton South. As the nation slowly slid toward civil war, Bickley put the KGC on the secessionist bandwagon. Most of this group were Copperhead Democrats and definitely pro-Southern. Bickley had created a monster, but it was also a chameleon that would change colors in a snap, confounding its master.[9]

There was a military element to the KGC. At the start of the War, 150 members participated in the seizure of the Federal Arsenal in San Antonio. Others formed part of the Confederate expedition to takeover the New Mexico Territory. Clearly the KGC could "bite."

The Copperhead political movement was seen to be intertwined with various subversive groups.

While there is some dispute it appears the Knights of the Golden Circle (KGC) morphed into the Order of American Knights (OAK) in 1863 and the Sons of Liberty (SOL) in 1864.[10] SOL was selected to try to make an emotional connection with the group of Revolutionary War fame. The bulk of the membership was made up of Copperheads and Peace Democrats, those who thought the war was terrible mistake, Washington was taking too much power and the country needed "peace at any price."

Whether it was the Copperheads, KGC, OAK or SOL, the aims differed depending on the viewer. Many in the North considered them all a pro-Confederate fifth column of murderous traitors ready to do the South's bidding at the drop of a hat. Others looked at them as not much more than glorified Masonic type organizations full of ritual and secret handshakes and little more. Certainly many members wanted the war to end and peace to return, but were not really pro-Confederacy. The leadership of the groups usually took a more war-like stance, often selling the Canadian agents on the powerful military capability of the organization, etc. This was especially true when Thompson was disbursing his secret funds for their support! It is fair to conclude that dependent on the time and place, these groups encompassed the range of capabilities, from benign backslappers to militant Southern irregulars.

While the leaders knew the sinister purpose of the groups, in the early days membership in some instances looked at them more from the viewpoint of belonging to organizations as innocent as the Moose or Elks. It didn't take long for their true colors to become apparent. In 1861 the KGC was openly recruiting for the Confederate Army in Illinois, and running guns and guerrilla raids in Iowa.

The true number of members in these groups was always questionable but in 1864 the Supreme Council of the SOL at a New York meeting claimed it stood between 800,000 and 1,000,000. Delegates claimed 125,000 in Indiana, 140,000 in Illinois, 108,000 in Ohio, 70,000 in Kentucky, 40,000 in Missouri and 20,000 each in Michigan and New York.[11]

In February 1864 the SOL elected miscreant congressman Clement L. Vallandigham "Supreme Grand Commander." Although Vallandigham later claimed he never knew the group was pro-Southern or did anything illegal, it is likely he was simply maintaining what presidents would later call "plausible deniability."

Members of the SOL came from every order of life and included judges, state and Federal legislators, doctors, lawyers, merchants as well as rank and file laborers and others from the lower rungs of society. For the folks at the bottom of life, the opportunity to belong to the same "secret" society as those at the upper end was very attractive, especially when the upper strata made certain to reach out to them. Of course the reason for this social evangelism was driven by the leadership's need to use the lower end folks for the dirty work. The coming SOL rebellion needed men willing to be the assault troops and that was the job of the lower end members.

Knowing the critical importance of attracting members from the lower classes, the leadership established an apparent degree of upward social mobility, something society as a whole largely denied to the non-elite. The KGC/OAK/SOL provided a "comfortable and genial" atmosphere to allow them to "qualify" for higher honors and status. For example there were three degrees for the SOL: First, the Temple; second the Grand Council and third; the Supreme Council.

Great effort was made to provide an illusion of secrecy. Using the Chicago temple as an example, a prospective member was escorted to the fifth floor as his sponsor made certain they were not followed or observed.[12] The applicant is left alone in a small room with a sliding peephole cut into a closed door. Approaching the door, the applicant gives three raps and the peephole slides open. He whispers the monthly password and the door opens and he enters into a large room where a group of prospective members are undergoing the rites of preliminary initiation. After completing this first ceremony, the new member is led to another room where a "Guardian" lectures him on more mysteries of the "holy order." Passing further up the chain he receives instruction from the "Ancient Brother." Then it is on to another room and more admonitions, now from another "Guardian" who warns against of terrible curses and horrible punishment should he ever reveal the secrets of the order. Finally he is received by the "Grand Seignior" who provides him with the secret sign of distress as well as more rants and raves of retribution should he fail to adhere to the dictates of the order. He is now a full-fledged member.[13]

The Temple degree was roughly analogous to a county organization; the Grand Council to the state and Supreme Council to the national government. During 1863 and 1864 the Supreme Council met nearly every month to hash out plans for action. To provide for military leadership the constitution named the Supreme Commander of the Supreme Council as also the commander-in-chief of the SOL's military forces when called to action. To assist him, each state had a Major General. Membership was reputedly so large in Indiana it had **four** major generals. The organization further provided each congressional district with a brigade, each county a regiment and each township a company. Every effort was made to arm the force with what ever weapons could be found. Illinois units were said to be especially well equipped with carbines and revolvers and in Indiana thousands of muskets and revolvers were in their hands. Other arms came from Nassau in the Bahamas to Canada and then smuggled to the SOL. A major general later claimed Indianapolis had a factory to manufacture various ammunition and hand grenades were made in Cincinnati. "Infernal" devices, real time bombs, using Greek Fire, were produced and assembled in Louisville, according to U.S. detectives. The infamous Confederate "Greek Fire" was a combination of bisulphate of carbon and phosphorus and could burn underwater. The bombs used a clockwork mechanism to determine the time of firing and could be secretly placed on boats or in buildings or other high value targets. Placing them in a trunk was a perfect way to smuggle them virtually anywhere without suspicion. Again according to the agent, the SOL used the devices to destroy two boats loaded with Union supplies in Louisville as well as other targets.

Leaders reputedly encouraged their men to enlist in the local militia to receive arms as well as important training. Once the rebellion came, the SOL members were supposed to desert bringing their weapons with them.

As an organization, the SOL worked against the Union in a number of ways. How well individual temples and members "did their duty" is debatable.

1. Aiding Union soldiers to desert and harboring those who did. This included providing them with money, clothing, food, and escape routes to safe areas including "skedaddling" to Canada or elsewhere or going over to the South. Perhaps even worse when Union officers apprehended deserters in Illinois, judges who were closet SOL members released them. A story is told of such judges arresting the officers for "kidnapping" the deserters! Instances were reported where Union patrols sent out to capture deserters in Indiana were fired on by the runners as well as SOL members of the civilian population. Northern recruiting officers were also attacked in Indiana. Of course when deserters "went over the hill" with their arms, ammunition and even horses, it was a big plus for the cause.

2. Discouraging enlistments and resisting the draft. They were especially active in trying to talk Northern recruits out of joining the army.

3. Circulating disloyal and treasonable publications. This was seen as a effective way to lessen or otherwise impact public support of the Northern war effort.

4. Communicating and giving intelligence to the enemy. Rebel spies, messengers and various emissaries were protected as they passed through Union territory. Given an age when all communication essentially had to be written, shielding couriers carrying important messages and other communications was vital to the war effort. One post war report claims Vallandingham kept up a constant correspondence with SOL leaders by the use of such messengers. Women visiting "relatives" within the other's line were a popular method of passing information. A timely report by a rebel spy indicating a movement of a Union force could prove critical to the South. The SOL made special efforts to pull intelligence from men working in telegraph offices, ferry boats, railroads, express offices, Federal military department headquarters, anywhere they could gain useful intelligence of Union plans and movements. If an in-place worker could be "turned," made into an SOL spy - great! If not, efforts were made to have an SOL member gain employment in the position. Couriers carrying vital supplies to the South such as drugs were also very important to protect from Union apprehension.

5. Aiding the enemy by recruiting for them or assisting recruiting. Southern recruits were hidden away as needed from Union forces and taken south on a regular basis. In theory every time a Confederate army moved into disputed areas, local men were encouraged to answer the call to arms.

6. Furnishing rebels with arms and ammunition. Confederate forces operating in the Trans-Mississippi area were a long way from normal logistic lines and whatever supplies could be smuggled south by the SOL were valuable. Women were especially adept at hiding small high value items like drugs and percussion caps on their person then infiltrating through the lines. See the Moon sisters in Chapter 9 for more details.

7. Cooperating with the South in raids and invasions. SOL members provided critical local support to Confederate raiders operating behind the lines, including food, shelter and guiding them to important targets.

8. The organization also worked as a disruptive force behind the lines, seeking to sabotage the Union war effort anyway possible.

9. Perhaps most important in view of the desperate plans of the South was to have the SOL and similar organizations "rise," literally revolt against the North. Such a revolution would have a devastating impact on the federals and an equally positive impact on the South.

It is entirely reasonable to look at the entire organization as a "shadow" government ready to step into the light of day when the present Northern government collapsed. Other historians considered it more as a paper tiger.

The organization was in all of the states having "disaffected" populations. In Illinois headquarters (aka "temples") were in Chicago, Springfield and Quincy; Indiana, Indianapolis and Vincennes; in Ohio at Cincinnati, Dayton and Hamilton (referred by some folks as the "South Carolina" of the North); Missouri at St. Louis; Kentucky at Louisville and at Michigan in Detroit which was a key link in the chain since it allowed easy communications with SOL president Vallandigham safely ensconced in Windsor just across the Detroit River in Canada. From his protected perch he could easily direct operations for the SOL as well as keep in close touch with his supporters.

Meetings were always held in secret, invariably at night and major cities excepted, in secluded places. Guards were placed on all of the approaches and only those men with the correct password were allowed to enter the meeting.

Thompson's rebels were not operating unsupported by the central government. For example there is a school of thought that claims Confederate general Sterling Price invaded Missouri in the fall of 1864 as a way of reinforcing a planned state uprising. In fact testimony during a subsequent military investigation claimed 50,000 men from Illinois and 30,000 from Missouri would combine with Price's estimated 20,000 to form an army capable of occupying and holding Missouri against Federal counterattack. The rising in Indiana, Ohio and Kentucky was supposed to be supported by Generals Breckenridge, Buckner and Morgan. Likewise it is claimed General Hood's dangerous position in northern Georgia, Alabama and Tennessee was taken for the same reason. Considering the relative weakness of the Southern armies and generally deteriorating military situation confronting the South, such bold dispositions could only have been taken by the direction of Jefferson Davis. All ultimately failed.

Price did invade Missouri on August 4, 1864 by direction of General Kirby Smith with the mission of threatening St. Louis. It was not the South's finest moment. As Price led his rag tag and self-styled Army of Missouri into the state things began to unravel quickly. His total strength was 12, 000, a far cry from the anticipated 20,000. On the plus side though, virtually all were mounted for mobility. Unfortunately the horses were all local captures instead of trained cavalry mounts thus affecting capability. Even worse, 4,000 of his men were unarmed, the intention being to capture arms from defeated Union forces. He was also doubtless (within some limits of credulity) "certain" of receiving a flood of recruits as promised by the SOL and many of them would bring their own arms. His logistic situation was critical with few rations or wagons to transport them. Living off the land to the greatest extent was vital. Even worse for his army, a shortage in horses meant he couldn't even bring all of his field artillery with him. A lack of artillery meant less combat power.

Crossing the border was initially successful but he quickly ground to a halt when hundreds of state militia constantly chewed away at his force. Outnumbered Federal soldiers under General Alfred Pleasonton fought well too, forcing Price into frontal attacks costing him hundreds of casualties he couldn't afford. In the end, the thousands of men the SOL promised never materialized and Price was driven 60 miles backwards in two days, deep into Arkansas and eventually all the way to Texas. Price's debacle was the South's last-ditch effort in Missouri and the Trans-Mississippi theater.

U.S. Canadian Efforts

The U.S. was also active in Canada in various secret efforts to defeat Southern projects. Secretary of State Steward initially had agents in place with two major objectives.

The first mission was to find a way to obstruct Confederate communications with Europe. The most popular method was via Bermuda, from the South to the island, then north to Halifax and east to Europe and the reverse in return. If the Canadian link could be broken, delayed or otherwise impeded, it was to the Union's advantage. The second task was to stop or disrupt any Canadian supply efforts to the South. Shoes were a particularly important item and a popular export from Canada to the South through Bermuda and/or Britain. Armies may move on their stomachs, but they march on their feet and no shoes meant a slower and less capable army.

As the war progressed, Federal agents and spies became more common in Canada and provided a wealth of information to the North. Often they worked through various U.S. Consuls allowing their reports to directly enter the official "pipeline" minimizing potential for interception. Many of the Union agents were doubles, Confederates willing to work both sides for cash or later advantage.

References

Colonel I. Winslow Ayer, *The Great Treason Plot in the North*, U.S. Publishing Company, Chicago, 1895, 26-28, 31-41, 47-50, 58, 90, 93.

Mark M. Boatner III, *The Civil War Dictionary,* (New York: David McKay Company, 1959), 409.

Wilifrid Bovey, "Confederate Agents in Canada During the American Civil War," *Canadian History Review*, Vol. 2, No. 1, (1921) 46-57.

Chicago Tribune, November 8, 1864.

The Confederate Secret Service and the Assassination of Abraham Lincoln - http://spitfirelist.com/for-the-record/ftr-691-the-confederate-secret-service-and-the-assassination-of-abraham-lincoln/.

Charge and Specification Against David E. Herold, George A. Atzerodt, Lewis Payne, Michael O'Laughlin, Edward Spanger, Samuel Arnold, Mary E. Surratt and Samuel A. Mudd - http://www.surratt.org/documents/dcharges.html.

Conspiracy in Canada - https://www.cia.gov/library/publications/additional-publications/civil-war/p37.htm.

Ollinger Crenshaw,. "The Knights of the Golden Circle: The Career of George Bickley," *American Historical Review*, Vol. 47, No. 1, October 1941, 23-50.

John S. Galbraith, "George Sanders, Influence Man for the Hudson's Bay Company," *Oregon Historical Review*, Vol. 53, No. 3 (September 1953), 159-176.

Wood Gray, *The Hidden Civil War: the Story of the Copperheads* (New York: Viking Press, 1942), 167.

David Stephen Heidler, Jeanne T. Heidler, David J. Coles, *Encyclopedia of the American Civil War: a political, social, and military History* (New York: W.W. Norton and Company, 2000), 509.

Hubbart , Henry Clyde, "Pro-Southern Influences in the Free West 1840-1865," *The Mississippi Valley Historical Review*, Vol. 20, No. 1, June 1933, 45-52.

New York Times, April 30, July 9, 1865.

Public Affairs, *Central Intelligence Agency, Intelligence in the Civil War,* (Public Affairs, Central Intelligence Agency: Washington, DC), 43-45.

William F. Raney, "Confederate Agents in Canada During the American Civil War," *Canadian Historical Review*, Vol. 2, No. 1, (1921), 46-57.

Felix G. Stidger, *Treason History of the Sons of Liberty,* (Chicago: Felix G. Stidger, 1903), Appendix A.

William A. Tidwell, *Confederate Covert Action in the American Civil War - April '65*, Kent, Ohio: Kent State University Press, 1995, 30-32, 35, 135, 155-159, 243.

Toronto Globe, December 5, 1864.

William A. Tidwell, *Confederate Covert Action in the American Civil War - April '65*, Kent, Ohio: Kent State University Press, 1995, 30-32, 35, 135, 155-159, 243.

War Department Collection of Confederate Records - (Record Group 109) 1825-1900 (bulk 1861-65) 109.13.3 (Other Records).

Robin W. Winks, *Canada and the United States - The Civil War Years,* (Baltimore: Johns Hopkins Press, 1960), 268, 275.

Footnotes

[1] David Stephen Heidler, Jeanne T. Heidler, David J. Coles, *Encyclopedia of the American Civil War: a political, social, and military History*, (New York: W.W. Norton and Company, 2000), 509.

[2] Wilfrid Bovey, "Confederate Agents in Canada During the American Civil War," *The Canadian Historical Review*, Vol. 2, Issue 1, March 1921, 46-47.

[3] Wilfrid Bovey, 47.

[4] Ayer, Colonel I. Winslow, *The Great Treason Plot in the North*, (U.S. Publishing Company, Chicago, 1895), 32.

[5] Some historians speculate they escaped by bribing a guard rather than by tunnel. The tunnel simply made a far better story.

[6] There is an argument that Grenfell was quitting the Confederacy and returning to England and merely was delaying in Canada to enjoy some hunting and fishing before departing for good. When he heard about the "action" coming in Chicago it offered too much adventure for him to ignore and he went along to see what would happen. Unfortunately, he would be swept up by the Union following the debacle suffering the inevitable penalty.

[7] *Detroit Free Press*, January 26, 29, 1861.

[8] As the name implies, the Electric Medical Institute studied electricity as a healing agent.

[9] Crenshaw, Ollinger. "The Knights of the Golden Circle: The Career of George Bickley," *American Historical Review*, Vol. 47, No. 1, October 1941, 23-50.

[10] Mark M. Boatner III, *The Civil War Dictionary*, (New York: David McKay and Company, 1959), 466.

[11] Ayer, 34.

[12] Local "lodges" were called "temples."

[13] Felix G. Stidger, *Treason History of the Sons of Liberty*, (Chicago: Felix G. Stidger, 1903), Appendix A.

CHAPTER SIX
PLOTS AND MORE PLOTS

Some historians question the seriousness of the plans to form a Northwest Conspiracy, free the prisoners from Camp Douglas and "burn" Chicago, claiming the various plots were mostly created by Republican newspapers and Union Army officers for self-serving purposes. And, of course, the SOL, OAK, KGC, Copperheads and related groups were really just harmless social and political organizations posing no significant threat to the North. At this late date, I believe arriving at a positive determination of truth is impossible. That said, what follows is taken from contemporary accounts, reminisces from participants and later historical texts. I believe it to be a reasonable treatment of what happened and <u>could have happened</u> had events worked out differently. If Southern leaders had been more energetic and imaginative, history could have been made.

The Camp Douglas Raid

The first covert action planned by Thompson's Canadian action group (Hines was apparently the designated agent in charge) was a raid on Camp Douglas, a large prison camp in Chicago in conjunction with a general uprising of the SOL in various "Old Northwest" states.

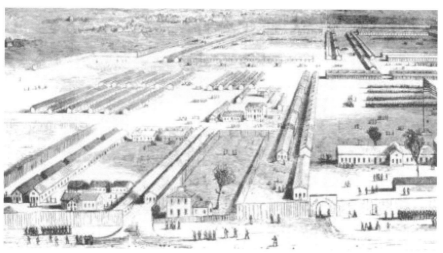

Camp Douglas was never intended to be used as a long term prison camp.

The camp was about three miles south of the city center and a couple of hundred yards from Lake Michigan. Since the land was owned by Senator Stephen A. Douglas, it was named for the benefactor. The camp was originally laid out in 1861 by the state Adjutant General as a mobilization point for Wisconsin units bound for the war. It was directly east of Douglas Square on 33rd Street, the eastern limit defined by Cottage Grove Avenue and the southern line by the northern boundary of the old Chicago University grounds. It also expanded into State Street and south to Hyde Park with various drill grounds and out camps. The main gate was on Cottage Grove Avenue.

It was never intended as a year-around facility but was forced into the role by the circumstances of the war. The initial prisoners arrived from General Grant's victories at Fort Donelson and Fort Henry in February 1862. A reporter for the *Chicago Tribune* was on hand to watch the captured Confederates arrive. Comprising mostly men from Alabama, Mississippi and Texas, they were particularly unprepared for the cold. "Their clothes had been intended for a warmer country and their frames were all unused to the cold… hence the prisoners looked pale and actually had attacks of ague chills as they stood waiting the preparation of their barracks. A more woebegone set of men it would be difficult for the reader to imagine. It may have been from exposure and low diet but they were all sallow faced, sunken eyed and apparently famishing."[1]

Since both sides routinely exchanged prisoners, the Southern soldiers were not expected to be at Camp Douglas long. When the exchange cartel finally broke down in

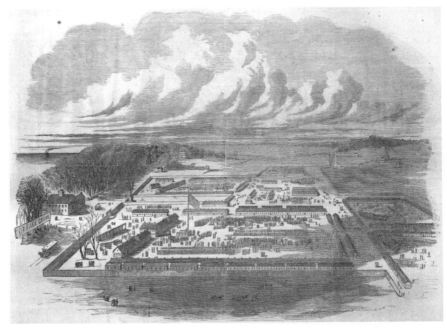

Camp Douglas looking south. Note how close the grove of trees are to the east, perfect cover for a quick assault on the prison.

the spring of 1863, Camp Douglas inmates and a stream of new prisoners were there for the duration of the war. Much is often made of the high death rate in various prison camps North and South. But when the general condition of the prisoners is considered, usually half-sick, poorly nourished, minimal clothing and demoralized, it is easy to understand. Mix in close quarters in poorly constructed barracks and a spark of disease like small pox or typhoid and poor sanitation (personal and group) and death is soon calling.

Built on a muddy bog with abysmal drainage, it was perhaps the unhealthiest prison camp in the North. The more troops quartered there, the greater the sanitation problem and greater the resulting health problem. Inspecting Union officers suggested abandoning the camp but the command staff thought it cheaper to improve conditions rather than giving up on it. Efforts to fix the multitude of problems were ineffective and between February 1862 and June 1865 nearly 4,000 prisoners died of various diseases including smallpox, diphtheria, dysentery, cholera and typhoid.

It also wasn't the most secure prisoner of war camp in the North and escapes were commonplace. Inmates even constructed a tunnel under the wall. Others were able to slip out on a variety of pretexts and fade away into the ever-changing Chicago population. Reputedly, some escaped through the help of Southern sympathizers in charge of distributing supplies sent from home. Escapees usually made their way back to the Southern lines, aided often by the SOL. The entire story of Camp Douglas is fascinating and too complex to include in this text.

To maximize the potential for Union confusion and panic the planned Confederate attack would take place on August 29, 1864 simultaneously with the Democrat National Convention in the city. The convention was originally scheduled for July 4 but since Lincoln's popularity was plummeting as the Union was unable to score decisive victories over the South, Democrat leaders wanted to delay as long as possible to let the Northern problems pile up. The more problems the Union and Lincoln faced, the better their nominee would look to the voters. Thompson and company weren't happy with the delay since they were desperately seeking a way to divert attention from Sherman's striking into Georgia and rolling up the Confederate armies as he drove inexorably to Atlanta. The horror of his famous March to the Sea wouldn't begin until November. They believed a successful rising could knock Sherman off his stride. For a while it looked like "D-Day" would be July 20, then August 16 and finally August 29. It was a clear conflict between the military necessity of diverting Sherman and the political importance of defeating Lincoln. Once August 29 was finally set in stone, the wheels for the Thompson - Hines operation were put in motion.

There were thousands of veteran Southern soldiers in Camp Douglas and comparatively few guards. If the penned up rebels could be set loose perhaps they could inspire a general uprising among the subversive SOL, OAK and KGC. At worst, the freed prisoners would create havoc requiring the North to commit large numbers of soldiers to restore order. It would also be disheartening for the Union. If the Army couldn't even keep enemy prisoners safely secured, how could they defeat the Confederates on the battlefield? It was a no lose opportunity for Hines and Confederacy.

Agent Hines was a slippery fellow, able to move about the North with little apparent difficulty. Reputedly, he used numerous aliases including those of a doctor, banker, teacher and French-Canadian exporter.

As with most Northern prisoner of war camps, the guards were members of the Veteran Reserve Corps formed in April 1863. Previously known as the Invalid Corps, it was constituted to make the best use of soldiers rendered unfit for active field service by wounds or disease contracted in line of duty, but who were still fit enough for garrison or other light duty, and by recommendation of their commanding officers, meritorious and deserving. By any standard they were not combat ready but still useful soldiers.

Considering the entire plan for creating a "Northwest rebel-lion," Chicago was a great place to start. Camp Douglas was poorly defended against an attack; the city had a strong Copperhead contingent, some estimates running to 5,000 and Illinois was a hotbed of anti-Union feeling, organizers claiming an SOL membership of 85,000 men; tactically, the city was a major center of commerce with several major rail lines reaching Chicago from numerous directions, the coming and going of various passenger and freight vessels adding another transportation dimension. A rising in the city would throw the industrial, banking and shipping industries into turmoil with national repercussions. The city was always crowded with transients so Southern agents would be invisible against the flood of others. The upcoming Democrat convention was a perfect cover for their scheme since attention would be focused on the raucous political theater until it was too late!

The Invalid Corps was a value asset for the Union, freeing soldiers for frontline duty.

Chicago was certainly a good location for the uprising for other reasons, too. The city was divided in many ways. Racial tensions ran high as evidenced by an 1862 race riot caused when white teamsters tried to prevent blacks from riding the city's horse

By the start of the Civil War Chicago was a burgeoning industrial and transportation center for water and rail commerce.

drawn omnibus system. City schools were also racially segregated. Further tension rose when a mob of 300-400 Irish attacked several U.S. Marshals after they arrested two men for failing to register for the draft.[2] There was also conflict over the *Chicago Times*, a Democrat Party "mouthpiece" loudly supporting the Democrat peace movement. The Army closed the newspaper down literally at bayonet point in June 1863. Democrat supporters responded by mobbing the Republican *Chicago Tribune*. Under pressure, Lincoln relented ordering the *Chicago Times* suppression to cease. Given the boiling pot of competing tensions, Chicago was a perfect environment for traitorous intrigue and revolution.

The Supreme Council of the SOL met in Chicago on July 20, 1864, at their "temple" on the corner of Randolph and Dearborn Streets known locally as "McCormick's Block." Earlier as the Order of American Knights, the SOL met on South Clark Street in a large building a marked by a sign emblazoned "Invincible Club Hall".[3] So as to not attract attention members always entered singly or in groups of two or three. Others stood quiet guard to assure against interruptions. The topic of the Supreme Council meeting were the plan for the anticipated rising. A major general of the SOL, a Colonel Barrett chaired the meeting in his role of Chief of Staff to the Supreme Commander. He stunned the members when he announced he was appearing as an official representative of the Confederate government and it authorized him to provide the SOL with $2 million (money captured supposedly from the Union Army) to help finance the coming operation. The funds would be used to purchase arms and ammunition.[4]

The Governor of Ohio was so concerned about the influx of arms to his state, including the very effective Henry rifles. He wired Secretary of War Stanton asking what he could do to staunch the flow. Arms salesmen were all over the state doing a land office business selling their wares to whoever had the money without regard to the end use.[5]

Chicago SOL members carefully compiled lists of the men, especially police and other officials who stood against them. When the rising came, they would be dealt with in their turn.

Careful watch was also kept on the Chicago Police and Provost Guard as well as any changes in the positions of the protecting artillery at Camp Douglas. When the time to strike arrived such minute data was vital.

The rebels kept a close observation on Camp Douglas. Freeing the prisoners was the key part of the overall plan so it was vital the attackers knew everything possible about the compound. In the days leading up to the convention they were distressed to see additional troops and artillery arriving and taking up key defense positions. They also had a spy in the telegraph office reporting every message of importance. None of the news was good for the cause. Clearly the Federals knew something of the rebel threat and were taking action to counter it. One of the Toronto Confederates later complained in a report to Clay that a "regiment was placed within the enclosure with the Confederates and 16 pieces of artillery were parked ready to open fire upon those defenseless men in case an attack was made."[6]

Quietly SOL members from Kentucky, Missouri, Indiana and Illinois slinked into Chicago, each taking pains to appear as a friendly Democrat conventioneer. Each man was to be ready to strike at a moment's notice. It was claimed many brought muskets hidden under straw in the beds of their wagons. Supposedly over a thousand of them were organized and officered, just waiting for the word to attack. SOL leaders claimed another six thousand were said to be in the wings, not brave enough to initiate action

A group of rebel prisoners bundled in blankets against the chill of Chicago.

themselves but willing to jump into the fray once the battle royal started. When the resulting riot was in full swing, they would be happy to join in the fun! With the breakdown of law and order, doubtless many local vagrants and criminals would willingly add to the mayhem. From the Confederate viewpoint the greater the carnage, destruction and pillaging, the better.

As the convention drew near thousands of men flocked to the city, delegates and others. Hotels were packed, private homes took in boarders and hundreds more used copious amounts of whisky to deaden senses enough to stretch out in the streets, a curb for a pillow. A few more belts of rot-gut whisky and blankets were dispensed with too! One local wag claimed, "Of all the God-forsaken, shaggy-haired, red-faced, un-shorn, hard-fisted, blasphemous wretches that have ever congregated, even at the gallows at Newgate, many of the visitors of the Peace Wing of the Democrat party were entitled to first consideration."[7]

Hines and the leadership group supposedly including Colonel George St. Ledger Grenfell checked into the Richmond House Hotel and set up shop, hanging a sign

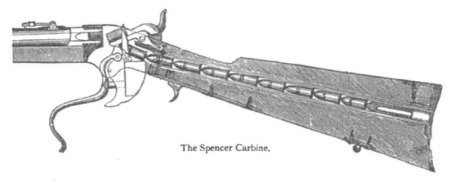

The Spencer Carbine.

The Spencer carbine could hold seven bullets in it's magazine and fire up to 20 per minute. The Henry carbine, a similar weapon, could hold 16 bullets and fire up 28 rounds in a minute!

"Six-shooters" like the Remington (and others) provided a quick burst of firepower to any force.

proclaiming "Missouri Delegation" over their rooms. It was scant disguise.[8] Grenfell was an English "soldier of fortune" who earlier served with General Morgan.[9]

Thompson also reputedly put out a call to the Southern men in Canada to assist, but was only able to find 75 volunteers.[10] The veteran soldiers from Canada were considered critical backbone to the insurrection and breakout. Hines in overall charge of the operation assembled his group in Toronto and made sure each man received $100 in cash, a train ticket to Chicago and a pistol with ammunition. Today we might view a pistol as scant armament for so dangerous a mission but in 1864 when nearly all firearms were single shot muzzle loading muskets and rifles, a five or six shot revolver was a powerful firearm. The revolvers could be viewed as the "Uzi" machine pistols of the day. The handguns were smuggled in from New York earlier. The number of revolvers in civilian hands was staggering. During the War the Colt company alone manufactured over 387,000, only half being purchased by the government.[11] The rest were out there - somewhere. The rebels were well armed, especially for urban fighting. Repeating rifles like the Henry or Spencer were relatively rare and even breech loading rifles uncommon outside of the military.

The men from Toronto arrived in Chicago in small groups of 8-10 and quietly checked into local hotels. Their role was a key one - to be the leadership cadre for the horde of SOL members said to be in the city. Clearly Hines needed the numbers the SOL offered but didn't trust their untested leadership, thus the need for his core Toronto contingent.

The Confederates hoped the Chicago action would spark rebels in other places, especially around prisoner camps at Camp Chase near Columbus and Camp Morton near Indianapolis to take similar offensive action. The greater the camp breakouts and city destruction, the greater the Northern response and greater the blow against the North.

Planning by Hines and his Copperhead legion was very detailed. For example all of the participants, both rebels and SOL supporters, were to wear red and white badges thus identifying them to compatriots. Their property would be also saved from destruction and looting by displaying a confederate flag. If everything worked the way they planned, the city would be a boiling riot of flames, rioting, destruction and murder. Knowing friend from foe was critical.

The Confederates and their minions were certain Camp Douglas could be taken with little trouble especially since the prisoners were kept informed of the plans as they developed. One of the daily visitors to the camp was the wife of a local judge who was also thought at the time a member of the SOL. Later charges against the judge were dropped, the traitorous actions of his wife being supposedly unknown to him. His wife's constant coming and going to the camp to provide baskets of food and warm clothing for the "poor Johnny Rebs" was a perfect cover to conceal her real mission of transmitting critical information to the prisoners and messages out. Any escape scheme needed the active and timely help of the prisoners. And as a "lady" and judge's wife she was above suspicion and a perfect conduit.

Camp Douglas wasn't a very secure compound, surrounded by a plank fence an inch and a quarter thick and a bare 12 feet high. A good strong push from the prisoners

General George McClelland was a bust as a military leader and politician.

would literally topple the walls. The boards were all nailed from the inside and a guard parapet ran three feet from the top of the fence on the outside. Looking at the camp critically it was designed to keep prisoners in not keep attackers from the outside out. It was very vulnerable to an outside assault. The camp was also within the city limits and easy to reach by streetcar. Various private buildings surrounded it too, including houses on the north side and a hotel on the east as well as other dwellings. The various structures provided cover for potential attackers and hidden positions for rebels to watch and track camp activities.

About a month prior to the convention, the SOL conspirators began to prepare in earnest. Many took trips out of the city to secretly practice with smuggled firearms. When the time for action came they wanted to be prepared.

But the plan went awry. In spite of strong financial support and firearms smuggled in to secret groups courtesy of Commissioner Thompson, Hines couldn't get the Southern sympathizers in Chicago to commit to an uprising. At the time of the convention it was assumed disgraced Union general George McClellan would be nominated by the Peace Democrats and he would easily defeat Lincoln in the fall. Since the delegates, many SOL leaders, thought McClellan was committed to take the North out of the war which would guarantee a Southern victory, why risk getting shot in a needless uprising? The Chicago scheme just fizzled into nothing.

Had they only known how McClellan would double cross them, the Copperheads would have been angry indeed. When the resolutions committee met under pressure from Vallandigham (the nominal SOL leader) it adopted a plank stating the Union was to be preserved but not by war rather by a, "cessation of hostilities with a view to an ultimate convention of the states or other peaceful means to that end, that at the earliest possible moment peace may be restored on

General Simon Bucker, CSA

the basis of a Federal Union of the States." Instead "Little Mac" accepted the nomination and later issued a letter repudiating the peace platform. He wasn't the Copperhead candidate he pretended to be! In retrospect they should have "risen" but the moment was past and golden opportunity lost.

The situation was made worse by the failure of Generals Price and Buckner to threaten or even seize St. Louis or Louisville. A Southern victory or even a strong threat would have greatly encouraged the SOL to rise in rebellion. The Southern general's failure to take effective military action helped doom the uprising.

General Sterling Price, CSA

The uprising took a further body blow when the *Chicago Tribune* published a complete exposé of the various SOL's secret handshakes, grips, signs, passwords, etc. To a point members were held up to ridicule. While hasty meetings were held to discuss changing the secret signs, there wasn't time before the "big show." Reportedly however many of the signs, passwords and rituals were later changed.

The capture and destruction of Atlanta brought the war home to many Southerners.

Colonel Benjamin Sweet adeptly defended against potential Confederate assaults on Camp Douglas and Chicago.

When Sherman defeated Bragg and handily captured Atlanta on September 2, 1864, Northern voters realized the war was well on the way to being won and the victory destroyed any chance of McClellan defeating Lincoln at the polls. The August opportunity for a Chicago-sparked insurrection was lost.

In spite of failing for want of committed conspirators, the plan was also doomed by a Union spy. Considered by the Confederates to be a loyal son of the South, he regularly kept Colonel Benjamin J. Sweet, the Union commandant of the Post of Chicago, informed of every nuance of the plan. One report claimed Union spies were so efficient every member of the Chicago SOL was identified!

Sweet's command was a large one in terms of geography including Madison, Wisconsin, southwest to Rock Island, Illinois, to Springfield and east as far as Detroit. Camp Douglas was part of his responsibility. He had full jurisdiction over everything relating to the military's affairs and various supply depots. Sweet was troop poor with a tremendous amount of responsibility but very few assets to protect it.

Sweet was appointed to the job in May 1864. Previously he commanded the 21st Wisconsin Volunteer Infantry Regiment and was thought mortally wounded at the battle of Perrysville, Kentucky, on October 8, 1862. The 21st Wisconsin was part of a Union force under Major General Don Carlo Buell that stopped Braxton Bragg's invasion of Kentucky. Although a tactical Confederate victory, Bragg was eventually driven back out of the state. When the battle started, Sweet was lying sick in an ambulance with malaria but he staggered out of his sickbed and bravely led his regiment into battle. The 21st was in the Army barely a month and was the greenest of the green. Although as well drilled as possible in the short time since their muster, they had never, "seen the elephant" as the popular Civil War expression went, and had yet to be blooded. Their first experience was devastating. By the end of the day, a third of the regiment was lost and Sweet twice wounded.[12] The first injury was a flesh wound to the neck but the second was a musket ball striking his right elbow and traveling up to his chest, a wound thought mortal. Although he eventually recovered, his right arm hung useless. Rather than accept a quiet mustering out as unfit for further field duty, he accepted transfer to the Veterans Reserve Corps and the command at Chicago. Given that he previously was an officer in the famous Iron Brigade, such fortitude was understandable.[13] Years later many of the older citizens remembered when he arrived to take command he was a pale young man of 32, "worn with long illness, his arm still painful."

His ace in the hole in Chicago was his intelligence network. The information his spies provided meant he was always a step ahead of the Confederates. When the attack on Camp Douglas became imminent, he shifted his men and artillery to counter any assault. One observer noted, had the rebels attempted an attack, there would not have been enough of them left standing to carry away their wounded. Sweet finally had his pleas for help answered on August 28 when he received a reinforcement of 1,200 short-term volunteers. They weren't really soldiers but looked like them and certainly at least could be used to bluff the SOL into thinking he now had real combat troops. It wouldn't be enough if the Confederates made a determined attack, but as a show of force, it did the trick. Even better, somehow the SOL were convinced Sweet's real troop strength was 7,000! Accurately counting soldiers was a difficult thing for amateurs to do correctly and the SOL leaders were nothing if not amateurs. When the hour for action arrived, SOL leaders blinked even as Hines fumed at their lack of courage.

Sweet was also astute enough to note a sharp upswing in the number of letters prisoners were sending home prior to the convention. Each man was allowed a one page letter each month but it was a task many men didn't bother doing. Suddenly every one was writing home and most of the pages were largely blank. A little detective work showed the letters contained secret messages all relating an expected change of fortunes! Clearly the men knew something was about to happen.

Confederate operational security was certainly less than optimal. In fact it was amateurish to the extreme. The entire plan to attack Camp Douglas had been laid out in detail during an earlier general meeting of the Chicago "temple" of the SOL. One of the planners carefully explained to all those present that two sides of the camp were most accessible and the west wall was clearly the weakest. Guns (presumably small caliber field pieces) were only on one side and attackers could approach the camp under cover of surrounding buildings. The attack would be quick, furious and successful. Spies soon relayed the details of the plan to Colonel Sweet.

The rebels also planned to take over the railroads entering the city, all dockyards, telegraph offices, public buildings and the like. In some instances SOL members had found employment in such critical places as railway yards, telegraph and post offices, even the office of the Provost Marshal.[14] When the rising came they were in a perfect position to seize and hold them. If Northern reaction was too strong, a torch would reduce the facilities to smoking embers. Should the carnage in Chicago spark a general rising across the old Northwest, arsenals at Indianapolis, Columbus, Springfield, Louisville and Frankfort would be seized and their arms and ammunition distributed to the SOL, further increasing their fighting form.

The infamous Confederate raider William Quantrill sacked Lawrence, Kansas, an act so barbarous even his Southern supporters disavowed it.

An artist's depiction of Quantrill's horrific destruction of innocent Lawrence.

It is worth considering that if the plot actually worked whether the horde of freed Confederate prisoners would have followed the orders of the SOL leaders or those of their military leaders is unknown. By regulation they should have responded to their own officers and not the civilian conspirators but in the heat of the inevitable confusion of escape all bets were off.

It is also confusing to evaluate how many of the new arrivals were supposed to be part of the plot. It is claimed the SOL had arms and ammunition for 10,000 men stored in the city, including carbines, revolvers and rifles. Supposedly, the arsenal was smuggled in over a number of months by ship and rail and carefully hidden in four different places in the city.

Doubtless Union men remembered the murderous Confederate raid on Lawrence, Kansas, the year before by the infamous Confederate bandit William Clark Quantrill. In the Lawrence assault, he and his "followers" burned a quarter of the town's buildings and summarily dragged out of their homes and murdered between 185-200 men and teenage boys. The killers who later formed the infamous James-Younger outlaw gang were members of Quantrill's mob. The James-Younger boys arguably received invaluable training in the finer points of outlawry from the master. Even Richmond was appalled by the brutal action of the Confederate force. Considering the organizational model of Quantrill's typical "raid," smaller groups of heavily armed "men" coming together from different directions and converging on the target, striking with extreme violence and showing no mercy, exactly the tactics the SOL rising was planning for Chicago, there was reason for concern regardless of how well the North thought they have thwarted the enemy.

Sweet also received information from Lt. Colonel Bennett H. Hill, the Assistant Provost Marshall of Detroit. Hill was a widely experienced officer. A graduate of West Point, he saw action in the Seminole War, Mexican-American War and field service in the Civil War.[15] It seems Hill received a letter from a man claiming to have secret information about a desperate plot against the Union and wanted money in exchange for the details. Hill ignored the letter as from a crank. He also received a second letter, ignoring it, too. Finally the man himself showed up in Hill's office and gave him sufficient information for Hill to report the details of rebel plans against Chicago and Camp Morton as well other particulars.[16] Apparently the man was one of the men detailed to go with Hines from Toronto. Hill instructed him to remain with Hines and report to Sweet in Chicago but when Hines reached Chicago, Federal agents noticed the informer wasn't with him. The informer never reported to any Union man again. There is speculation the raiders learned of his treachery, killing him in retribution. Investigators think he may have been a man named Smith who kept a hotel in Windsor frequented by rebels and picked up the information from his "guests." The game of spy and counter spy is never kind. Regardless of what happened to the turncoat, he provided additional warning and details of the scheme unfolding allowing Sweet to prepare and ultimately take counter action.

After pondering the reports provided by Hines in Chicago, Thompson pulled the plug on the entire operation. By day three of the Democrat convention it was clear to him Federal countermeasures were too strong and the thousands of SOL troops promised by their leadership were not ready to fight. If he ordered the attack without an overwhelming force sufficient to guarantee success, he risked a complete failure the South could not afford. By this point in the war his potential was nearly the last arrow in the Southern quiver. He couldn't afford to waste it. With little option, Thompson prudently called the operation off. Roughly a third of the 75 men from Toronto returned to the city. The rest went to Southern Illinois to either train local SOL or return to the Confederacy.

As a way of at least demonstrating their political relevance before their departure for various homes, many of the SOL marched in a massive torch light parade down the streets of Chicago. The head of the SOL in the state and the Chief of Staff of the Supreme Commander led the procession. It was certainly an example of high political theater and political impotence.

Regardless of the Chicago situation though, Hines and his crew also planned a simultaneous uprising in Indianapolis. However, a Union counterspy in the SOL ratted out the plot and the local Federal commander arrested the five leading conspirators, his quick action defusing the scheme. The Indianapolis Provost Marshal also reportedly seized 26 boxes of arms and ammunition secreted in a room in the newspaper basement. The shipping papers indicated the boxes contained "stationary" while individual crates were marked "Sunday School Books." After breaking the crates open, they found 24 were filled with 25,000 rounds of revolver ammunition and the remaining two with 350-400 pistols. All were hauled off to the Federal arsenal for safe-keeping. The next

Union spy Felix Stidger was a key part of getting inside of the SOL hierarchy.

day a careful search of a nearby room found six more boxes containing additional arms and ammunition as well as the invoices for the arms factories in the North that provided them and a list of city SOL members. Clearly the conspirators were ready for a bloody uprising!

The Union spy was 31- year old Felix Stidger, an unobtrusive Kentuckian dry goods store owner who managed to worm his way into the highest echelons of the SOL in Indiana and Kentucky. He was considered so loyal to the cause he was appointed Secretary of the Copperheads in Indiana! When he had enough damning information he reported to the Union military commander in Indiana but with the clear knowledge his life was forfeited if his treachery was discovered.

In order to coordinate the rising Hines, the field commander of the Confederates supporting the rebellion, journeyed to Louisville to meet with Stidger. The "eyeball to eyeball" meeting went well and the usually suspicious Hines apparently trusted Stidger completely. The spy's reports proved devastating to the Copperheads in Indiana. When the Federals finally pulled the plug on the conspirators they arrested over 100 of them, all as the direct result of Stidger's good work! Union troops made certain to arrest Stidger with the rest of the conspirators to provide him with cover since he continued to gather useable intelligence while in jail with his "friends." It wasn't until he appeared in court to testify for the Union his true role was revealed. All of the Copperhead leaders were found guilty of treason and awarded the ultimate punishment but President Johnson commuted the sentences with the intent of national reconciliation.[17]

The Johnson Island Debacles

There were two serious plots to free the soldiers from the prison camp at Johnson Island on Lake Erie. The first never got to execution stage before being cancelled but it spawned the second plan, which actually was set into motion and long captured the public imagination. Before we get to the two plans, understanding the target is important.

Johnson Island was selected late in 1861 as a perfect site for a prisoner of war camp, specifically sized to hold 2,500 officers. It is an old axiom of war when prisoners are captured it is best to separate officers from the enlisted men. Without officers to lead and organize them, the men were usually far easier to manage as well as more likely to be convinced to provide useful intelligence. Johnson Island was a particularly good

Colonel William Hoffman, a very experienced officer was the Union Commissary-General of Prisoners.

site since it allowed easy access by ship for supplies and Sandusky Bay provided protection from the full fury of Lake Erie winters. The fact it was an island added another layer of difficulty to any escape attempt.

South Bass, Middle Bass and Kelley Island, all off shore in Lake Erie, were also considered as possible locations but their closer proximity to Canada and therefore potential escape, was thought too great a risk. The large winery on Kelley Island was also seen as an unacceptable temptation for Union guard troops! Ironically, Colonel William Hoffman, the Union Commissary-General of Prisoners, the officer who ultimately recommended placing the prison at Johnson Island to the Secretary of War, used the steamer *Island Queen* as his search vessel.[18] Colonel Hoffman also visited Detroit, Toledo and Cleveland as possible sites. He was a veteran officer, a graduate of West Point

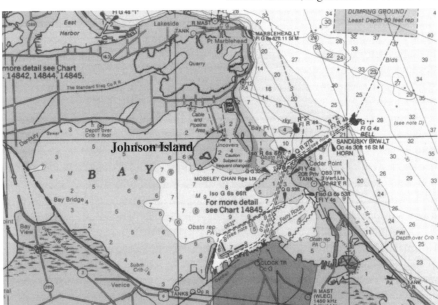

Johnson Island was just off Sandusky, Ohio. At various times it was called Johnson, Johnsons and Johnson's Island.

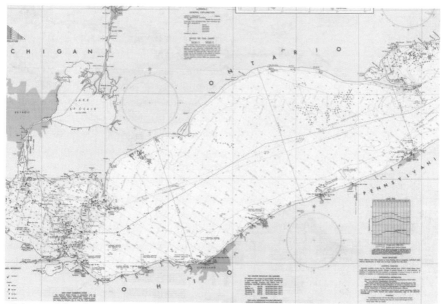

Johnson Island was not too distant from Canadian territory including Pelee Island.

with action in the Seminole War, frontier Indian fights, Mexican-American War and early Civil War, retiring in 1870 as a brevet Major General.[19]

Large stands of wood on the 16.5-acre island also provided the raw materials to build the camp and fuel for heating. Prisoners were kept in a dozen two-story frame buildings surrounded by a 15-foot high wood stockade. In addition there were latrines, hospital, wells, mess halls, etc. Another 40 buildings were outside the walls including stables, barns, quarters for the guards, and other ancillary structures. The camp opened for business in April 1862.

A total of roughly 15,000 prisoners passed through the camp during the war, reaching 3,200 men as the peak. On exception, some Confederate enlisted men were held in the camp as were a few Union deserters and political prisoners. Remarkably, it had the lowest mortality rate of any prisoner of war camp on either side, only about 200 men lost due to disease. Considering the tough Lake Erie winters and often terrible (sick, wounded, ill-fed and poorly clothed) condition many of the prisoners arrived in, it was an enviable record. Many of the dead are buried in the small camp cemetery.

The original guard force was known as the Hoffman Battalion named after Colonel Hoffman, Union Commissary-General of Prisons. It was a very small force consisting of four companies recruited in the local area. By September 1862 its strength was a mere 718 men. When six more companies were added in January 1864, it was designated the 128th Ohio Volunteer Infantry Regiment (OVI) with a strength of roughly 1,300 men.[20]

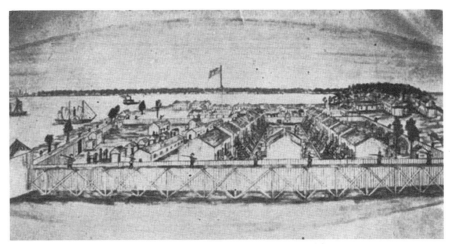

The prison camp at Johnson Island was well suited for it's purpose.

The first commander was Lieutenant Colonel William S. Pierson, a Sandusky lawyer. He was known as a good officer, the only complaint from superiors being he was too kind to the prisoners. When the unit was increased to a regiment Colonel Charles W. Hill, the Ohio Adjutant General, took command.

While it is natural prisoners would not like their guards, the Confederates were especially disdainful of theirs. First of course, the Yankees scrupulously enforced camp rules resulting in the death of one prisoner when he failed to obey them. The majority of the guards were not combat veterans but had enlisted specifically to be a member of the guard regiment. In addition, they were given a cash bonus and exempted from field service. Chances were they would never experience a shot fired in anger! The Confederate combat veterans were insulted by being ordered around by such men.

That said, both the Hoffman Battalion and the 128th OVI did furnish detachments for service elsewhere in the War in locations as far flung as western Virginia in 1862 and Southern Ohio against Morgan's raiders in 1863. These deployments were "in extremis," troops were desperately needed and regardless of the 128th being a guard regiment, it was time to give them a chance to "see the elephant."[21]

During the various escape scares the island was reinforced with other units including elements of the 12th Ohio Cavalry, 24th Artillery, 1st Ohio Heavy Artillery, 1st Brigade of 3rd Division 6th Corps. In addition, the island was used as a rendezvous and instruction site by several Ohio regiments prior to war deployment. Seeing all of this military activity was very discouraging to the prisoners. Not only did it largely prevent their escape but it clearly showed the great strength of the North. While they knew every available Southern man was fighting at the front (or so the "Lost Cause Legend" would have them believe), the North was able to quickly deploy such powerful forces to the island at seemingly the drop of a hat!

An unusual incident broke the cold monotony of camp life in the winter of 1864. One of the prisoners gave birth to a "bouncing baby boy." Since no females were held at Johnson Island, it was clearly a case of a "secret soldier" finally showing herself! Females masquerading as males were not ucommon.

Sometimes tension among the prisoners sparked into violence. In February, 1865, one prisoner murdered another. The reason is unknown but rather than committing the killer to a court martial, Federal authorities arranged to transfer him South for appropriate action.

The camp was ordered closed on June 8, 1865.

Escapes

As expected given the circumstances of capable men crowded together with little to occupy their time or minds, escape planning was a common activity. The officers applied their full intellect and leadership experience to the problems of not only how to get out of the compound but perhaps more important, what to do afterward? They knew organization was critical. Major General Isaac Trimble, the ranking Confederate officer in the camp, assumed overall command of the planning and execution and other officers placed in charge of each prison building. Together they formed the prison "escape" committee charged with directing and approving all escape efforts.

The men could literally "storm" their way out, tearing down the walls and overwhelming the comparatively few guards. The viability of this method depended on the number of guards on the island. As the war progressed, more guards were assigned to the camp, decreasing this option. There was also the quieter way of just bribing the guards to look the other way, allowing a few men at least to hot foot it out of the camp.

Outside the wall there was still the challenge of getting off the island. In the winter they could walk across the frozen bay. During the rest of the year it was possible to seize the small steamer used to run back and forth to Sandusky. On reaching town they could capture a larger steamer and run for freedom in Canada. Assuming a prison population of 2,500 men and the maximum of 500-800 men on a large steamer, at least three and likely four steamers were needed. Sandusky's population was roughly 25,000 but wasn't expected to offer any particular problems to the escapees.

Instead of fleeing to Canada, they could also travel overland as a military force to Southern lines in Virginia, Tennessee or Georgia after moving through Pittsburgh or Kentucky. They would need to find horses, wagons for the ill, weapons and food but given good luck, it was possible. At best they would be an armed rabble but also a dangerous one capable of causing huge disruption in the Union rear area.

Men tried numerous ways to escape. One group of enterprising rebels tunneled from their barracks under the wall only to be greeted by several guards when the dirt covered diggers finally burst from their dark and dank cavern into daylight. Doubtless an inmate passed the word to the warden about the attempt. One of the same group tried again using a different approach. Seeing the guard driving the garbage wagon into camp was too drunk to remain conscious for long the prisoner waited until the trooper sat down under a tree and soon passed out. The prisoner quickly threw the soldier's overcoat on, hopped on the wagon and drove out the front gate only to be stopped just short of freedom when the boozy guard woke up enough to yell an alarm.

One Louisiana lieutenant was especially resourceful. After cobbling together a musket from a length of wood, old tin cans and the handle of a soup ladle, he obtained a Union uniform from a hospital worker and tried to march right out of camp! His ploy almost worked until a sharp-eyed officer noticed he had no cartridge belt, which led to his apprehension.[22]

Some attempts were successful. In October 1864 Captain Robert C. Kennedy of the 1st Louisiana Infantry supposedly went over the wall with a homemade rope, stole a small skiff and eventually reached safety in Canada via crossing at Buffalo. It took nearly a week for the guards to discover the escape since brother officers kept answering for him at roll call. Later Kennedy would be infamous for his role in trying to burn down New York City with firebombs.

A mass escape of between 25-30 men was tried during the month of December 1864. The stampede overwhelmed the gate guard and in spite of numerous shots fired, some of the prisoners reached freedom on the mainland. A local farmer, alerted by the sharp reports of the rifled muskets, grabbed his trusty double-barreled shotgun, marched out of his house and promptly rounded up the runners.

Military Executions

Johnson Island was also the site of several military executions. After being convicted by military court martial in Cincinnati of recruiting for the Confederacy within Union lines and carrying messages for the South, two Kentuckians, Captains William F. Corbin and Thomas J. McGraw, were hauled off to the island for "death by firing squad." While death is death, execution by firing squad is considered honorable, as opposed to hanging reserved for heinous crimes such as treason and murder.[23] Corbin's sister pleaded with President Lincoln to commute her brother's sentence but he rejected her appeal.

The order was carried out on May 15, 1863 with full military precision. The entire guard battalion less duty troops and the firing party formed up facing Sandusky Bay in a hollow square formation facing inward with the east end open. The two unfortunates arrived in a wagon sitting forlornly on their own coffins. The post chaplain followed the wagon and a military guard under the command of an experienced sergeant flanked it. The regimental band blaring out the somber tones of the "Dead March" was immediately behind. Once the procession reached the designated spot in front of the massed battalion, the Kentuckians and their coffins were unloaded. Meanwhile the band halted, the bandmaster aligning it facing the point of execution. After the pine boxes were carefully arranged on the ground the men sat on them and the chaplain read a short statement from the men thanking the post commander, his officers and soldiers for the kindness shown them during their stay and forgiving all enemies and accusers. The Post Adjutant then ceremoniously read the official proceedings including sentences.

The soldier sits blindfolded on his coffin awaiting the deadly hail of bullets.

The post's Acting Provost Marshal marched out the 16-man firing detail, halting it centered on the prisoners before ordering a facing movement to provide a clear and direct firing direction.[24] Once the detail was properly aligned and the chaplain offered a short prayer, the Adjutant blindfolded both men who were still seated on their coffins. He likely also pinned a white piece of paper over their hearts to provide a clear target for the firing detail. He then positioned himself near the band.

The 16 man firing detail was aligned with eight men for each prisoner. Prior to drawing their muskets the Adjutant loaded each one personally making certain that one of the eight (two in the 16) was loaded without a musket ball. The loading was done out of sight of the firing party. The muskets were then racked and issued to the soldiers in random order allowing for two sets of eight. This meant no shooter knew for certain that he fired the killing shot. It is likely the Adjutant or the Acting Provost Marshal reminded the soldiers they were just doing their duty, however disagreeable it might be.

When all of the participants were in proper position and prepared, the Acting Provost Marshal raised his right arm, palm facing front and fingers tight. In response the firing party brought their muskets silently up to their shoulders. When the officer lowered his arm, the soldiers took careful aim. When he ordered "fire" 16 rifled muskets spat hot lead and the two Kentuckians fell to the ground dead. He then commanded "order arms," "right face" and "forward march" moving the firing detail back to barracks, replacing the muskets in the racks randomly. A ration of whiskey for a distasteful job well done usually followed.

After a quick examination by the post surgeon and an official proclamation of death, the men were laid into their boxes. A sharp command from the officer in charge reformed the battalion and it moved off to the dirge of the "Dead March." So ended traitor's deaths![25]

Interviewed long after the War was over, an old-timer who was the assistant quartermaster at the camp, recalled two other prisoners were executed "for atrocious treatment of Southern Unionists." However, there is no official record of the event.

At least one Union soldier was also executed by firing squad at the island. Private Reuben Stout of the 60th Indiana Volunteer Infantry convicted of desertion and murder by court martial. Ominously he stated at his court martial he was seduced by the siren call of the infamous Knights of the Golden Circle, the same group that figured so prominently in the Southern hope for a Northwestern Conspiracy. Regardless of the feeble excuse, he was on the wrong end of justice. As the act was certainly treason, he should have been hung as opposed to shot, but justice can be fickle.

Approximately 500 men were shot or hung by both sides during the War. Union and Confederate Articles of War were nearly identical concerning execution for various military crimes. During the early part of the conflict both sides tended to treat deserters with leniency but as the War dragged on and the desertion rate skyrocketed, especially in the South, more draconian measures were instituted. One of the most disreputable mass executions was ordered by Confederate Major General George Pickett as Commander of the Department of Virginia and North Carolina. In February 1864 he approved hanging twenty-two prisoners of war, soldiers of the 2nd North Carolina Infantry, a Union unit. He claimed they were deserters from the Army of Northern Virginia.[26]

Johnson Island Planning

None of the various Johnson Island plans worked in the tactical sense but they did have collateral success in scaring the Great Lakes public, shipping interests and governments, local, state and Federal.

Plan 1

The first plan to free the prisoners at Johnson Island was apparently conceived by Lieutenant William H. Murdaugh of the Confederate Navy in February 1863. Murdaugh previously was a lieutenant in the U.S. Navy giving up his sworn duty by bolting south when the war started. He achieved the rank of commander before the end of the war.[27]

The plan he developed was imaginative and reflected the type of action the South needed to turn the Great Lakes into a bloody battleground that could divert Union attention and affect the Federal war effort. He knew the only U.S. Naval vessel on the Great Lakes was the gunboat *USS Michigan* and if she could be somehow captured or at least neutralized, opportunities for causing mayhem in the Union rear area were terrific.

Commissioned in 1844, the 165-foot, 685 gross ton *Michigan* was the United States Navy's first iron-hulled warship and performed a critical role in Great Lakes security during the Civil War. Although by no means a powerful "battleship," by virtue of being the only real warship on the Great Lakes, she was the key to any plan. With the outbreak of the war her armament was upgraded consisting of a 30-pounder Parrott rifle, five 20-pounder Parrott rifles, six 24-pounder smoothbores, and two 12-pounder boat

Lt. William H. Murdaugh developed the original scheme to free prisoners at Johnsons Island.

howitzers. Her normal complement was 88 officers and men.

Other than her potential for direct combat intervention, the ship also served a vital "show the flag" mission, reinforcing the power of the Federal government to folks who might otherwise be tempted to "stray." For example, on July 28, 1863, following the deadly riots in New York City, Commander John C. Carter commanding *Michigan* reported from Detroit, "I found the people suffering under serious apprehensions of a riot... The presence of the ship perhaps did something toward overawing the refractory, and certainly did much to allay the apprehensions of the excited, doubting people." In August 1863, the warship did the same duty in Buffalo.

Murdaugh proposed purchasing a small steamer in Canada and manning her with a crew of roughly 50 men with the public purpose of embarking on a mining expedition to far off Lake Superior. His crew would be armed with revolvers and cutlasses and homemade torpedoes (mines or bombs) built out of blasting powder and small iron buoys. The mining story was a perfect cover story for a boat filled with roughnecks and blasting material. A generous supply of turpentine, gunpowder and fuses would provide the means to burn Northern cities and destroy the aqueduct at Rochester, Erie Canal locks at Buffalo, the Ohio Canal locks and Illinois and Michigan locks at Chicago. He even targeted the Soo Locks at Sault Ste. Marie, Michigan.

Key to the plan was capturing the *Michigan*. With the powerful warship in Confederate hands, all of the lake ports were open to destruction. She could bombard Tonawanda, Detroit and Cleveland and destroy any lake shipping that blundered across her bow. Once the men on the small steamer took the *Michigan*, the original ship could act independently thus multiplying the actual damage and the panic manifold. When the word spread the *Michigan* was on the loose under the Stars and Bars, Federal shipping wouldn't dare to leave port. The economic impact would be devastating.

When he mentioned the plan to two fellow lieutenants, they too immediately recognized the potential, perhaps excited by the prospect of the great adventure such a plan offered as opposed to the routine of normal naval life. As they pushed the proposal "up the chain" of command it met resistance at every level until it reached the Secretary of the Navy Stephen Mallory, who recognized the great upside it offered for little risk. However, a lack of money, estimated at a mere $25,000, temporarily shelved it. Finally the money was found and three young officers, now joined by a fourth friend were ordered to hold themselves ready for action. A scratch crew made up of sailors from the scuttled *CSS Virginia* (of *Monitor - Virginia* fame) was also designated. Suddenly the mission was scrapped. Jefferson Davis, the President of the Confederacy, was concerned it could potentially upset relations with the British if it was perceived Canadian (British) neutrality was somehow trod on. At the time Britain was diplomatically "ignoring" the private construction of two Confederate ironclad raiders in British ports. Since the two vessels were considered vital for Southern interests, nothing, especially not a hair-brained scheme to hijack a Federal warship and use it to attack shipping in the Great Lakes, could be allowed to impact it.[28]

In August 1863 Secretary of War James A. Seddon and Secretary of the Navy Stephen R. Mallory reconsidered the imaginative scheme and directed Navy Lieutenant Robert D. Minor to de-

CSA Secretary of War James A. Seddon.

velop a variation with the goal of freeing the prisoners on Johnson Island. Minor was a veteran of the ironclad *CSS Virginia*.[29]

The two British built raiders were now at sea and captured Confederate officers were piling up at Johnson Island. That Mallory advocated such a daring plan is in line with his character. Prior to secession he was a U.S. Senator from Florida and chairman of the Committee on Naval Affairs. During his chairmanship naval technology was evolving quickly and he strongly advocated ships of the U.S. Navy should be as capable as those of Great Britain and France, then the foremost navies in the world. He also wrote and pushed a bill through Congress requiring compulsory retirement of officers not meeting professional standards. Given the tenor of the times, when senior Army and Navy officers became living fossils, it was a remarkable feat![30]

The new plan was soon drawn up and approved. A budget of roughly $111,000 was provided and a cover story concocted that the entire 22-man "crew" was going to England was circulated. Given the success of the Confederate ocean raiders, sending additional sailors to England was logical and didn't attract comment.

How many people were aware of the real plan is questionable. Certainly Lieutenant Minor and a Lieutenant B. P. Loyall and the mission commander Lieutenant John Wilkinson knew the details. Of course, Mallory and Seddon were in the loop too but

CSA Secretary of the Navy Stephen R. Mallory.

the rest of the men thought they were going to England. Given the state of Confederate security it is logical to assume Northern spies picked up at least the broad outline on the real task.

Early in October the crew successfully ran the Union blockade off North Carolina's Cape Fear and reached Halifax, Canada. Dividing into two parties they took the train to Montreal and checked into small, quiet rooming houses to avoid attracting attention. The group was augmented in Canada by 32 additional men, all escaped prisoners arranged for by Confederate agents. Whether any of these new men were in fact Northern agents is unknown but not unlikely. Since Wilkinson was planning on 180 new men joining in Canada, he was certainly disappointed. Counting the 22 he brought with him from the South his group only numbered 54, very small for the big plans he intended. Considering that the number of men was critical in the assault, his decision to continue with the mission was questionable. Seizing the *Michigan*, even with great subterfuge, required a sudden and overwhelming assault and that meant maximizing the number of men in the assault force.

Their next hurdle was to communicate with the prisoners at Johnson Island to let them know of the plan and to be prepared for action at a moment's notice. A carefully coded message was passed to prisoner Brigadier General James J. Archer through the personal columns in the *New York Herald*. D-day was shortly after November 4. Archer commanded the Texas Brigade in Lee's Army of Northern Virginia and was captured at Gettysburg.[31]

The original plan was to board a steamer at Windsor (on the opposite side of the river from Detroit), overpower the crew and use it to reach the island. The prisoners would have already overwhelmed the guards and could be quickly taken to Canada and freedom. Other captured steamers would make the evacuation all the quicker.

Fate intervened when a Canadian named McQuaig was introduced to Wilkinson by a trusted Tennessee blockade-runner. McQuaig told the officer that steamers to Windsor were too few to be reliable and it was better to develop another plan.

Meanwhile the group sent a spy to Sandusky to evaluate the target. He reported back the *Michigan* was anchored directly off the prison about 200 yards out and there were reportedly 400 troops in the guard battalion. The only artillery consisted of two small howitzers, one of which was mounted on the ferry used to run between the island and Sandusky. Overall the camp was well defended since the *Michigan* had arrived at Sandusky in late October. She spent the summer cruising the lake on recruiting duty but also stopped at Buffalo and Detroit to provide a "calming" presence in the event of draft riots.[32]

Concurrently, the raiders were busy accumulating arms and ammunition including 100 Colt revolvers and two small 9-pounder cannons.[33] Ammunition for the Colts was easy to acquire but since purchasing cannonballs would raise suspicion, they substituted iron dumbbells. In point of fact, the dumbbells were similar to naval "dismasting" shot used to destroy the rigging of sailing vessels during a close in engagement. Butcher knives would substitute for cutlasses and grapples were common enough in commercial fishing and salvage that purchasing a few from different sources caused little comment. The grapples were needed to haul the steamer alongside the *Michigan* after she lay alongside with way on.

The final plan was to board one of the steamers running from Ogdensburg, New York, to Chicago masquerading as a group of mechanics and laborers traveling to work on the city's waterworks construction projects. To this end a passage was purchased

The USS Michigan *sometime after the Civil War.*

for a group of 25 "laborers" to Chicago with the other raiders intending to board in small groups along the Welland Canal.[34] A smaller group was to meet the steamer at St. Catherine's on the Lake Erie end of the canal with a number of boxes labeled "machinery" containing the guns and ammunition.

Once the steamer was out in the lake and well into American waters, the raiders would reveal themselves and overpower the steamer's crew. After mounting the two 9-pounders, the steamer was to head directly to Sandusky reaching the *Michigan* at the break of dawn and after accidently colliding with her and grapples thrown, the raiders were to rush aboard, overwhelm the crew and seize her. Once secure, the men would load the *Michigan's* guns with a charge of grape and train them on the prison headquarters, demanding the surrender of the guard force. Given the overwhelming firepower of the *Michigan,* Wilkinson was certain the prison commander had no option but to surrender. Using the captured steamer and *Michigan*, plus the half dozen boats usually moored at Sandusky, it would be an easy matter to carry the prisoners to freedom in Canada barely 40 miles distant.

The raiders were so sure of success, the St. Catherine's group went to the port to wait the anticipated arrival of the rest of the men on the Ogdensburg steamer. Then their world collapsed when they learned Secretary of War Stanton had telegraphed Great Lakes mayors on November 11, warning of a Confederate plot to raid port cities. It seems the Governor-General of Canada had learned of the Confederate plans and concerned with the potential for a diplomatic disaster between the U.S. and Canada, quietly passed a warning to Washington. He also sent a representative to keep watch on the canal for any suspicious activity. Stanton already had reports from the Provost Marshal of Detroit that Confederate supporters would use two captured steamers to attack the prison camp within two days. Stanton's spies were sending a stream of information, some true and much false making sorting it out very difficult and the "word" from the Governor-General certainly helped clarify the reports. Stanton's telegram of the possible raids electrified the port mayors and with all on guard, Wilkinson and his men could only abandon their scheme. Their whole plan depended on the powerful element of surprise. Without it they were literally dead men!

The Union Army immediately dispatched a battery of 10-pound rifled artillery to Johnson Island as well as 500 newly raised troops. Sandusky militia as well as units from surrounding areas also reported for duty. The rifled artillery was especially useful since it was far more accurate and had a greater range than the smoothbore Napoleons in popular use. The rifled guns were directed at the channel and Napoleons positioned to rake the prison to "discourage" escapes. An approaching enemy vessel would have a very nasty surprise when the rifles opened up and the prisoners equally shocked when the Napoleons roared out their double charges of canister![35]

As an added measure, the commander at Detroit dispatched the steamer *Forest Queen* down to Lake Erie to patrol for Confederate raiders. Although unarmed, she could provide warning of an attack. Likewise he pressured his Canadian spy network to find out whatever they could about the plan. The *Forest Queen* came back empty handed with no evidence of preparation for a raid.

Parrot rifles (rifled artillery as opposed to smooth bore Napoleons) were very effective field pieces.

To keep a diplomatic lid on the affair, the Canadian Prime Minister met with the Mayor of Buffalo and Department of the East Army Commander Major General John Dix. To assure Buffalo was well protected, Dix had earlier reinforced Buffalo with a regiment of militia. Dix was greatly concerned since the Buffalo militia units were only partially armed and the state arsenal with 3,000 stand of arms and 20 pieces of artillery was practically unguarded! There also wasn't ammunition available for the artillery. Prior to his dispatch of additional militia, the total guard was only 30 men from the Invalid Corps. Stanton's warning added credibility to many rumors and when a report surfaced about a planned attack on Detroit's Belle Isle from Windsor in 1864, 1,000 men were set to chopping down enough trees for a hasty defensive barricade. Another force was at Erie building defensive fortifications for the harbor.[36]

Once it was clear the Johnson Island scare was over, the militia was dismissed and some of the regular troops transferred out but clearly the local guard force needed to be increased against potential future "scares."

Regardless of what actually happened, Great Lakes newspapermen had a field day with publishing misleading and outright false information about the episode. No story was too wild or outrageous for the papers.

One said an ironclad steamer was on the way from Canada to capture the island, free the prisoners, burn Sandusky and then attack shipping. Another claimed the channel was protected with "torpedoes," the Civil War term for what today we call mines. If the raiders succeeded, there would have been havoc on the lakes.

The attempt on Johnson Island was actually a near thing. After the war ended one of the former prisoners was supposedly told by Confederate Secretary of War Sheddon that had the raiders had two more days before Stanton sent out his eleventh hour warning, the attack on the island would have been made.

In spite of knowing what was planned, however, the Canadians took no action against the Confederate force in country. Clearly the Canadians were playing the middle of the field, but with a strong bias to the Confederates. The raiders later "exfiltrated" from Canada and arrived safely in Wilmington after again running the Yankee blockade.

According to Wilkinson, it was a Canadian named McQuaig who betrayed them. Apparently McQuaig concluded if the plan succeeded his own fortune was in jeopardy, including possible imprisonment or exile. Being faint of heart, he folded and told all to the Canadian authorities who passed the warning to the Northern Secretary of State.

There was a later report that the real impetus to rescue the Southern officers was because Johnson Island was a deliberately arranged Northern death trap for the prisoners. The argument went something like this. The officers were from the south and used to warm weather. By placing them in a prison so far north, exposed to the harsh winter winds and temperature, they were clearly going to perish. It was, in effect, inhumane to place southerners given the "deadly" environment. Therefore, all efforts were needed to try to rescue them from such a cruel and certain death.

Given the gift of hindsight it is easy to see the daring plot failed through an abysmal lack of security. Too many men knew about the plan and as result, the word leaked. The old adage about the "need to know" wasn't only ignored it was sliced, diced and mulched. The result was inevitable failure.

Another scare popped up in January 1864 and, of course, it was the result of an irresponsible press report. Supposedly, 2,000 - 3,000 Confederates had gathered on Point Pelee, Canada, about a dozen miles north of Sandusky. Apparently the plan involved their marching across the frozen lake and storming the camp. When a violent storm reputedly broke up the ice, the planned attack was abandoned. Regardless of the mind-boggling foolishness of the idea, the Army did establish a lookout in a house on the peninsula near Marblehead Lighthouse to keep a watchful eye on the lake, frozen or not.

Another scare was revealed by a Toronto newspaper in July 1864. Details were not provided but apparently enough credence was given to cause the *Michigan* to lay off the prison "just in case."

Plan 2

How the second scheme hatched is open to some speculation but one of Thompson's first actions on arrival at Montreal was to ask a Confederate naval officer details about the *Michigan*. As the only real U.S. Navy strength on the Great Lakes, her capture or at least neutralization was critical to Southern naval operations on the lakes. When the first Confederate naval officer proved unequal to the job it was passed to agent Charles H. Cole, a 38-year old captain in the Southern army. One observer said Cole was 5-foot, 7-inches tall and weighed about 135 pounds. He was further distinguished with long red hair, long drooping mustachios and beady little grey eyes. He was not a man who would blend into a crowd. Cole soldiered with the famous Confederate cavalry General Nathaniel Bedford Forrest before being captured. Sent to Johnson Island as a prisoner, he escaped in July, 1864, thus he had first hand knowledge of the camp's weaknesses and operations. Cole also claimed to hold a commission as a lieutenant in the Confederate Navy, a skill that may have recommended him to Thompson.

Cole, agent John Y. Beall and a young army officer named Bennett Young spent two weeks doing a careful evaluation of the *Michigan* and her influence on the maritime aspects of the Great Lakes. Their report to Thompson was replete with opportunities for the South.

They reported Buffalo was virtually undefended, only a single regiment of the Invalid Corps guarding the city. Since the regiment was performing hospital duty and guarding various supplies including ammunition and artillery, it was hardly positioned for immediate reaction to a Confederate armed threat.

In Cleveland, they claimed to have toured a government iron foundry producing cannons being sent to Sandusky, Milwaukee and Chicago.[37] Cole also noted various sailing directions around Cleveland.

The next stops were Detroit and then Chicago. Cole paid special attention to the new and bigger tugs in use on the Lakes, estimating them at 175 tons, single propeller, ten knot speed and capable of hauling enough coal for 36 hours of running. Perhaps more important, he noted each tug could carry two guns, a larger one on the stern and a smaller one on the bow. Armed tugs were common along the east coast. It would have been a small matter to bring a 12-pound Napoleon on the stern deck with a 3 or 6-pounder on the bow. Thinking ahead to the potential of attacking Camp Douglas, he related the tugs could easily cross the offshore bar, enter the river and use their guns to destroy bridges and shoot up other

John Y. Beall lead the unsuccessful Philo Parsons *raid on Johnsons Island.*

Grain elevators were easy target for arsonists.

targets as long as their ammunition lasted. The city was defenseless. Milwaukee could be attacked the same way. Detroit was also open to such water borne assaults, even more so considering deep water allowed tugs to run close inshore. Sheboygan was unprotected, too, and as a major grain supplier was a good target. The guns at Mackinac Island offered a fine command of the Straits but it was unclear whether he was aware that the garrison at the fort had long been withdrawn. He opined Lake Erie and Ontario offered good prospects for Confederate success, but the city of Erie was a difficult location to enter due to the long protecting arm of the Presque Isle Peninsula. Of course none of these opportunities for lake attack could be possible if the powerful guns of the *Michigan* were defending.

Seeing the huge opportunities the destruction or capture of the warship offered, Thompson's men began to build their concept of operations. As the plan developed,

Cole reportedly became "friends" with Commander John C. Carter, captain of the *Michigan*, with the idea of bribing him but it became apparent the veteran officer could not be bought. Thompson evidently liked Cole's report and placed him in charge of the land side of the operation and assigned agent John Y. Beall to assist him. Although he saw active duty as a soldier, Beall was later commissioned as a sailing master thus providing a critical skill for the *Michigan* plot.

When Beall first reached Canada and reported to Thompson, he supposedly asked to be allowed to start privateering on Lake Huron. Given the amount of shipping on the Lakes, much of which was transiting Lake Huron and the many small islets, bays and coves on the Canadian side all providing excellent locations to hide until the "heat" was off, it was a good choice. Instead, Thompson decided to use him for the Johnson Island mission.

During a meeting in Sandusky, Cole and Beall cobbled together a plan that was essentially a variation of Murdaugh's scheme. In short, agents would slip out of Canada, seize a Lake Erie steamer, use it to capture the *Michigan* and in turn attack and free the thousands of Confederate officers in the Johnson Island prison camp. The horde of prisoners backed up by the *Michigan's* powerful guns, would capture other ships, tear up port cities, destroy railroads and bridges and, in general, create havoc in the entire region. Once they heard of the success at Johnson's Island, the SOL in other port cities, especially Cleveland, would rise up and seize local steamers and set out as part of a fleet of Confederate privateers capturing and destroying Union shipping across the defenseless Great Lakes. Without the *Michigan's* awesome firepower, the Union would be utterly prostrate to even minimally armed rebel raiders. Perhaps even more important, the psychological effect would be devastating, literally shutting down shipping across the Great Lakes. Wild tales of desperate and bloodthirsty Confederates sinking ships and murdering their crews would gain a fearsome notoriety regardless of their accuracy especially as promulgated by the newspapers. While technically the raiders could be considered privateers, it is likely the Union would have called them pirates and acted accordingly.[38] There was even the opportunity to extort tribute from lake ports and shipping not to destroy them. Gold has a certain value all of its own!

Key to the scheme was the *Philo Parsons*. The 222-ton steamer was built in Algonac, Michigan, in 1861 to serve the passenger and freight trade between Detroit and the western Lake Erie Islands to include Sandusky and intervening river ports. In 1866 she was "sold Chicago" running between the city and St. Joseph with stops at Grand Haven and Muskegon. She was cut down to a tug in 1870, but had a short career as she soon started to come apart at the seams. Instead of an expensive rebuilding, she was abandoned in the north branch of the Chicago River and left to rot away. She was destroyed in the Chicago Fire of 1871.[39]

The plan went into action on September 19, 1864 when agent Bennett G. Burley boarded the *Philo Parsons* in Detroit with about 40 other passengers.[40] Burley was another agent with a dashing background. After being captured during a raid along the coast of Maryland, he was locked up at the Fort Delaware prison just below

The Philo Parsons *was an innocent passenger and freight steamer before she became the center of the Confederate plot.*

Philadelphia. He claimed he escaped by making his way down a drain and swimming underwater for 25 yards finally emerging into the Delaware River. After a time he reached Toronto and fell in with Thompson and company. Burley knew Beall from his work on the Chesapeake.

After the *Philo Parsons* started down river Burley convinced the captain to make an unscheduled stop on the Canadian side at a little town called Sandwich where four fellow agents boarded. The number of men was evidently less than expected since later one of the *Philo Parsons* testified he heard one of the Detroit men say, "Where are the rest of them?" One of the four new men replied, "They didn't come."

Beall and about 20 men boarded the small steamer at her next stop at Amherstburg again on the Canadian side of the Detroit River. They also carried aboard an old large, black trunk tied together with rope. Unknown to the captain, it was filled with weapons for the raiders. The captain of the *Philo Parsons* thought they looked like "skeedaddlers" (aka military deserters) from Ohio who had hid out in Canada until the pressure was off. Such low-lifes were common enough to cause little comment. None of the raider groups showed any apparent recognition of the others. All acted as perfect strangers.

As the steamer churned her way down river and into Lake Erie some of the agents morphed into very pleasant and friendly folks, mixing well with other non-agent passengers, even turning sheet music pages for ladies "tickling" the ivory of the ship's parlor piano! It was all very pleasant.

Scheduled stops were made at North Bass Island, South Bass Island, Middle Bass Island and Kelley Island as expected. Passengers came aboard and others departed, freight was loaded and unloaded as normal.

At 4:00 p.m. she hauled out of Kelley Island bound for Sandusky and her date with the *Michigan*. Or at least that's what the Confederate raiders thought.

About a quarter of an hour later, Beall entered the wheelhouse and put a pistol to the head of Mate DeWitt Nichols and brusquely told the startled man the boat was now under his orders. He stated, "I am a Confederate officer. There are 30 of us, well armed. I seize this boat and take you as prisoner. You must pilot the boat as I direct."

Breaking open the trunk and arming themselves with revolvers and hatchets, the crew ran up the "stars and bars" on the steamer's jack-staff and after roughly searching them for weapons, the male passengers and crew were herded at gunpoint below decks. Not all the men went willingly, but a couple of pistol shots sped them on their way. One sailor claimed each of the raiders brandished two revolvers and a belt and holster held a third.

One of the *Philo Parsons* crew remembered seeing one of the raiders, "…run after the fireman with a cocked revolver in his hand, shouting to him to go down the main hatch or he would shoot him. The fireman escaped and the man turned to me and made the same order. I told him to "go to hell" and he shot at me, the ball passing between my legs as I was ascending from the main to upper deck."

The women were placed in the cabin, a far more comfortable place than the stifling hold. In keeping with Southern "chivalry," women were not searched, accepting their word they were not armed. None the less, several women broke down and cried, dejected from their shocking treatment. The entire take over of the steamer took less than half an hour.

By 5:00 p.m. the steamer was eight miles off Cedar Point and bound for the entrance to Sandusky Bay. Whether the *Michigan* was in plain sight anchored off the prison camp or not is questionable. It was now that one of the engineers told Beall the ship didn't have enough fuel to run the eight hours he wanted after seizing the warship! His only choice was to come about and return to Middle Bass Island, the nearest location with a stock of cordwood.[41]

The unexpected return of the steamer to the island created confusion among the residents. When men who normally refueled the ship learned she was under the control of the raiders, they refused to load her. At least until the agents "encouraged" them with a few well fired shots!

Among the startled folks on the island was the *Philo Parsons'* captain, 58-year old Sylvester F. Atwood. As normal he left the boat once a week when she stopped upbound for Detroit. Since he lived on the island, it gave him a chance to visit his family and also gave the Mate an opportunity to run the steamer on his own and gain some valuable experience. Once he debarked he saw nothing of her until a bit after 7:00 p.m. when (in his words) a little boy, "came running much frightened, (saying) they were shooting there and killing his father and said the *Parsons* had come. I immediately started for the dock, saw a number of men running about there, went up and asked them what the hell was up. Three or four pistols were at once pointed at me and I was ordered aboard the boat. I refused to go and replied that I was captain of that boat and myself. Two of them shoved me onto the plank and I walked aboard. They followed me to the cabin and I saw the crew and passengers sitting there guarded by men with pistols."

The cordwood loading was interrupted when the small 173-ton steamer *Island Queen* suddenly appeared inbound to the same dock the *Philo Parsons* was moored. The *Island Queen* ran from the Bass Islands to Sandusky every morning, stopping at

The Confederates attended to sink the Island Queen.

Kelley Island and returning every afternoon. It was strictly a boring milk run and nothing ever happened. However, this time was different. As the captain closed the last several feet to the dock the raiders suddenly appeared preparing to board and seize her. Sensing the danger, the steamer's captain tried to haul off but was unable to do so in time. The rebels had her! In the confusion, one of the raiders fired at the *Island Queen's* engineer, the ball passing his nose and through his left cheek and ear! The raiders didn't want the small steamer, but they couldn't let her go. Her passengers were quickly forced off at gunpoint and into the *Philo Parsons* hold with the others. Included was a contingent of 25 or so soldiers mustering out of service. Without arms or ammunition, they could offer no resistance. When the refueling was finally finished, 108 or so of the captive passengers and crew were put ashore and warned not to contact anyone for 24 hours. There were only three houses on the island, which were used to shelter the women. Men had to fend for themselves. Several spent the night in a haystack, later saying they were "fairly comfortable."

Sometime after 8:00 p.m. the *Philo Parsons* took the *Island Queen* in tow and headed back for Sandusky and destiny. About halfway between Kelley Island and Middle Bass Island the raiders opened the sea valves on the smaller ship and cut her loose.[42] If they thought she was going to the bottom of Lake Erie it was another error in a long line of errors. The opened valve let too little water in too slowly and she drifted ashore off nearby Pelee Island. Within a week she was back on her regular route.

Free of the *Island Queen*, refueled and ready for action, Beall headed the steamer around for nearby Johnson Island. The *Michigan* remained at anchor just off the camp.

As the *Philo Parsons* came up to Marblehead Light at the end of peninsula, the wheelman warned the Confederates it was too dangerous to run the narrow channel into Sandusky at night. All it took was a small error and they would be aground.[43] There was also the problem of a lack of a signal from the *Michigan*. The raiders were looking for a sign the warship was rendered harmless by Cole or at least cause a distraction sufficient to allow the *Philo Parsons* to run up along side. The signal could have been a rocket launched from Johnson Island or from the cupola of the West House Hotel. Were the officers "tampered" with or the crew drugged or drunk as planned? When no signal came, the Confederates assumed the worst - she had somehow been alerted and was waiting for them with guns manned and run out!

It is worth considering if the strange antics of the *Philo Parsons* herself put the *Michigan* on alert. Since the warship spent a lot of time anchored off the prison her crew were very familiar with the movement of shipping, especially a scheduled boat like the *Philo Parsons*. Her punctual arrivals and departures were something they could set their watches by. When she started to come in to the bay earlier, only to suddenly turn around and head back into the lake, the crew must have taken note and wondered what was up. For the Confederate plan to work they needed complete surprise, which meant everything had to appear as normal as possible until the very last second when the trap was sprung. Her hasty and unexplained earlier action meant things were no longer normal. To an alert lookout something was up!

Beall wanted to continue with the mission regardless of the uncertainty about Cole and the *Michigan*, but his crew literally mutinied and refused to make such a dangerous gesture. Regardless of his pleading, the scared men wouldn't budge. Reluctantly he ordered the steamer about and set a course back up the Detroit River. Beall later told Thompson that, "if it had not been for these mutinous scoundrels I could have run that boat on these lakes for two weeks, burning and destroying all the vessels we met with before the Yankees could have made us take to land."[44] What Beall was saying was the *Philo Parsons* could have been the raider herself and caused great damage before the *Michigan* would have caught her.

The passengers and crew marooned on Middle Bass Island remember seeing the *Philo Parsons* plowing northward under a full head of steam around 1:00 a.m. on the 20th. As the ship made her way up the Detroit River, Beall asked *Philo Parsons'* crewmen about the numerous downbound ships they met. When they told him they were in Canadian waters, Beall replied it was a "good thing for them else he would board them."[45]

Between 4:00 and 5:00 a.m. the steamer reached the small Canadian town of Malden and entered the British channel. About three miles above Malden, she sent a yawl ashore with goods stolen from the steamer.[46] A little further upstream she landed all of the remaining passengers and crew save three dropped off on Fighting Island about 8:00 a.m.

When they reached Sandwich, the raiders moored to the dock and unloaded more goods stolen from the steamer, including mirrors, chairs, trunks, bedding, furniture and even her piano! Why the Confederates decided to "burgle" the *Philo Parsons* is unknown. It certainly reduced what could have been argued was an honorable act of war to common thievery. The underlying cause may simply have been a lack of good discipline. The earlier "mutiny" reinforces this reasoning. The Confederates didn't just make off with the furniture, they also stole the ship's money in gold and greenbacks from the clerk. After taking everything portable of value, they cut her injection pipes (in effect opened her sea chest, the piping for engine cooling water from the lake) allowing her to sink dockside. Their effort at sabotage was as effective of the whole raid at least in terms of breaking out the prisoners. Damage was so minimal she was back in service four days later! As a further illustration of the premise, "when things go bad, they really go bad," a Canadian customs officer arrested the men removing the goods from the ship for importing without a license! However after a quick arraignment before a justice of the peace, the raiders were released. Northerners saw such light treatment as more evidence of Canadian support of the South

The Union requested formal extradition of the raiders identifying the crimes as piracy, robbery and attempted murder. Legal scholars argued the seizure technically wasn't piracy since the *Philo Parsons* and *Island Queen* never left either U.S. or Canadian waters. Piracy could only be committed on the high seas, in international waters. The other charges were valid, but Canadian cooperation proved elusive and nothing ever happened to the formal request. Again the North saw the outcome as clear proof of Southern support by Canada.

Examining the plan it was clear to make it work the raiders needed to fully "case the joint," learn as much as possible about the prison at Johnson Island, movement of guards and particularly the *Michigan*. As an escapee, Cole was perfect for the role and he spent much of August and September in Sandusky lodging in the West House Hotel directly across the bay from the prison and warship. He had a clear view of both from his rear window. The hotel was five stories and relatively new, built in 1857 by one of the same contractors who built the prison. It was torn down in 1919.

Cole proceeded to ingratiate himself with the local citizens, the island guard force and crew of the *Michigan*, claiming he was the secretary of the Mount Hope Oil Company of Harrisburg, Pennsylvania. He opened accounts in local banks and made frequent use of the telegraph office. Both helped establish his "cover." He also spent much time in the local saloons and such places as gentlemen of business may often gather to socialize. He freely paid for drinks not only for his new civilian friends but his military ones too whether Army or Navy. He became everyone's best buddy!

It was surmised on the night of the attack Cole was to entice the *Michigan's* officers as well as those from the camp to an afternoon of "wine and women" at a party ashore where they would drink heartily of drugged wine while enjoying the attention of the fair sex. Leaderless, both ship and camp would be easy prey for a determined assault by the raiders. There was also a rumor Cole had suborned one of her engineers to disable her machinery at the critical hour. Regardless of Cole's intentions, by policy Captain Carter only allowed one line officer off duty at a time so the ship would have been well officered.[47]

In the subsequent investigation it was suggested the Confederate plan could have been to set fire to the *Parsons* as she approached Sandusky Bay. Reputedly she had 25 barrels of coal tar as part of her cargo and the raiders brought fire starters (balls made out of burlap, grease and camphene) with them. Seeing the flames, *Michigan* sailors would have rushed to the rescue of the passengers and crew in their boats which the raiders would have easily captured, filling them with their own men and returned to the gunboat. The men left on the *Michigan* would have assumed it was their own crewmen coming alongside with the passengers and crew from the burning steamer. Instead a gang of bloodthirsty Confederates who would come swarming over the rail!

However, Cole's work was for naught. It seems Captain Carter was suspicious of him from the start and assigned one of his gunners mates, 24-year old John Wilson Murray to tail him. Murray was hardly an experienced detective but he certainly had spunk and enthusiasm and in the end was able to ferret out the plot against the *Michigan*.

Murray was born in Scotland but moved to New York with his family when he was five years old. He enlisted in the Navy in 1857 thus was an experienced sailor when the War broke out. He found he liked detective work and following the War was employed as a special agent for the Navy Department before joining the Erie Police Department in 1868. Finding the grass greener on the other side of the border he emigrated to Canada, becoming the Head of Detectives for the Canadian Southern Railroad and later the Provincial Detective of Ontario.

Murray first went to Detroit to confer with Lieutenant Colonel Bennett H. Hill, Assistant Provost Marshall for Michigan. Details of the *Michigan* - Johnson Island plot were very murky, but Hill apparently thought Vallandingham was involved in it, or at least was the best lead they had. Wearing civilian clothing Murray crossed the river to Windsor and "staked out" his home waiting to see who came and went.

Murray identified one of the frequent visitors as Charles H. Cole, a known Confederate agent. When Cole left Windsor, Murray was on his tail all the way to Montreal and the St. Lawrence Hall Hotel, notorious as a Confederate meeting place where Cole linked up with "Irish Lize." Murray later wrote, "She was an elegant looking lady, big and stately, a magnificent blonde, with clothes that were a marvel to me." The contrast with Cole was striking. "She was big, stout and fine-looking; he was a little, sandy haired fellow, but smart as lightning." More about Irish Lize later.

He followed Cole and Irish Lize through various American and Canadian cities taking careful notes of their every activity. They finally arrived in Sandusky about June 20, 1864. Murray reported back to Captain Carter all he had found out. Clearly something was up.

It also seems Cole's part of the plot unraveled further when the entire scheme was ratted-out to the North by a Confederate turncoat. Apparently a Southern deserter somehow connected to the design reported the plot to the Assistant Provost Marshall at Detroit on September 17, two days before "D-Day". He related once the Confederates had the *Michigan* they would control the Great Lakes for months, halting shipping and attacking port cities. The ex-Confederate claimed some of the *Michigan* sailors, including officers, had been "tampered" with and agreed to support the plot and the attack would come soon. The Provost Marshall telegraphed a warning to Captain Carter of the *Michigan*, who vouched for his men completely, disbelieving any would turn traitor. He trusted his *Michigan* crewmen were all loyal. The deserter returned to the Provost Marshall the following day with more details. The attack would be made using the steamer *Philo Parsons* and the raiders would come across from

Windsor, boarding her in Detroit. The deserter then faded away into history. Who he was remained a mystery. The Provost Marshall quickly went down to the dock and gave the *Philo Parsons* the once over, concluding she was too small to be of any real danger. He wired another warning to the *Michigan*, again cautioning some sailors had "gone over." As the result of the warnings, the *Michigan* and her men were fully prepared for whatever came their way. When they saw the strange movements of the steamer it must have set alarm bells off.

After talking the matter over with the commander at Johnson Island, on September 19th, Captain Carter sent an officer with several members of the Army Provost Guard to Sandusky in a ship's boat. Leaving most of the crew at the launch, the Navy officer and several others walked to the hotel where Cole was known to live. Finding him in his room, the officer invited Cole to return with him to the ship. He said Captain Carter was reluctant to allow his officers to attend Cole's party. Perhaps if Cole spoke to him he could change the captain's mind. Seeing the whole plan collapsing if he couldn't get the officers off the *Michigan*, Cole agreed to try.

Before leaving, however, Cole invited the Navy officer as well as an accompanying Army officer to have a good swig of whisky. The Navy officer, thinking it could be poisoned, demurred explaining he had a chaw of tobacco in his mouth. Although after Cole took a big gulp of the whisky, the officer relented and took a shot of the red-eye too as did the Army officer.

Cole then said he needed to go to the bank to withdraw some cash and, playing along, the Naval officer accompanied him. To protect the officer from any of Cole's tricks, the boat's coxswain secretly followed dodging from lamppost to lamppost. The Army officer remained behind, perhaps enjoying a snort or two of whisky.[48]

Finishing the banking, Cole and the Navy officer returned to the hotel room where all enjoyed a few more drinks and after a time headed back to the boat.

As soon as they reached the *Michigan's* boat, the Navy officer pushed Cole into it, and jumped in after him. The crew standing by on the oars immediately shoved off and pulled for the ship. On reaching the *Michigan*, Cole was promptly arrested as a spy. Carter's men nabbed Cole just in time, as his bags were packed for Toronto and hotel charges paid in full.

Cole proved to be a very careless spy. A quick search of his person and hotel room provided a treasure trove of incriminating evidence. They found papers showing he was a captain in the Confederate Army and took the oath of allegiance to the U.S. as a condition of parole. His present actions against the Union were a clear violation of his parole. Retribution for parole violators could be harsh! Numerous letters showed he regularly corresponded with Southern sympathizers at Windsor, Niagara Falls, Toronto and other Canadian cities. He also had $600 in cash and ten certified checks totaling $5,000. Each was drawn on a Montreal bank doubtless, from Thompson's secret account. What he alleged was a simple business telegram about, "30 shares of Mount Hope Oil wells" the Union knew really meant 30 agents were aboard the yet to arrive *Philo Parsons*! Once the Union officers revealed that they knew about the plot, Cole gave up any pretense of innocence and provided a flood of details.

Cole reported additional reinforcements were coming to Sandusky by the 5:30 p.m. train. With little time to spare, a platoon of 35 soldiers was quickly dispatched to town to prepare a proper "arrival." While no additional agents were found on the train, a number of Sandusky residents implicated by Cole in the plot were rounded up by the soldiers. It turned out after later investigation the "Sanduskyites" were innocent. Cole simply gave names to "muddy" the waters following his arrest. A later train also proved empty of Confederate agents.

Initially, local resentment against the Sandusky men Cole named ran so hard there was strong talk about giving them a good and fair lynching! Hearing the comments, one of the traitors reputedly broke down in tears as he was dragged to the island prison for interrogation.

After learning the details of the plot from Cole, the crew of the *Michigan* waited patiently for the raiders to approach peering anxiously into the dark night looking for the steamer. Captain Carter ordered steam up in his boilers to allow a quick response as needed. If the *Philo Parsons* attempted a boarding action she was in for a very big surprise! He would doubtless wait until the last possible moment when the *Philo Parsons* was close aboard before his guns spewed death on the raiders. A single "broadside" from the gunboat would have smashed the steamer into kindling.

Meanwhile aboard the *Michigan,* Captain Carter knew what Cole had revealed under questioning but certainly was unsure of what was true and what was misinformation. The statements about additional agents coming into Sandusky by train proved false. But he knew the information about the *Philo Parsons* was apparently true. She hadn't arrived on schedule, which was ominous. Likewise, John Brown Jr., son of the infamous abolitionist, met with Carter earlier and related seeing the strange antics of the steamer, including towing the *Island Queen.* Brown had a vineyard at Put-in-Bay on nearby South Bass Island. Since Captain Carter had orders to keep his ship at Johnson Island to guard the prisoners, he did not have freedom of action to just desert his station. Regardless, he considered the threat of the *Philo Parsons* sufficiently grave to exercise his initiative and leave his guard point off the camp and steam to the open lake and determine what was happening. Colonel Hill, at the camp, agreed with Carter's decision. Offensive action was needed.

At dawn the *Michigan* hauled anchor and headed into the lake. Her first stop was Kelley Island where the folks ashore were unsure if the raiders succeeded or not until they recognized sailors on the deck of the *Michigan.* It was at the island Captain Carter learned for certain the *Philo Parsons* and *Island Queen* were captured. She continued on through the islands searching for the *Philo Parsons.* Finding the *Island Queen* aground off Pelee Island, she sent a squad of sailors aboard and arrested one of the raiders inadvertently left aboard. Fully cognizant of his duty to guard the prison, Captain Carter returned to the island and anchored. He was confident the immediate danger was past.

Meanwhile the commander at Johnson Island was busy, too. He telegraphed his superior with the news of the attempted attack as well as provost-marshals and commanders at Detroit, Monroe, Toledo, Cleveland, Painesville, Ashtabula, Conneaut,

Erie, Dunkirk and Buffalo, warning all to be on guard against additional assaults and to warn any steamers they could. Clearly he didn't know where the raiders went or what their plans were. They could have returned to Canada for reinforcements, seized additional boats or suddenly attack other ports. To guard against their return to Sandusky, he also quickly established a battery of four 20-pound Parrott rifles at a point commanding the entrance to Sandusky Bay. The quiet was shattered when the guns began firing to determine the range as well as train the infantry crews. The Parrotts were powerful weapons. Far more accurate than the more common smoothbore Napoleons, a 20 pound Parrott could fire her projectile over two and a half miles.

Hill was unsure when the *Michigan* would return from her lake reconnaissance and cognizant of the need to protect both the camp and city against an attack, he commandeered the 115-foot steamer *General Grant* into Federal service. After strengthening her deck with additional timbers, he intended to mount a couple of 20-pounder Parrotts and a 12-pound howitzer with a small infantry force. Given her likely opponent, at best a captured lake steamer like the *Philo Parsons*, the tug would have been a formidable weapon. However, before the guns were brought aboard the *Michigan* returned and the plan was scrapped.

Sparked by the shock of the *Philo Parsons* attempted raid, the Union immediately considered rushing the completion and arming of a steam Revenue Cutter already under construction. Working night and day she could be ready in ten days. Several commercial propeller steamers could also be chartered and armed quickly with guns to augment the force.

When the dust finally settled, all the raiders escaped except Cole and Commissioner Thompson wrote Confederate President Jefferson Davis asking for his intervention. According to Thompson, Cole was, "an escaped prisoner and having never returned to his own country since his escape was legitimately within the enemy's lines." It was an argument the North didn't agree with.

Cole may have been apprehended alone but he operated with a rental wife registered as "Mrs. C.H. Cole," aka "Annie," "Anna Brown," "Belle Brandon" or "Irish Lize." It seems Cole also spent more time with his "wife" than needed for this cover, taking her to Philadelphia for example was hard to justify for his mission.

Since Thompson provided Cole with $4,000 in gold and greenbacks, he had plenty of cash to spread around entertaining *Michigan* officers, officers and men from the guard force and local businessmen as well as himself and Irish Lize. Among his "business expenses" were a brace of fast horses and a chartered yacht. According to the detective, Murray, Cole was a great favorite of the crew of the *Michigan* and Army officers on the island for constantly sending out boxes of cigars and cases of wine for their enjoyment and, of course, in recognition of their service to the country.

Cole's character from his army days wasn't stellar. An officer from his old regiment stated his reputation for truth was, "bad and he would not believe him under oath." He was held for a time at Johnson Island, his old "alma mater" of sorts, then transferred to Fort Lafayette in New York Harbor before eventually being discharged once the war ended.

Prisoners wiled away time in the cold stone cells of old Fort Lafayette.

Irish Lize (Annie) later returned to Sandusky with a letter for the Union commander from Thompson extolling Cole's innocence. After a supervised visit to Cole she was clapped up in the county jail as an important witness. In later testimony Annie was identified as Emma Bison, aka Annie Brown, not only Cole's mistress but also working as a messenger between he and Thompson. She reputedly met Cole in Buffalo where she was working as a prostitute. Interrogators said she was a good-looking young woman with fortitude and intelligence.

Cole later claimed the *Michigan* officers and Johnson Island Army officers were to be entertained at a grand dinner at the Seven Mile House seven miles outside of Sandusky where they would be taken captive by he and his men. One story says the officers would be killed in cold blood and women of Sandusky given over to the insatiable lust of the just released prisoners. Another says at the height of the party, Cole was to slip away and dash back to Sandusky and take his yacht out to the harbor entrance signaling the *Philo Parsons* all was clear. The raiders would then run up to the warship where Beall and his swashbuckling crew would board and subdue the leaderless Union sailors. Other steamers in port would be quickly swept up and the combined fleet would transport the prisoners to Point Pelee, Canada, and freedom.

Another Scare

It is easy to understand the good citizens of Sandusky as well as the prison guards were nervous indeed following the botched Confederate attempt. When the local paper later reported city saloons were filled with tough characters from Canada, it was surmised they were in town to somehow breakout the prisoners. Sixteen of the suspicious miscreants were "rounded up" by the police and hauled off to the camp for questioning. Doubtless "Miranda Rights" were not part of their processing prior to their being closely interrogated. A group of soldiers from the camp patrolled the city on watch for more potential roughs as well as any potential saboteurs or arsonists. Setting the town ablaze would be perfect cover for breaking out the prisoners. To provide a longer term safety solution, a Sandusky vigilance committee was soon carefully keeping an eye on things.

Another Rumor

Whether it was a case of nervous federals or Confederates planting rumors, in October, 1864, the word spread there were 18,000 stand of arms ready in Canada to be taken across the lake to Toledo, Sandusky or Niagara Falls (Buffalo, NY) to arm either covert members of the SOL or Confederates freed from Johnson Island. Supposedly, a fleet of fishing boats was held in readiness for bringing them across Lake Erie or Ontario. The rumor was substantial enough to bring the *Michigan* into Toledo where her crew searched a number of likely warehouses without success. Additional reports claimed there were 2,000 rebels waiting at Point Pelee or the mainland nearby to raid the U.S. As with previous alarms, evidence proved elusive. But all the rumors caused a Northern reaction, which to a point affected the Northern war effort.

Yet Again a Scare

Another spate of rumors of Confederate attack occurred in early November 1864. The U.S. Consul in Toronto telegraphed warnings of pending action when his agents discovered what they claimed was another plot to attack American Great Lakes ports. Troops in Detroit were immediately put on full alert, issued arms and readied for immediate action. Canada was just across the river, barely a mile distant and a sudden attack by Confederates assaulting across the water was not beyond the possible. Buffalo was another especially vulnerable port. Canada was also just across the Niagara River and a quick gray clad rush could tear up the vulnerable city as well as exit of the vital Erie Canal knocking out lock gates and generally closing the waterway. By any assessment, Buffalo was an easy target for a determined Confederate assault. Perhaps most surprising, the city was wide open to a sabotage. A well placed explosive charge could wreak havoc. A ship borne assault from Port Colborne, only 15 miles distant could flank Union defenders and burn down the important grain elevators. There were also claims of light signals between the Canadian side of the river and the U.S. By contrast, Detroit was far less of a valuable target. Although there were shipping and rail lines, it didn't present the same return on attack Buffalo promised.

Target - Vermont

Although Vermont is far removed from the Great Lakes, the planning for the raid was done by the Canadian Confederate mission, thus I included it in this text.

Thompson's team didn't waste any time after the Johnson Island debacle to attempt another strike. A bare month later on October 19, 1864, about 20 raiders wearing civilian clothes led by Lieutenant Bennett Young of Kentucky crossed the border and traveled 15-miles south to St. Albans, Vermont. Agent Thomas Hines was apparently involved in the raid's organization, but took no active part.

Young was a cavalry officer who earlier served with General John Hunt Morgan. He was captured in July 1863 during Morgan's ill-conceived raid into Ohio and imprisoned at Camp Douglas. After escaping from Camp Douglas, he made his way back to the Confederacy via Holcomb's escapee "pipeline" to Wilmington aboard a blockade-runner.

Lieutenant Bennett Young lead the disastrous attack on St. Albans,Vermont.

Morgan's raid was highly publicized and struck deep into Indiana and Ohio running from June 11 to July 26, 1863, covering over 1,000 miles but the timing was horrible. The fear the raid could have ignited in the North was negated by the Union victories at Gettysburg and Vicksburg. In

Morgan's catastrophic raid into Ohio resulted in the loss of nearly his entire force.

Morgan actions in sacking many of the towns and villages he passed through alienated Southern supporters contributing to his defeat.

comparison, Hunt's campaign was seen as a pinprick. It did, however, pull thousands of Union troops from the battlefield to contain the attack and limit damage and it created apprehension in several states. However, Morgan overreached his objective and the deeper he went, the more his route back to the South was blocked by Northern units until he was finally trapped and obliged to surrender what was left of his command. Given the constant combat he was forced into by pursuing and blocking Northern forces, his force was greatly reduced when he finally gave up. Perhaps even worse, his undisciplined troops freely stole food, horses and pretty much anything that struck their fancy as they moved north, greatly antagonizing the pro-Southern supporters they robbed. In the end, his raid was both a military and political disaster. That said, many folks in the South considered him a hero and others in the North feared his aggressive action.

There is some thought Confederate Secretary of War James Seddon had sanctioned Young's plan of action in Canada and had ordered him to return to Canada and scout the towns along the American border, free to sack and burn those most exposed. According to Seddon, "It is but right that the people of New England and Vermont especially, some of whose officers and troops have been foremost in these excesses (in the South), should have brought home to them some of the horrors of such warfare." Clearly an important component of their plan was to make the raid some kind of "retribution" for supposed Union actions in the South. Regardless of Seddon's involvement, Confederate Commissioner Clay issued Young the order to attack and burn St. Albans.

The value of the attack was psychological. If sleepy little St. Albans could be laid waste, could not other border communities suffer the same fate? How could these very vulnerable communities be protected?

Confederate reconnaissance showed St. Albans was a perfect target for a raid. It wasn't overly large, about a mile square and not likely to have too strong of a local citizen reaction force and a major railroad ran through it. Since it was also within reasonable distance from the Canadian border, escape back to safety was relatively easy. Perhaps most important, it had three banks in the center of town within a block of each other! The banks were important to the Confederate plan.

The raiders arrived in town in civilian clothing in small groups attracting no particular attention. Some arrived by train and others on horseback. All checked into hotels and kept a very low profile.

The town was quiet when they struck, rounding up local citizens herding them to the town square. With most of the locals accounted for, the rebels quickly robbed the banks of roughly $200,000, but their plans to burn down the town with homemade Greek Fire was unsuccessful. Although a few buildings earned scorch marks, the fire-bombing effort was a dismal failure destroying only an old woodshed. After stealing some horses, they beat a hasty retreat but only after killing one of their pursuers.

The townspeople of St. Albans didn't roll over and play dead as the raiders were certain they would. Rather, once they realized what was happening and the dire peril their town was in, rifles came off the walls and hot lead began to fly in the general direction of the Confederates. It was hardly a disciplined and military response, but it was a galling fire and enough to cause the raiders to quickly gallop for the border.

Robbing banks like common criminals reduced the attack to one by common criminals.

Those who arrived by train and needed mounts stole them from the local livery. Young didn't plan on the "citizen militia" or the leadership of Captain George P. Conger, an Army captain on leave. His hastily organized posse harried the Confederates all the way north and even beyond the border.

It seems the Union had some knowledge before of the attack provided by double agent Robert Montgomery. Unfortunately, as sometimes typical in the shadowy world of spies and counter spies, he only knew the general outlines of what was going to happen. A Vermont town was the target, but not which one or when? If the Union flashed a warning to all towns, the Confederates would know there was a spy in their midst. So as not to compromise their asset, the North did not react.

The raid caused great consternation all along the northern border. Previously, the area was a quiet backwater with no possible direct threat from the enemy. Now, in a single stroke, it was laid bare to Confederate attack. If they could assault St. Albans and nearly burn it down (with the non-working Greek Fire) then they could do it anywhere! Citizens demanded protection.

The legislature in Montpelier, Vermont's capital, quickly adjourned when they heard the news of the attack with some members falling in with local militia companies to defend the city. Other cities called out their militia, too. In the first moments after the news of the assault flashed across the border-states it was feared it was part of a massive Confederate invasion from Canada or even the long feared British invasion in support of the South. In response to the St. Abans attack, an under strength infantry battalion with two field pieces reached the city by morning. Rumors, of course, ran rampant. One claimed Confederate raiders seized a steamer on Lake Champlain and using their feared Greek Fire would soon be attacking and burning lake front cities.

The attack reverberated across the northern tier of states. Ogdensburg, Buffalo, Cleveland and Detroit all felt the shock of sudden vulnerability to Southern attack. Port cities solidified plans to repel anticipated invasion from Canadian territory. Arms and ammunition were stockpiled and militia units drilled in preparedness. Some Great Lakes businessmen also urged the Governor of Michigan to beef up protection given to various locks and canals including the vital locks at Sault Ste. Marie.

Enraged by the mild Canadian reaction to the attack as well as the criminal action of the raiders, Union General John A. Dix, Commander of the Military Department of the East, ordered troops to destroy the rebels, pursuing them into Canada if necessary. Unknown to General Dix, Captain Conger had already pursued the raiders into Canada and nabbed several including Captain Young. Before the Americans could withdraw with their captives, a British major appeared and warned them of the dire international consequences of the violation of Canadian neutrality, convincing Conger to surrender them to him. Reluctantly Young and his companions were given over to the British major and the Americans withdrew.

In retrospect, Dix's pursuit order could have spelled disaster for the Union had Lincoln not quickly cancelled it. Having Northern troops swarming over Canada in search of ghostly raiders could have incited a major reaction from Britain acting to defend her sovereignty. It could have well ignited a frontier war pulling Imperial troops into the fray. The South would have had the British - U.S. war it always wanted and all from a very minor pinprick raid!

By now the Canadian government was becoming less than pleased with the overt actions of the supposedly covert Confederate agents. The Canadians tracked down and arrested 14 of the raiders, but refused to immediately hand them over to the U.S., instead trying them in a Canadian court. The charge was violating Canadian neutrality laws but the trial was also to decide if they should be extradited to the U.S. Young and his men claimed they were only soldiers following orders issued by their government to raid St. Albans. The U.S. and Vermont claimed the raid was a violation of the Webster-Ashburton Treaty of 1842, specifically article 10 involving extradition for criminal offenses.[49]

The infamous George Sanders of the various Lincoln plots helped defend the raiders, claiming their attack was part of a general plan to assault numerous Northern cities in a effort to draw Union forces away from the battlefront. Clement Clay, however, later distanced himself from supporting the attack, supposedly disgusted by the bank robberies. There are a couple of ways to look at his post raid actions. First, if the raid was directly planned from Canada, it was a clear and very public violation of Canadian neutrality and at this stage of the war even Canada realized the chance of Confederate success was fast fading so why back a loser? Second obtaining cash in the form of Yankee greenbacks was very important for the clandestine operations Thompson and Clay were running. They were always in need of funds. But once the raiders were caught and the attack was a fizzle rather that a powerful blow for the South, it was best to, "disavow any knowledge of your action." While Clay authorized the operation, he didn't specifically authorize the robbing of banks thus making the act a crime rather than an act of war. There was lots of wiggle room.

The first "trial" ended in an egregious piece of legal flim-flam. The Canadian judge ruled that since the C.S.A. and U.S. were at war and no crimes were committed in Canada, he had no authority to hold the prisoners or extradite them to the U.S. Rubbing salt in the wound from the Northern perspective, he also stated the raid was commendable and justifiable. Seeing the absurdity of the judge's decision, the Governor General of Canada immediately ordered the raiders arrested again, charging them with violation of the new Canadian Neutrality Act. But again from the Northern viewpoint, the decision showed Canada's clear Southern bias. By the time the rebels arrived in Toronto for a second trial, the war was over and all were released.

A major outcome of the raid was the movement of the U.S. Congress toward abrogating the Rush-Bagot Treaty limiting naval vessels on the Great Lakes. Northern newspapers clamored for withdrawing from it as well as the 1854 Reciprocity Agreement. The Senate voted to withdraw and gave Great Britain the required six months notice. Included in the bill was the authorization for six new armed Revenue Cutters for the Great Lakes. This action sent a strong message to both the British and Canadians resulting in increasing Canadian pressure on the resident Southerners to prevent the Canadian Confederates from using Canada as a base for U.S. attacks.

Seeing the positive result of the action, Secretary of State Seward quietly withdrew the action allowing the status quo to continue.

Again - Camp Douglas

The fertile minds of the Canadian Confederates never stopped bubbling with ideas. When the rebels left Chicago following the Democrat convention debacle most of them assumed any plan to break out the prisoners at Camp Douglas and other camps and indeed spark a general northwestern conflagration was dead. Captain Hines and a few of the leaders thought differently. They soon hatched a watered down scheme following the general outline of the first. To assure a competent command structure was in place once the plot exploded, several rebel general officers were even brought to the Great Lakes area to take charge, according to a rebel prisoner later taken in Chicago.

And like the previous scheme, SOL leaders may have hoped for General Hood to push on Nashville, General Buckner on Louisville and General Price on St. Louis. The three simultaneous campaigns would inspire members in the area to rise up, join up with the attacking forces, drive the Yankees away and either pull Kentucky, Tennessee and Missouri, perhaps even Indiana and Ohio, too, into a Northwest Confederacy. It was, of course, only a pipe dream. By 1864, Southern armies were worn out and incapable of sustained offensive action. They could still defend and even bite back, but were unable to withstand determined Union attacks. Admiral Farragut had captured the port of Mobile, (remember "damn the torpedoes, full speed ahead) and General Sherman marched into the once mighty bastion of Atlanta on September 2. The landscape had changed. The South was fast crumbling.

As in the previous scheme, the SOL leaders oversold their support, telling Hines this time there, "would be no holding back." The Confederate captain did his best to assure himself it was true, including participating in secret planning sessions of the SOL. To help widen the insurrection, one of the Confederate leaders even went to Missouri to help organize and arm SOL guerillas there.

As with the earlier plan, the rebels needed cover to conceal the influx of soldiers and SOL members. They chose Election eve, November 8, 1864, as D-Day. Chicago would be crowded with folks and the rebels would be lost in the mob. To assure they were invisible to the watchful Union, Southern sympathizers met them at various train stations and carefully stashed them at various safe houses throughout the city.

Later, Union agents claimed many of the men arriving in Chicago were from southern Illinois counties and to all appearances were, "vagabonds, cut-throats, felons, bounty-jumpers and deserters."[50] They were strangers even to the SOL men. Instead of quartering at respectable hotels and rooming houses, they reportedly found their way to various vice dens and criminal resorts. Of course, Chicago being Chicago, finding such places wasn't very hard! It was thought by the Northern agents many of the new arrivals were the same men in the city for the aborted rebellion at the Democrat convention.

Should the rebellion happen as the Southern leaders hoped, it was expected banks would be a prime target. Given an option, taking the gold was always a good idea.

One of the Chicago SOL leaders commented to a questioning supporter the new arrivals were in town to, "vote and to fight," and, "by God they will vote early and often and they will fight." The fighting part might be in question but given Chicago's election reputation voting early and often wasn't an issue.

SOL emotions were running extremely high. According to a government agent, in a secret October meeting members proposed raising a bounty of $50,000 for whoever would assassinate President Lincoln. Perhaps it was an idle piece of rhetoric but it clearly showed the level of hatred against Lincoln and the Union. As in most of the SOL story, separating fact from wishful thinking is difficult.

Others were less mysterious. During the evening of November 3, hundreds of local SOL members gathered in their hall in Chicago. Known locally as the "Invincible Club," it was the scene of many a tirade against the Union and those arraigned against the south. On this occasion arms, and ammunition were given to members as well as instructions for the coming rebellion. One of the leaders reported two full regiments of SOL were ready and "well disciplined" and a third nearly complete. Each regiment would have equaled roughly a thousand men. Speakers were certain all of the Copperheads would rise up as one, not only in Illinois but also throughout the entire region.

After much debate, members decided how to tell friend from foe. When the rebellion began. Members would wear a McClellan badge on the left breast attached by red and white ribbons.

Further, runners were set to report results from every polling station direct to headquarters and that the imported voters would cast their ballots with one hand while holding a revolver in the other. According the some members, the Invincible Club from Philadelphia was also in town and prepared to help with their votes, too!

The rebels were well armed, having all of the guns and ammunition secreted from the earlier planned uprising still available for use. It included boxes of rifles, cartloads of pistols said to be already loaded, holsters, cases of cartridges and even light artillery. They would not fail for lack of firepower.

Again, it was a Confederate spy who, "spilled the beans" on the secret plot. Keeping his eyes open and ear to the ground, as well as being fed reports from loyal citizens, he wrote his commander that Chicago, "is filling up with suspicious characters, some of whom we know to be escaped prisoners, and others who were here from Canada..." To be certain his messages got through, he sent them by trusted couriers, fearing conspirators might intercept telegrams. Colonel Sweet, Commandant of the Post of Chicago, certainly knew or at least strongly suspected, rebel agents were in the telegraph office so any messages were likely to be at least read if not "lost" before being sent.

The plot was also compromised when a Union spy in Toronto passed the word to the U.S. Consul who in turn notified Secretary of State Seward in Washington. Seward telegraphed the mayors in various Northern cities warning of a "...conspiracy on foot to set fire to the principal cities in the Northern States on the day of the Presidential election."[51] Watchfulness was critical.

In the words of Colonel Sweet, the rebels, "intended to make a night attack on (him) and surprise this camp, release and arm the prisoners of war, cut the telegraph wires, burn the railroad depots, seize the banks and stores containing arms and ammunition, take possession of the city, and commence a campaign for the release of other prisoners of war in the States of Illinois and Indiana, thus organizing an army to effect and give success to the general uprising so long contemplated by the Sons of Liberty."

Colonel Sweet was especially vulnerable since he still only had comparatively few men to guard roughly 9,000 prisoners at Camp Douglas. His roster for November 6 showed he had 736 men present for duty. Sixty of the men were acting as city Provost Guard, looking for deserters and protecting key points. Others were involved in quartermaster work.[52] In the end there were only 500 men left to guard the prisoners. This meant two shifts of 250 men each, a ridiculously small number to guard nearly 9,000 rebels.

Making the job more difficult, the prisoners had already heard the rumors of a coming attack so they were not only restless, but ready for action, too. Neither were his guards front line combat troops who could be relied on should the city burst into flaming riot. They were all Veteran Reserve Corps. The best troops and officers were in the field, not detailed to guarding remote prison camps.

His agents continued to keep him abreast of the Confederate plans. Whether it is a case of Southern security being that bad or perhaps feeling there was nothing the beleaguered colonel could do to prevent the plan's success isn't known. Perhaps the rebels were over confident of triumph. Regardless of why, Sweet was inside of the rebel decision loop.

One of the double agents Colonel Sweet used was a paroled prisoner Lieutenant John T. Shanks, a 22-year old Texan who had earlier served with in infamous Morgan.[53] His character may not have been the best as one source claims he was "thief, forger,

traitor, spy, liar, perjurer and a coward."[54] Shanks was employed as what today would be called a "trustee" working in the prison office. According to legend, he fell in love with a well off young Chicago widow who regularly brought fruit and cigars to the prisoners. Seeing a chance to "turn" Shanks into a spy, the camp commander before Sweet allowed him to visit his widow in Chicago under guard in exchange for his information of activities in the camp. When Sweet took over command, he continued the arrangement since it provided him with a pipeline to prisoner plans.

Although Shanks wanted to take the oath of allegiance to the Union, his request was refused by U.S. authorities. After five prisoners escaped from Camp Douglas, a not uncommon occurrence,

John T. Shanks enabled Colonel Sweet to penetrate the SOL.

Colonel Sweet decided to see if he could use Shanks to locate some of the men who he suspected were being hidden by Chicago Judge Buckner S. Morris and his wife, both supposedly infamous SOL supporters. His wife was very active in distributing various sundries to the prisoners including clothing and food. Doubtless the colonel dangled the reward of taking the Federal oath to Shanks as well the continuance of the widow's romance. Shanks agreed to help him. After Sweet made the arrangement with the camp trash hauler, Shanks was "allowed" to escape hidden in a wagonload of garbage. It was a "put up" job all the way but worked well.

Following the colonel's instructions, on November 3 Shanks went to the home of Judge Morris where he claimed he was an escaped prisoner needing help. Could he be hidden with the other escaped men? Everyone in camp knew the judge was a friend of the South. While he learned nothing about the other escaped prisoners, the judge's wife gave him one of her husband's suits to replace the worn and obvious clothing from camp and $30 in traveling money. After expressing his gratitude, Shanks left the judge's house.

It wasn't long before Shanks met the colonel at his downtown office and handed over $30 the judge's wife gave him to help with his own escape. (I assume he kept the suit). Now the colonel had the "goods" on another conspirator!

Sweet was too smart an officer to let Shanks off on his own. He had U.S. Secret Service agent Tom Keefe trail him all the time. Keefe had earlier been following Hines from Toronto to Chicago but lost him in the crowd on arrival. He went to Sweet to brief him on what he had learned about Confederate plans when the colonel talked him into following Shanks just to be certain.[55]

Shanks wasn't finished with his espionage work. He also went to the Richmond House Hotel and reported to Grenfell, telling him he was an escapee from the camp and a loyal son of the South. Grenfell apparently completely believed him, briefing the spy in detail on the plan to attack Camp Douglas as well as how the whole operation was financed from Canada! With clandestine operators like Grenfell it is easy to see how the whole plot unraveled.

Secretary of State Seward also sent Colonel Sweet one Maurice Langhorne, another "turned" Confederate, who was

British soldier of fortune St. Ledger Grenfell was caught up in the foiled Confederate Chicago plan.

knowledgeable about those working from Toronto. As suspects were later rounded up, Langhorne personally identified many as Confederate agents from Canada.

Secret Service agent Keefe either through Colonel Sweet or alone, also recruited a local vendor of patent medicines, one I. Winslow Ayer, to join the SOL. As expected from a patent medicine hawker, his medical knowledge was minimal although he claimed to have graduated from a reputable university and medical school, his diplomas were considered forgeries. Ayer didn't need much convincing as apparently he was "making the rounds" of Union officials offering his services in exposing the conspiracy for a large reward. Doubtless he was paid for his efforts, but the usual rate as opposed to the bonanza he expected. Spies are usually not savory characters, so Ayer certainly fit the mold. Ayers later wrote a book, *The Great Treason Plot of the North*, detailing his adventures. Regardless of his morals, Ayer kept Keefe and Sweet informed of the SOL plans as they developed.

From all his sources, Colonel Sweet determined the Confederates planned to strike on November 8, the night before the election. Fires would be set in different parts of the city to distract attention and railroad offices and yards would be seized and held against any Federal counter attack. Grabbing the railroads and telegraph would prevent authorities from wiring for help and holding the train yards prevented their arrival when the call finally was heard.

Breaking out the Camp Douglas inmates was vital to the plan and the rebels intended to strike during the dark of night. Confederate agent Hines assisted by Grenfell, estimated their assault force would be approximately 1,200 men strong, made up of men they brought from Canada and "butternuts" from southern Illinois but the bulk would be SOL members, many from out of town. All were reportedly well armed.

Supposedly, the attackers would be divided into five groups. Grenfell would keep one with him as a general reserve to be committed where most needed. His group also carried a large supply of arms to provide the prisoners with instant firepower. A second group of roughly 200 men under the command of J.T. Shank, the Union spy, had the mission of attacking the main gateway and causing the bulk of the guards to focus on them. The three remaining groups would assault the remaining sides of the camp, tearing down the flimsy wood walls. With the walls down, the guards fighting the assault from the gate would be taken from the rear forcing a general surrender. Once the additional arms were issued to the prisoners, it was "Katy bar the door" for Chicago![56]

The attackers planned to assemble at a small wooded area not too distant from the camp. So as not to attract attention, the raiders were to approach it singly or in small groups. When they were fully prepared they would spring from the woods and attack all sides simultaneously for maximum shock effect. The actual assault signal was to be a red or blue rocket fired high enough to alert the prisoners, who forewarned of the attack, would assault simultaneously from the inside of the camp.

Colonel Sweet was certainly concerned with the security of the camp, especially regarding the civilian structures so close to the wall. One that gave him particular concern was a building on the south side locally known as the "Douglas House" or

Camp Douglas was ripe for a Confederate-SOL attack.

derisively as the "Douglas University." It was a well built structure a mere 100 feet from the wall. He knew 50 to 100 men dug into the building and armed with rifles could command the entire camp. Rooting the rebels out of the building would be difficult and deadly. To counter the threat, Colonel Sweet stationed two of his guard companies (roughly 100 men) around it until the threat was over.

Once the prisoners were freed and organized, small detachments would rendezvous at Court House Square flooding into the city cutting telegraph lines, seizing railways and otherwise disrupting government functions. They would rapidly be reinforced by thousands of SOL and capture the various arms, warehoused and city artillery. Other armed bands would rob the banks, loot stores, plunder homes of Union men and burn railway stations, piers, grain elevators and public buildings. The city's few fire lines would be destroyed to prevent the firefighters from responding.[57] The greater the destruction the better!

However, Colonel Sweet seized the initiative striking first on the night of November 6/7 arresting rebel leaders and Sons of Liberty officials as well as, "106 bushwhackers, guerrillas, and rebel soldiers."[58] Included in the haul were a local judge and a "brigadier general" of the SOL. Some of the men were apprehended by soldiers suddenly appearing at their front doors. In other instances, the Chicago Police did the honors. All were quickly bundled off to cells in Camp Douglas for safekeeping. Losing the leaders literally cut the head off the Copperhead/SOL snake.

One of the key rebels Sweet's men arrested was the infamous Colonel St. Ledger Grenfell, nabbing him in his Richmond House Hotel room. After locking him in leg irons, they hustled him to the paddy wagon and eventual imprisonment. Sweet's spy, Shanks, was put in the same cell with Grenfell in an effort to see if he could weasel out any incriminating evidence from him.

News of the arrests shot through the SOL ranks freezing any disloyal acts fast. The colonel's men also recovered 142 shotguns and 349 revolvers, along with thousands of rounds of ammunition from collaborator's homes near Camp Douglas. The arresting troops and police had to literally batter the door down to get into one house. In another instance, when word was hurriedly sent to a member's home to get rid of the hidden firearms, his wife assisted by other women tried to smuggle them out concealed under their hoop skirts. Regardless of the Confederate belles' efforts, Federal agents found the contraband.

In a public show of force Colonel Sweet reinforced the Army guard in Chicago by mobilizing a force of 250-mounted militia and arming them with the confiscated pistols. Seized shotguns were issued to the guards at Camp Douglas where they could prove very useful in the event of a breakout attempt! A rifled musket took a single attacker down. A shotgun with double "00" buckshot was deadly out to 20 yards blowing a hole through an attacking mob. The very visible troops protecting public buildings and armed citizens patrolling the streets placed a chilling damper on the planned insurrection.

A detailed map of Camp Douglas was claimed concealed in one of the arrested conspirators clothing, damning evidence of raider intentions.

When word of Colonel Sweet's actions reached the members of the SOL, it was like an electric shock! As it was clearly apparent a spy in their midst was the cause of the counterstroke, suspicions of who it was ran rampant. No one could be trusted! Surely the authorities knew each and every member and all were in dire danger of arrest. The Copperheads deserted the SOL like rats fleeing a sinking ship. The first man to run was supposedly one Doolittle, one of the designated leaders of the attack on Camp Douglas. Others with key assignments suddenly found reason to be elsewhere. It turned out one of the SOL brigadier generals had unknowingly employed a government spy to go to his home and instruct others how to manufacture cartridges!

Hines, the real brains behind the planned Camp Douglas attack managed to escape capture. When the word spread of the wave of arrests, he fled to the home of a local SOL member and literally hid in a bed mattress. When Federal troops searched the home they failed to find him.

Of course the city's Republican newspapers trumpeted the foiling of the great conspiracy and the Democrat ones howled with outrage. Doubtless, truth was squeezed between them.

Eight of the high value prisoners, including Colonel Grenfell, were sent to the McLean Barracks in Cincinnati for trial by military commission. The McLean facility wasn't much, just a small military prison modified from an old building. The prisoners were arraigned on two major charges: conspiring to free the prisoners at Camp Douglas and conspiring to lay "waste and destroy Chicago." Hines was tried in absentia.

When judgments were announced on April 18, 1865, the results of the trial were mixed. Of the eight prisoners, one of the men, Charles Daniels, managed to escape from his guard and another, Benjamin Anderson, committed suicide. A third was considered crazy and not tried. Two, Judge Buckner Morris and a Vincent Marmaduke, were acquitted while Charles Wash and Richard Semme were pronounced guilty but later pardoned. The heaviest blow fell on Colonel Grenfell. He was sentenced to death by hanging. After a flood of requests for clemency President Johnson commuted the sentence to life in prison at Fort Jefferson on the Dry Tortugas.[59] Given Lee's surrender at Appomattox on April 8, justice was likely tempered with recognition the war was for practically purposes, nearly over.

The end result of the second Chicago uprising was nothing - the Confederates were defanged and took no action. Score one more for the Union. But the potential for success was real. If they had been able to literally keep the secret, blood could have run in Chicago streets and chaos in the Union rear!

Burning - New York

As with the St. Albans raid, New York City wasn't in the Great Lakes area either, but the planning was also done by the Canadian Confederates and it was part of the overall scheme to disrupt the Northern rear area. On a more ominous note, it was clearly an act of pure terror with questionable military value.

New York's rise to prominence as a port city was significantly enhanced by the completion of the Erie Canal in 1825. Linking New York City via the Hudson River with Lake Erie and, therefore, the entire Great Lakes opened the city up to international importance as a shipping center. Now the entire bounty of the rich Great Lakes could flow to the city for shipment to countries around the world and the products of the world, including immigrants, poured into the Great Lakes. It was the proverbial "two way street" with both ends becoming the richer.

After failures at Johnson Island, Chicago and St. Albans, the Confederate commissioners in Canada looked hard for a target that could assure success, one that would strike fear across the entire North. They decided to burn down New York City.

Eight Confederate agents were given the job of turning New York into a funeral pyre. Lieutenant Robert Cobb Kennedy was in apparent command. Kennedy was considered a skilled officer based on his two years at West Point before he quit the academy. Due to his experience at West Point, he was given a lieutenant's commission in the Confederate Army. His field experience was excellent, wounded at Shiloh and after recovering, campaigning with the Army of Tennessee for two years. He later transferred to General Joe Wheeler's cavalry division supporting General Braxton Bragg's forces. In October, 1863, he was captured while carrying dispatches during the Chattanooga campaign, ending up a prisoner at Johnson Island.

Rather than just run around the city trying to start fires with matches like normal pyromaniacs, Confederate arsonists used special containers of what was often generically called "Greek Fire" Its origins go back into deep history and can be traced to an incendiary weapon used by the Byzantine Empire in the 7th Century.

The version the Southern agents used was cobbled together by a chemist in New York City and involved a composition of phosphorous and carbon bisulphate. Supposedly, the leader of the saboteurs picked up a valise filled with 12 dozen four ounce glass vials of the devilish concoction from the chemist. As long as the containers

The Confederate attempt to burn down New York City was an act of pure terrorism.

were sealed, they remained inert. Once the tops were removed or if the container was smashed, the devilish mixture would burst into flame on exposure to air.

The leader, in turn, distributed the vials to his accomplices in convenient carrying satchels and the dastardly operation was underway. Each of the agents rented rooms in a series of city hotels, left an open bottle in each room (some in closets) closed the door and left. The intended result was major fires in 19 hotels, and other locations. Given a little luck, much of the city could be reduced to a smoking ruin.

During this period, local newspapers were filled with stories of Sherman smashing his way through the heart of Georgia and Sheridan laying waste to the Shenandoah Valley, so the Confederate agents were anxious to extract revenge on the North. Burning down New York would be perfect!

One of the terrorists later described his actions. "In the evening of November 25th, (1864) I went to my room in the Astor House at twenty minutes after seven. I hung the bedclothes over the foot-board, piled chairs, drawers and other material on the bed, stuffed newspapers into the heap and poured a bottle of "Greek Fire" and quickly spilled it on top. It blazed instantly. I locked the door and went downstairs. Leaving the keys at the office as usual, I passed out. I did likewise at the City Hotel, Everett House and United States Hotel. At the same time Martin operated at the Hoffman House, Fifth Avenue, St. Denis and others. Altogether our little band fired nineteen hotels. Captain Kennedy went to Barnum's Museum and broke a bottle on the stairway,

Quick action by the authorities prevented the fires from becoming serious.

creating a panic. Lieutenant Harrington did the same at the Metropolitan Theater and Lieutenant Ashbrook at Niblo's Garden." The fires, however, never really "caught" and were soon extinguished. While panic reigned for a short period, when it became apparent the city wasn't going to be consumed by flames, life settled down to normal. The mission was another Confederate failure.

The terrorists did everything right to get the results they wanted except in an effort to hide the fires from early detection they closed the doors and transoms over the room doors. Since fire needs oxygen, their action effectively damped the blazes and at worst the rooms were scorched but the fires never really caught.

Robert C. Kennedy

The arsonists quickly fled town and back to safety in Canada. The New York newspapers rightly exploited the despicable act and the city offered a reward of $5,000 for the apprehension of any of the terrorists.

A month after the debacle, Federal agents nabbed Kennedy while he was trying to slip from Canada to Richmond. The first leg of this route was on the Grand Trunk Railway to the Canadian side of the Detroit River, then a ferry to St. Clair, Michigan, and on to Detroit. When Kennedy walked out of the Detroit station to stretch his legs, two New York City detectives grabbed him. The Confederate tried to fight his way free but was knocked to the ground and secured with iron bracelets before they dragged him to a cell in the Detroit House of Correction and then on to the Mulberry Street Police Station in New York. He was

Some of the hotels targeted by the Confederate for destruction.

Fort Lafayette was built on a small rock island lying in the Narrows between the lower end of Staten Island and Long Island, opposite Fort Hamilton.

such a truculent prisoner, trying to bribe the guard to allow him to escape among other actions, he was soon hauled off to Fort Lafayette Prison.

On January 15, 1865, Kennedy was tried by military commission, found guilty and sentenced to death. His appeal to Lincoln for clemency was denied in view of the heinous intent of his act. After confessing to his role in the New York terror plot, he claimed, "I know that I am to be hung for setting fire to Barnum's Museum," he said, "but that was only a joke." No one laughed.

On March 25, 1865, he was walked to the Fort Jefferson scaffold and positioned carefully over the trap door, his manacles were removed, arms bound tightly to his chest, legs bound together to preclude movement and a black hood slipped over his head. The noose was adjusted around his neck and knot placed behind his left ear as custom and science required. After the verdict was officially read, he blurted out, "It's a damn lie." When the officer in charge dropped his arm, his assistant pulled the trap lock and Kennedy was launched into eternity. His body swayed for a few minutes before the surgeon pronounced death, then cut down.[60]

Target - Railroad

Commissioner Thompson was nothing if not resilient! It was try, try and try again for the Confederate Canadian station chief. As a result of his continued efforts to free Southern soldiers from Northern prisoner of war camps, especially from Camp Douglas and Johnson Island, Federal authorities decided to move some of the "high value"

General Trimble was one of the South's better officers.

prisoners to more secure facilities. In this instance, Fort Lafayette in New York City. Among the generals scheduled for transfer were Major General Isaac Trimble, Brigadier General John R. Jones and General John Frazer. Trimble was captured at Gettysburg after "going up the hill" with Pickett's Charge and losing a leg in the action. All three were valuable officers needed by the Confederates, either to lead troops broken loose from Yankee prisons or at least for their morale and propaganda value.

Thompson ordered two of his senior agents previously involved with the firebombing of New York to develop a new plan keyed to freeing the generals. The new scheme was simple. As the generals were being transferred to New York by rail, they would "rob" the train of the officers!

Since the train ran from Sandusky to Buffalo with stops at Erie, Pennsylvania, and Dunkirk, New York, there was opportunity to infiltrate agents at both middle stations. John Beall, one of the agents involved in trying to seize the *Michigan* and break the prisoners out of Johnson Island was brought into the design as a key player. On December 13 and 14, 1864, the raiders crossed the border to the U.S. from Fort Erie, Ontario, to Buffalo. On the night of the 14th, they huddled up in a room in the Hotel Genesee for the final operational orders.

The following morning both groups of agents took westbound trains, detraining at Erie and Dunkirk as planned. They would patiently wait for the eastbound train carrying the prisoners, board it and on signal, surprise the guards, seize their weapons, decouple the passenger coaches, cut the telegraph wires and run on to Buffalo. To aid in disguise, the generals would dress in clothing taken from passengers.

When the generals failed to arrive on the expected train, the raiders returned to Buffalo but posted an agent to keep the train station under close watch to alert them if the targets arrived without notice. After several days of waiting, the generals failed to appear.

Desperate to do something, the following day the raiders moved several miles west of Buffalo by sleigh and planted an iron rail across the tracks. In theory the rail should derail the train and they could use the wreckage to break open the express car and steal the money. Express cars always carried money. If the generals were aboard they could dust them off and take them along on their escape. The train came rumbling through on schedule at 5:00 p.m. and ran smack into the rail knocking it off into the surrounding fields. Unsure of what happened or what they hit, the engineers braked the train several hundred yards away and climbed down with lanterns glowing bright against the snow covered ground to see what was wrong.

Here the raiders lost their nerve. Instead of attacking the train according to plan, the raiders ran for the hills and Buffalo. It was almost like kids playing a Halloween prank. Most of them immediately crossed the border to Canada but Beall and two others stopped at a restaurant just short of the international bridge for a meal and fell asleep. When Federal agents threw the cuffs on them, they were still rubbing sleep out of their eyes. Justice was quick. Beall was tried and convicted as both a spy and a guerrilla then hanged on February 24, 1865.

Target - Germ Warfare

Certainly the most despicable act of attempted Confederate terror was promulgated by a Kentucky medical doctor named Luke Pryor Blackburn. The doctor had been in Bermuda supposedly treating victims of a yellow fever epidemic. Since he was purportedly an expert in the disease there was nothing unusual about his humanitarian actions, at least until the U.S. Consul in Bermuda learned that Blackburn was collecting victims' sweat-soaked clothing, sheets and blankets and secretly shipping them to Canada where the boxes were to be distributed to various Northern cities for distribution to the poor. By outward appearances it was just a simple act of Christian charity. A special box was even made up for Abraham Lincoln and identified as from an admirer.

There is little doubt Blackburn believed that yellow fever could be transmitted by victim clothing thus distributing the clothing to the poor in densely packed cities would help a yellow-fever epidemic spread across the North. The knowledge that the disease was actually spread by the bites of Aedes aegypti mosquitoes was still far in the future. Yellow fever was a very real terror weapon. An epidemic in Bermuda before Blackburn's arrival involved 3,000 cases and over 500 deaths. The implications of it running rampant through a tightly packed military camp were obvious, or in a densely populated city were horrifying.

Thompson was rumored to have funded the operation to the tune of $200,000. The Confederate agent in Toronto charged with distributing the boxes apparently had a change of heart over the pure despicability of the plan and told all to the U.S. Consul in Canada. It was one thing to target soldiers with collateral damage to civilians but to deliberately attack innocent children and women was truly despicable.

Since Bermuda was a British colony as was Canada, the consul preferred charges of, "conspiracy to murder in a foreign country," resulting in Blackburn's arrest in May of 1865 and a subsequent trial in Canada. He was acquitted for an imaginary lack of evidence but since the war was over, small note of the affair was paid in the general euphoria of peace.

Blackburn faded into the hills of Kentucky later to emerge as governor, proving the adage, "you can't keep a good mass-murderer to be down." In an

Doctor Luke Pryor Blackburn

apparent effort to rehabilitate his despicable Civil War reputation, the words, "the good Samaritan" are cut into his gravestone. Go figure.

The Northeast Conspiracy

The Confederates certainly had an active collective imagination for plotting against the hated Yankee. One of the stranger plans involved stretching Union attention and resources over a very wide area.

While records are not clear who "imagined" the operation, it was Canada born and accepted the premise it would be a great advantage to create as much confusion in the North as possible when the anticipated August "rising" was underway in Chicago. Not only would Northern leaders be confused over what was really happening, it would also dilute their military reaction.

The scheme went something like this. General Morgan would lead a strike force of roughly 5,000 men heavy with field artillery on a seaborne assault on Maine! The force would be delivered to the state by eight fast blockade runners who would afterwards slip back to a Southern port (by this time in the war most likely Wilmington). Morgan and his men would subsist off the land as Sherman did on his "March to the Sea" through Georgia. Morgan was to divide his force into five columns and keeping each within supporting distance of the others, cut his way through the state burning and looting Federal and State property, as well it assumed, appropriate civilian belongings to bring the fullest effects of war deep into the North. If Sherman made Georgia howl, then Morgan could make Maine howl!

The Confederate armed steamers *CSS Tallahassee* and *CSS Florida* would cooperate in what today would be called a "combined arms" operation by shelling coastal cities, especially Portland, creating additional confusion and panic.[61]

How far along the actual operational planning proceeded before sinking of its own weight is unknown but starting in May and running for a couple of months, local Maine fisherman reported there were many so-called artists along the shoreline painting various scenes of the coast. Given the high visibility a period photographic operation would have created and the common sight of artists on the picturesque

One of the end of war schemes involved General Morgan leading a 5,000 man invasion of Maine.

shore, this was an excellent and imaginative way to capture information. Was it Confederate intelligence gathering or just Maine paranoia?

Supposedly, a Confederate headquarters was established in St. John's, Quebec, to facilitate local planning and execution and several rebels were sent from Richmond to assist in the endeavor. Escaped Confederate prisoners also fell in around the planning cell. Once again the Confederates ignored the basics of secret operations, they talked openly about their plans, bragging of what was going to happen! The U.S. Consul in St. John's soon heard rumors and duly passed them on to the Secretary of State who relayed them to the Secretary of War. Telegrams flashed out from Washington and the Maine coastal cities and governments were alerted to the operation. The "Great Northeast" raid was dead.

Incredibly, on July 16, 1864, three of the men involved with the planning cell, apparently on their own, decided to raid the Maine town of Calais just across the Canadian border. Their target was the Calais bank. Again it was Confederate loose talk that killed the effort. When the raiders reached town they were met by an armed bank staff and a local sheriff with a posse mounted and ready to strike. The rebels quickly surrendered and were hustled off to the county jail.

Launching the full attack on Maine was predicated on the Confederacy being able to assemble the required soldiers with all supporting equipment as well as the sealift to transport them to the assault site. At this point in the war, collecting what was needed was virtually impossible.

If, and it is a very big if, the Confederate raid on Maine had been launched, in my opinion, several things were likely to have happened.

1. Sneaking a single blockade runner past the Union ships was comparatively easy. Slipping an entire fleet of transports plus presumably some armed escorts would have been impossible. There likely would have been some losses to the Confederate forces in the near shore area from U.S. Navy attacks and if the fleet continued the mission it is likely additional strikes would have severely depleted them. Ships filled with soldiers were always fat targets for naval gunfire!

2. Assuming at least some loss occurred from Union Navy action, what impact would it have had on the force? History teaches seaboard assault forces were rarely "combat loaded," placing troops and equipment on vessels in the order they will be needed ashore and divided among the fleet so that the loss of a ship or ships does not destroy the total force capability. For example, putting all the ammunition on a single ship, or all the artillery, or all the command and staff, etc.

3. Confederate naval experience was predicated mostly on single ship operations, blockade runners and raiders operating alone in distant waters. Fleet operations including sailing discipline, tactics and signaling, were virtually never done and the Maine force was an invasion fleet in every sense. The lack of experience would have greatly impacted efficiency regardless of Union Navy intervention.

4. Assuming the fleet arrived off the Maine coast in good condition, it would have had to seize a port to facilitate unloading. An invasion force of 5,000 men plus artillery

The Confederate invasion force would have been severely tested by the Union Navy.

train, horses, mules, quartermaster train and associated supplies could not have come ashore over the open beach, especially one as predominately rock bound as Maine.

5. Given the experience of other seaborne assaults through history, there would have been considerable confusion in unloading troops and gear in the proper combat order and priority. The force would likely not have reached the beach ready to fight.

6. Allowing a week for unloading and sorting out the force once ashore is reasonable.

7. The Union Navy would not have been idle. It can be assumed every floating warship would have been sent after the Confederate fleet, and likely would have trapped them wherever the unloading was being conducted.

8. Given the communications structure along the Maine coast (telegraph, train, coach, coastal steamer and other vessels), notice of the Confederate landing would have quickly reached Washington.

9. The North likely would have been alerted to the assault based on the contact with the Union Navy during the initial breakout. Clearly this was an invasion force so the only question was where? Troop strength would have been estimated by the number of ships. A quick Union steamer would have run ashore to the nearest telegraph office flashing the intelligence to Washington. In turn Washington would have alerted all northeastern ports (based on the direction of travel) of the potential assault.

10. If the port selected for seizing was alerted to the potential assault beforehand and had a fortification that could quickly be manned by militia, other troops or even townspeople, additional problems would be created for the Confederates. Seaboard assaults of fixed fortifications were rarely successful. Likewise Maine Militia units quickly emplacing artillery on shore could wreak havoc with the capture and unloading

process. All the defenders had to do was delay, buying time for the arrival of stronger Federal forces.

11. Assuming the Confederates were able to get ashore in some semblance of order, divide themselves into the five columns and strike out for inland targets, they were a thoroughly expendable force. An extraction by sea as in Dunkirk would have been impossible given the overwhelming strength of the Union Navy.

12. The further inland the soldiers marched, the more and more Union Army strength would oppose them and the more they would be denied replenishment of needed rations and supplies. It would have been a repeat of British general Johnny Burgoyne's disastrous march south from Montreal during the American Revolution. The Confederates hoped for just the opposite, that the disaffected including, local SOL members, would flock to the "colors" adding to the strength. It was wishful thinking.

13. On the Confederate plus side, regardless of what point the Confederate force ceased to exist as a functional fighting force, it would have thrown the North into panic! How long the panic lasted and what ultimate effect it could have had on the war is the unknown. If the near certain loss of the 5,000 men plus equipment and the likely loss of most if not all of the fleet was worth the resulting panic, was the political question.

A Last Gasp of Hope

As the weakened walls of the slavocracy came tumbling in, Thompson's fertile Canadian team reportedly hatched one last desperate plan. It required Lee's crumbling Army of Northern Virginia to break out of the defensive positions it held around Richmond and dash north, first feinting at Washington to fix the Northern Army in position, then moving rapidly up the Shenandoah Valley toward Philadelphia, take Pittsburgh and set up a temporary base at Wheeling while sweeping up the 100,000 plus soldiers kept in Northern prisons. Simultaneously, Joe Johnston's army was to move quickly up from the south and join Lee, building a combined force approaching 100,000 men, plus freed prisoners. Along the way every effort would be made to secure as many horses as possible to increase the army's speed and mobility.

As Lee moved north, he would destroy railroads and bridges to delay Northern pursuit. Grant and Sherman would, of course, try to run Lee down, so speed was of the essence.

Lee would then pivot his force to the east, assuming good defensive positions with his flanks anchored on Lake Erie and the Ohio River and Appalachian Mountains. Meanwhile, additional reinforcements from the west would arrive in the form of SOL volunteers. While sitting behind his strong defensive line, he could release a large mounted force to cut through Ohio, Indiana and Illinois creating more havoc. Other Confederate forces under Kirby Smith and Nathan Bedford Forrest could make their way up from the southwest to join Lee sweeping up more Southern prisoners, adding to the aggregate strength.

While Lee, striking northward, would have left the South utterly defenseless should the plan have worked, he would have been loose in the Union rear with an army invigorated with the newly released prisoners.

Would Grant have broken his armies smashing into Lee's new strong defensive positions? Or would he have fixed him in position and starved him out? Lee was far from any logistic base and while the countryside would have provided some supply, it was tenuous at best and arms and ammunition would have been critically short.

While it might seem to be a fool's plan given the abysmal state of the Confederacy, it was also a last most desperate gamble to snatch victory from the rapidly closing jaws of defeat. Would it have changed the war, given the South a chance to win? Certainly not, but it could have prolonged the slaughter a while longer to no one's advantage.

By the time the plan was conceived and formulated, it was too late. Lee had surrendered at Appomattox and the war was essentially over. It was just one more lost Confederate opportunity.

The Ill-Fated *Georgian*

If Commissioner Thompson was disappointed by the failures of his various Canada launched plots, he didn't show it, continuing to "soldier on" with new plans even as the roof of the Confederacy was crashing down on his ears.

Since he couldn't manage to capture the *Michigan* to use as a Great Lakes raider, he would simply buy his own ship and equip her as needed! Thompson's *Georgian* plan was essentially just a variation of the earlier one developed by Lieutenant Murdaugh of the Confederate Navy in February 1863.

The *Georgian* was the perfect ship for Thompson's purpose. She was a heavily built 130-foot, 377 ton passenger and package freight propeller constructed in 1864 at Port McNicoll, Ontario, at the mouth of Georgian Bay's Severn River. The term "propeller" referred to her use of a propeller instead of sidewheels. To disguise Thompson's involvement, the actual purchase from the Potter yard was masked by George Wyatt and A.M. Smith. Both were Southern supporters. The propeller in turn was sold to Thompson for about $17,000.[62] John Bates, an old Mississippi River pilot from Louisville, Kentucky, was to be her captain. Her lone drawback was speed, her 70-horsepower engine only capable of driving her at about 8 miles per hour.

"Disinformation" or providing a believable cover for the *Georgian* was important so the "word" was put out she would be used in the lumber trade, hauling cargoes between upper lake timber mills and down lake markets.

Ships in the lumber trade typically had several important characteristics, which also would be valuable as a privateer. She was heavily built to handle the expected lumber cargoes but also had a shallow draft to work over shoals and low water. As a privateer, a stout construction was critical to support deck guns as well as allow her to ram opponents as needed. The light draft gave her the ability to run and hide in the shallows of Lake Huron's Georgian Bay, going places the big and deeper draft *Michigan* could not. Georgian Bay was a wild and desolate place, offering many small islands and coves where she could hide. If used boldly, and with luck, she could paralyze lake traffic and even bombard port cities as opportunity presented. If she could capture a few smaller vessels, it would be easy to imprison their crew, replacing them with a few good *Georgian* men, drop a small gun aboard and send them out to raid commerce, too! The Union's problem would grow ever larger and more difficult, the more Rebel raiders were on the loose.

When the rumors spread about the real purpose of the *Georgian,* the lakes were again thrown into near panic. The *Philo Parsons*, incident St. Albans, Chicago, et.al., all gave credence that the Canadian Confederates were a real threat and growing! It wasn't about what did happen. It was fear of what COULD happen that set everyone on edge. But if Thompson thought he could

Philo Parsons *participant Bennett G. Burley was also involved in the* Georgian *plot.*

quietly introduce the *Georgian* into her new role as a commerce raider without anyone being the wiser, he was sadly mistaken. Northern spies were well aware of her and spread the word of her intended purpose.

Thompson apparently closed the purchase of the *Georgian* on November 1, 1864, at Port Colborne on the Welland Canal. A day later, she was in Buffalo to have her propeller repaired. Her Canadian officers denied any knowledge of the nefarious plans for her, even when dockside rumors circulated she was heading for Johnson Island to free the prisoners.

Supposedly, Captain Bates told a Confederate "friend" in Toronto about his plan to load cannon and small arms to use the ship as a privateer. The *Michigan* would be his first target. Unfortunately for Bates, the "friend" relayed the conversation to the U.S. Consul in Toronto, who in turn passed the information "up the chain." If the Union entertained any doubts about the mission of the *Georgian*, they didn't any more.[63]

It also seems that Bennett G. Burley, laying low from his escape from the *Philo Parsons* disaster, was in Guelph, west of Toronto, working at a local foundry casting cannon for the *Georgian*. Later investigation showed a 14-pounder had been shipped via the Grand Trunk Railway to Collingwood on Georgian Bay likely intended for the steamer. A gun carriage and other supplies were awaiting shipment to Spanish River, a small out of the way settlement hidden behind Manitoulin Island in northern Georgian Bay. Spanish River was the perfect place to hide the *Georgian* far from prying eyes.

The necessary munitions were later shipped in two barrels and a large box marked "potatoes" to Sarnia, Ontario, at the north entrance to the St. Clair River, since the

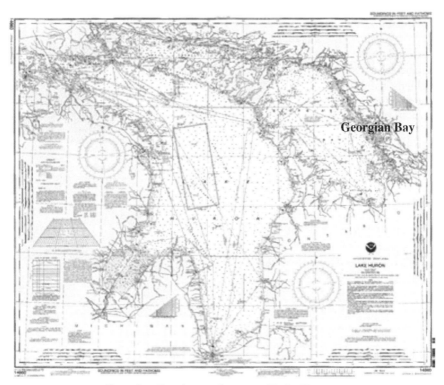

Georgian Bay, just to the east of Lake Huron.

propeller had already left, for some reason they were forwarded to Lexington, Michigan, on the west shore of Lake Huron where U.S. Customs agents recovered them.

Mayor Fargo of Buffalo didn't buy the *Georgian's* claim of innocence, telegraphing the captain of the *Michigan* with her location and extolling the threat. Navy Secretary Gideon Welles followed up with instructions to the *Michigan's* captain that the propeller be seized on the barest excuse and legal niceties need not apply. Mayor Fargo, "one-upped" Welles by arming a couple tugs with guns and commissioning them as the, "Buffalo Navy." Soon after four combat regiments marched into town to provide further defense. Given the city's very vulnerable position with Canada just across the river and vital Erie Canal terminus, such measures weren't entirely paranoid. Unwilling to concede the initiative local police boarded the propeller at first opportunity searching for weapons or other evidence of her true intention. Finding none, they reluctantly let her leave port on November 3 bound for Port Stanley, Ontario (midway down Lake Erie) for repair to her screw. Apparently repairs were not completely successful or perhaps problems with the propeller were just a cover for future operations.

After clearing Port Stanley, the *Georgian* stopped at Amherstburg on the Canadian side of the Detroit River for a couple of days on the way up to Lake Huron. Her arrival

Mounting cannon on tugboats was seen as quick way to increase defenses for port cities.

greatly alarmed Detroit officials who anticipated soon seeing her steaming across the river with guns blazing.

Just after leaving Amherstburg, U.S. Customs boarded and searched her, too, but found nothing suspicious. Not long after, a couple of hastily armed tugs under the control of Lieutenant Colonel Hill, the Assistant Provost Marshall of Detroit, stopped her, too, and searched but came up empty.

Her propeller must have remained a problem since when she reached Sarnia on November 11, Captain Bates went ashore and ordered a new one be sent to Colling-wood. Replacing the propeller would likely have meant drydocking and more lost time. Canadian authorities searched her again without finding anything unusual so she was released to continue her trip.

All the while the *Georgian* was steaming merrily along as a potential piranha of the Lakes U.S. diplomats were pressuring the Canadian government to take final action against her. When she reached Collingwood the Canadian government again inspected her but found nothing suspicious save her problematic propeller. The captain, of course, protested she was innocent and bound for Georgian Bay to be rigged for the lumber trade. The captain of the *Michigan* later related, "it was given out that she was going into the Saginaw lumber trade, but this was a blind. She has not carried a pound of freight or earned a dollar in legitimate trade since she fell into her present owner's hands." Perhaps remembering the important work gunner Murray did for him during the aborted *Philo Parsons* plot, Captain Carter was able to have two of his men surreptitiously join the *Georgian* crew. What they learned and how effectively they were able to relay information to him is unknown but having men on the inside is always good.

After the propeller was replaced at Collingwood, she started north to Bruce Mines also on Georgian Bay for winter lay-up but later returned to Collingwood. By this point the *Michigan* was shadowing her so perhaps her threatening presence dissuaded her from continuing on to the remote northern port. Regardless, the Canadians claimed they had no legal reason to impound her. At least the thick ice of the northern winter would lock her into port until spring.

Thompson was later moved to whine to Confederate Secretary of State Judah Benjamin on December 3, 1864 that, "the bane and curse of carrying anything out in this country is the surveillance under which we act. Detectives, or those ready to give information, stand at every street corner. Two or three men cannot interchange ideas without a reporter." Certainly this was true concerning the *Georgian*.

All winter long the U.S. pressured the Canadians about the *Georgian*. She clearly was a threat to the U.S. and just as clearly was going to use Canada as a base in violation of the Canadian law. Canada needed to take action!

By spring it was all a moot point. The Confederacy was only a rapidly fading nightmare. On April 7 the Canadians finally impounded the ship. A detailed search of her discovered documents relating to the use of the infamous Greek Fire including launching burning projectiles at other ships.

Union officials concluded one plan involved using her to capture American fishing boats as a quick way to build a Confederate Navy on the lakes. Given small Confederate crews, the fishing boats could range far over the lakes capturing and destroying Northern shipping. A later examination of records revealed a letter from Thompson to the Secretary of War relating it was his plan to, "have a boat on whose captain and crew reliance could be placed and on which arms could be sent to convenient points for arming such vessels as could be seized for operations on the lakes." Clearly she was intended to be a Great Lakes privateer.[65]

With the war over the *Georgian* was sold commercial and sailed for 23 years before smacking an ice floe in Georgian Bay while towing the schooner-barge *Gold Hunter* and sinking. So ended the tale of the Confederate "Pirate Ship."

Confederate Saboteurs

There is some evidence there was a plot intended to be executed in the Spring of 1865 that would have sent small parties of Confederates to the Union Great Lakes ports armed with various "infernal machines" (aka bombs initiated with timing devices) to destroy critical targets. The scheme was supposedly discovered by a spy code named (Fides) working for Mayor William G. Fargo of Buffalo.[66] The U.S. Consul in Toronto confirmed the reports adding the saboteurs would use Canadian passports. There was a similar claim a "Reverend Steward" was organizing men as saboteurs including freed Negroes to launch similar attacks.[67] Intriguing as this information is, little detail has been discovered or verified. But as in each of these stories, the POTENTIAL of what COULD HAVE BEEN is significant.

John Wilkes Booth and Canada

During the trial of the Lincoln conspirators following the assassination, it was revealed Booth made at least one trip to Canada and met with at least some of Thompson's men. The meeting took place in October 1864 but details are sparse. Union double agent Robert Montgomery later testified it involved a plot to kidnap Lincoln, exchanging him for the release of Confederate prisoners. The sudden influx of new soldiers would give the South new energy to continue the war. The kidnapping was to happen in March 1865 but when the President changed his travel schedule it fell apart. Lee's surrender on April 7 made the entire idea obsolete but apparently set in motion Booth's assassination plan.

References

Adjutants General of Ohio - http://www.sos.state.oh.us/SOS/elections/electResultsMain/
Historical%20Election%20Comparisons/Adjutants%20General%20of%20the%20State%20of
%20Ohio%201803%20-%20present.aspx.

Atlantic Monthly, July 1865.

"Biographic Sketch of the Late Gen. B. J. Sweet - History of Camp Douglas." A Paper Read
before the Chicago Historical Society, Tuesday Evening, June 18th, 1878, by William Bross,
A. M., Lieutenant Governor of Illinois^ 1865-9.

Wilifrid Bovey, "Confederate Agents in Canada During the American Civil War," *Canadian
History Review*, Vol. 2, No. 1, (1921) 46-57.

Canadian Archives, "Fides" Reports to Mayor Fargo About Confederate Plots, RG 7, G Series
6, Volume 14, 725-726, November 30, 1864.

Civil War Hangings and Other Executions -
http://www.footnote.com/page/762_civil_war_hangings_other_executions.

Conspiracy in Canada - https://www.cia.gov/library/publications/additional-publications/
civil-war/p37.htm.

Chicago Tribune, November 8, 1864.

Conspiracy in Canada - https://www.cia.gov/library/publications/additional-publications/
civil-war/p37.htm.

O. Edward Cunningham, "In Violation of the Laws of War," *The Journal of Louisiana
Historical Association*, (Spring 1977), 189-201.

Detroit Free Press, September 20, November 4,1864.

Catherine Lynch Deichmann, *Rogues and Runners, Bermuda and the American Civil War*,
(Bermuda National Trust, 2003), 73-74.

Encyclopedia of the American Civil War: a political, social, and military History.
By David Stephen Heidler, Jeanne T. Heidler, David J. Coles, W.W. Norton, NY 2000, 1562.

Encyclopedia of Chicago, Civil War - http://encyclopedia.chicagohistory.org/pages/2379.html.

Fort Lafayette - http://www.mycivilwar.com/pow/ny-fort_lafayette.htm.

Mayo Felser, "Secret Political Societies in the North During the Civil War," *Indiana Magazine
of History*, Vol. XIV, No. 3, 1918, 183-286.

Charles E. Frohman, *Rebels on Lake Erie*, Columbus, The Ohio Historical Society, 1965. 49.

Wood Gray, *The Hidden Civil War; the Story of the Copperheads*, (New York: Viking Press,
1942), 138, 183.

James M. Gillispie, *Andersonvilles of the North, the Myths and Realities of Northern
Treatment of Civil War Confederate Prisoners*. University of North Texas Press, Denton,
Texas, 2009, pp. 153-166.

Harper's Weekly, April 5, 1862.

James C. Hazlett, *Field Artillery of the Civil War*, (Cranbury, New Jersey: Associated
University Presses, Inc. 1983), 226-227.

William Hoffman - http://www.aztecclub.com/bios/hoffman.htm.

John Bell Hood - http://www.mycivilwar.com/leaders/hood_john.htm.

James D. Horan, *Confederate Agent, A Discovery in History*, (Crown Publishers, Inc.: New
York, 1990), 16; 21; 61; 87; 97-98; 113-117; 156-157; 187.

Island History, Civil War Garrison - http://www.johnsonsisland.org/history/war_guards.htm

Erik Heyl, *Early American Steamers Volume III*, (Erik Heyl: Buffalo, 1964), 285-286.

Bern Keating, *The Flamboyant Mr. Colt and His Deadly Six-Shooter,* (New York: Doubleday and Company, 1978), 205.

Oscar A. Kinchen, PhD, *Confederate Operations in Canada and in the North, a Little Known Phase of the American Civil War,* (North Quincy, Massachusetts: The Christopher Publishing House, 1978), 94-95, 131, 134-135, 152, 155, 181, 190-192.

Frank L. Klement, Dark Lanterns, *Secret Political Societies, Conspiracies and Treason Trials in the Civil War,* (Baton Rouge: Louisiana State University Press, 1984), 205-208, 216-217.

New York Times, December 5, 1864; March 25, 26, April 30, July 9, 1865, November 21, 1886.

Middle Bass Island - http://www.middlebass.org/Wine_Islands_of_Lake_Erie.shtml.

Francis Trevelyan Miller, ed., *The Photographic History of the Civil War, Volumes One and Two,* (New York: Thomas Yoseloff, 1944), 1.

Military Executions During the Civil War - http://www.encyclopediavirginia.org/Military_Executions_During_the_Civil_War.

Minor, Robert D. - http://www.lva.virginia.gov/public/guides/connavy/ship_results.asp.

Murdaugh, William H. - http://www.lva.virginia.gov/public/guides/connavy/ship_results.asp?page=10&ship=.

John Wilson Murray, *Memoirs of a Great Canadian Detective, Incidents in the Life of John Wilson Murray,* (Toronto: Collins, 1977), x-xi, 11-19.

Adam Myers, *Dixie and the Dominion: Canada, the Confederacy and the War for the Union.* (Tonawanda, New York: Dunham Press, 2003), 26-27, 35, 57-59, 85-88, 139-143, 168, 184-185.

Philo Parsons, *Dictionary of American Navy Fighting Ships,* http://www.history.navy.mil/danfs/cfa7/philo_parsons.htm.

"The Plan to Rescue the Johnston's (sic) Island Prisoners, Captain Robert D. Minor's Report," *Southern Historical Society Papers,* Volume XXIII, January - December 1895, pp. 283-290, Richmond.

Public Affairs, Central Intelligence Agency, *Intelligence in the Civil War,* (Public Affairs, Central Intelligence Agency: Washington, DC) 43-45.

Price's 1864 Missouri Expedition - http://www.missouridivision-scv.org/price1864raid.htm.

Edwin B. Quiner, *The Military History of Wisconsin,* (Chicago: Clarke and Co. 1866), 323-325.

Regimental History, Wisconsin 21st Infantry Regiment - http://wisconsin2.tripod.com/21sthist.html.

Bradley A. Rodgers, *Guardian of the Great Lakes: the U.S. Paddle Frigate* Michigan, (Ann Arbor: University of Michigan Press, 1996), 82-86.

Frederick J. Shepard, "The Johnson Island Plot; An Historical Narrative of the Conspiracy of the Confederates in 1864 to Capture the U.S. Steamship *Michigan* on Lake Erie and Release the Prisoners of War in Sandusky Bay," Buffalo Historical Society, 1906, 8.

St. Albans Raid - http://nightlightreadings.blogspot.com/2010/05/st-albans-raid-confederate-raiders-turn.html.

Stephen Z. Starr, *Colonel Grenfell's Wars, The Life of a Soldier of Fortune,* (Baton Rouge: Louisiana State University Press, 1971), 134-135; 161-162; 183-191.

Felix G. Stidger, *Treason History of the Sons of Liberty,* (Chicago: Felix G. Stidger, 1903), Appendix A.

James M.Stradling, "The Lottery of Death," *McClure's Magazine,* Vol. 26, November 1905, 94-101.

William A. Tidwell, *Confederate Covert Action in the American Civil War - April '65*. Kent, Ohio: Kent State University Press, 1995, 30-32, 35, 135, 155-159, 243.

Toronto Globe, December 5, 1864.

Robin W. Winks, *Canada and the United States - The Civil War Years,* (Baltimore: Johns Hopkins Press, 1960), 301-303, 308-310.

Ayer, I. Winslow, The Great Treason Plot in the North. U.S. Publishing Company, Chicago, 1895, 26-28, 31-41, 47-50, 58, 90, 93, 96-97, 100, 119, 125-127, 140, 167.

Yankee John Murray vs. Charles Cole - http://us-civil-war.suite101.com/article.cfm/yankee-john-murray-vs-charles-cole—-the-johnsons-island-plot.

Footnotes

[1] *Harper's Weekly*, April 5, 1862.

[2] Gray Wood. *The Hidden Civil War; the Story of the Copperheads*, (New York: Viking Press, 1942), 138.

[3] Whether the Invincible Club hall was later used in subsequent schemes is unclear. There is some thought the Invincible Club hall may have been synonymous with the local Democrat club.

[4] How true the $2 million story is is debatable. The bulk of the finances to support the SOL came from Thompson in Canada.

[5] Wood Gray, *The Hidden Civil War; the Story of the Copperheads,* (New York: Viking Press, 1942), 183.

[6] Lt. Young's Report of the Fiasco at Chicago, Clement C. Clay Papers, National Archives, Toronto, September 2, 1964.

[7] Newgate was an infamous prison in London, England.

[8] There is dispute whether Grenfell was with Hines at this point or not. It is a small detail given the scope of the story: Colonel Sweet, the commander at Camp Douglas believed Grenfell was still Morgan's Chief of Staff (Wilfrid Bovey, "Confederate Agents in Canada During the American Civil War," *The Canadian Historical Review*, Vol. 2, Issue 1, March 1921, 54).

[9] See Chapter 7 for more detail on Colonel Grenfell.

[10] *The Great Treason Plot* claims 200 men (page 129).

[11] Bern Keating, *The Flamboyant Mr. Colt and His Deadly Six-Shooter*, (New York: Double-day and Company, 1978), 205.

[12] Regimental History, Wisconsin 21st Infantry Regiment - http://wisconsin2.tripod.com/21sthist.html.

[13] The Iron Brigade initially consisted of the 2nd, 6th, and 7th Wisconsin Volunteer Infantry Regiments, along with the 19th Indiana, and was later joined by the 24th Michigan. The all-Western brigade earned its famous nickname during battle action in September 1862 when withstanding attacks from Stonewall Jackson's superior force and in fact pushing the Confederates back. When Union General McClellan saw the action commented, "They must be made of iron" and thus was born their famous moniker.

[14] Established in July 1862 the Bureau of Provost Marshal General of the U.S. provided for Assistant Provost Marshals in each state charging them to supervise enlistments, checking enemies of the government and keeping the Provost Marshal General in Washington fully informed of local conditions. Although not responsible to the state governors, Assistant Provost Marshals were to cooperate with them. In addition each congressional district had a subordinate

Assistant Provost Marshal and counties Deputy Provost Marshals. Armed assistance came from Army Departmental commanders as needed, primarily by the Invalid Corps.

[15] Mark Mayo Boatner III, *The Civil War Dictionary,* (David McKay Company: New York, 1959), 401.

[16] Camp Morton was a prisoner of war facility at Indianapolis.

[17] The trials were held after Lincoln's assassination.

[18] The same vessel would figure prominently in a later escape attempt.

[19] Boatner III, 404.

[20] Island History, Civil War Garrison - http://www.johnsonsisland.org/history/war_guards.htm.

[21] "See the Elephant" was an expression used by Civil War soldiers meaning going into combat.

[22] Frederick J. Shepard, "The Johnson Island Plot; An Historical Narrative of the Conspiracy of the Confederates in 1864 to Capture the U.S. Steamship *Michigan* on Lake Erie and Release the Prisoners of War in Sandusky Bay," Buffalo Historical Society, 1906, 9.

[23] Civil War Hangings and Other Executions - http://www.footnote.com/page/762_civil_war_hangings_other_executions/

[24] Typically a reserve firing party of six soldiers per prisoner is also provided in the event a "coup de gras" is needed. In this instance it appears one was not part of the ceremony.

[25] Shepard, 8.

[26] Military Executions During the Civil War - http://www.encyclopediavirginia.org/Military_Executions_During_the_Civil_War

[27] Murdaugh, William H. - http://www.lva.virginia.gov/public/guides/connavy/ship_results.asp?page=10&ship=.

[28] Shepard, 16.; One of the raiders was the *CSS Alabama* which during her career was responsible for destroying 65 Northern merchant ships valued at $6 million before finally being destroyed by the *USS Kearsarge*.

[29] Minor, Robert D. - http://www.lva.virginia.gov/public/guides/connavy/ship_results.asp.

[30] There is some question whether Murdaugh was involved in the new plan or not.

[31] Boatner III, 23.

[32] See Chapter 1 for more details of the *Michigan's* previous activities.

[33] How the cannon were to be smuggled onto a vessel is a mystery. The length and weight varied with style but ranged between 250 pounds and 1,350 and four to six feet in length. Carriages only added to the problem.

[34] The Welland Canal cut the Welland Peninsula and allowed vessel traffic to bypass Niagara Falls and travel between Lakes Ontario and Erie.

[35] Canister shot was made up of a hollow filled with iron or lead balls about the size of today's golf balls. The effect was like firing a very large shotgun, blasting away a huge swath of death to troops at the wrong end of the cannon!

[36] Shepard, 19.

[37] I have not found a record of a government or private foundry in Cleveland producing any artillery. Perhaps they confused it with foundries in Cincinnati.

[38] A privateer was private warship authorized by a country's government by letters of marque to attack foreign shipping during wartime.

[39] Erik Heyl, *Early American Steamers Volume III*, (Erik Heyl: Buffalo, 1964), 285-286.

[40] Also often spelled Burleigh.

[41] It is hard to understand Beall's decision to return for fuel considering he had sufficient to make Johnson Island and seize the *USS Michigan*. And with the warship as escort he could leisurely refuel at Middle Bass Island (or anywhere else) without interference from anyone.

[42] In theory the open valves would flood the holds sending her to the bottom of the lake.

[43] Given it was reportedly a bright moonlit night, the Marblehead Light was fully functional and a very well known port and channel to the steamer's crew, I suspect this was "disinformation" spread by the helmsman.

[44] Ayer, I. Winslow, *The Great Treason Plot in the North*, (U.S. Publishing Company, Chicago, 1895), 56.

[45] In my view the crew hoodwinked Beall about the ships being in Canadian waters. Beall at best a nominally capable navigator, was unaware of the border else he would have realized it was in what today's military would call a "target rich environment." Beall wanted to take no overt action in Canadian waters lest he disturb the benign attitude of the British.

[46] A yawl is a ships small rowing boat not to be confused with a lifeboat.

[47] A "line" officer, aka a "deck" officer was one capable of commanding or fighting the ship as opposed to an engineer officer, surgeon or supply officer all of whom were specialists.

[48] Shepard, 37.

[49] The Treaty resolved numerous several border issues between the United States and the British North American colonies, including the location of the Maine-New Brunswick border; set details of the border between Lake Superior and the Lake of the Woods, confirmed the location of the border (at the 49th parallel) in the westward frontier to the Rocky Mountains; called for a final end to the slave trade on the high seas, to be enforced by the U.S. and Britain and confirmed terms for shared use of the Great Lakes.

[50] Ayer, I. Winslow, *The Great Treason Plot in the North*, (U.S. Publishing Company, Chicago, 1895), 74.

[51] *Detroit Free Press*, November 4, 1864.

[52] Quartermaster activities are varied but include involving supply functions.

[53] Some sources identify Shanks as a captain and former Texas Ranger.

[54] Stephen Starr, *Colonel Grenfell's Wars, the Life of a Soldier of Fortune,* (Baton Rouge: Louisiana State University Press, 1971), p. 187.

[55] Keefe, T.H. "How the North-West Was Saved." *Everybody's Magazine*, Vol. II, 1900, 82-91.

[56] The expression "Katy bar the door" and similar variations means impending disaster, watch out and get ready for trouble.

[57] Ayer, 167-168.

[58] Some sources state the arrests were made on November 7 the confusion likely caused the hour and that there were multiple units performing the mission.

[59] Frank L. Klement, *Dark Lanterns, Secret Political Societies, Conspiracies and Treason Trials in the Civil War,* (Baton Rouge: Louisiana State University Press, 1984) 205-208, 216-217.

[60] *New York Times*, November 26, December 2, 1864, March 25, 26, 1865;

[61] The *CSS Tallahasse* was built in London supposedly for the Chinese opium trade but instead was used as blockade runner between Bermuda and Wilmington, N.C. until the Confederate Navy purchased her, converting her into an armed cruiser. On her first raid she sank 26 Northern merchant vessels and captured seven others on the Atlantic coast. Running short of coal, she put into Halifax on August 18, 1864, refueled and evaded a Northern blockading flotilla and returned to Wilmington.

After a colorful career and several name changes, she ended up in Britain at the end of the war and in August 1866 was awarded to the Union in partial compensation for her depredations on shipping.

The CSS *Florida* was also British built but her intended function was always that of a commerce raider. She departed England in March 1862, refueled and loaded arms, ammunition and other supplies from a pre-staged tender in Bermuda intending to start raiding immediately. However a yellow fever epidemic virtually wiped out the crew and she was forced to run the blockade into Mobile, Alabama for a crew refit. She put to sea in January 1863 and created havoc amongst Union shipping off North and South America, eluding Union warships sent to run her down. Refueling in Bermuda she sailed to France for a refit, then on to the West Indies, Canary Islands and finally Bahia, Brazil arriving in October 1864. By international law she was safe from Federal attack in neutral waters, so her captain took half his crew ashore. However, when the captain of the USS *Wachusett* found her virtually defenseless, he wasted no time in attacking and capturing her during a brilliant night action, Brazilian protests not withstanding. The U.S. Navy court-martialed the captain for ignoring the law, finding him guilty of the charge. The Secretary of the Navy wasted no time in setting the conviction aside and the officer went on to an excellent career.

The *Florida* captured 37 prizes during her career but met her end in November 1864 when rammed and sunk by a U.S. vessel. It is likely it was a deliberate "accident" since the court ordered her returned to Brazil (and the Confederate Navy) since the capture was illegal. Rather than see this travesty happen, Admiral Dixon Porter arranged the unfortunate accident. No ship, no return!

[62] There is some thought Thompson gave the money to Dr. James Bates, her later captain to make the purchase through Colonel George Denison. All of this was intended to hide the real ownership; Wilfrid Bovey, "Confederate Agents in Canada During the American Civil War," *The Canadian Historical Review,* Vol. 2, Issue 1, March 1921, 50.

[63] Oscar A. Kinchen, PhD, *Confederate Operations in Canada and the North, a Little Known Phase of the American Civil War,* (North Quincy, Massachusetts: The Christopher Publishing House, 1978),116-117.

[65] Adam Mayers, *Dixie and Dominion: Canada, the Confederates and the War for the Union,* (Toronto: Dundurn Press, 2003), 132-135.

[66] William G. Fargo was mayor from 1862 to 1866 and from 1868 to his death in Buffalo, he was president of the American Express Company.

[67] Oscar A. Kinchen, PhD, *Confederate Operations in Canada and in the North, a Little Known Phase of the American Civil War,* (North Quincy, Massachusetts: The Christopher Publishing House, 1978), p. 181.

CHAPTER SEVEN
END
GAME

Thompson's Failure

In terms of the major objectives, Thompson's Canadian mission failed. There never was a "rising" of disaffected northern states, prisoners were never broken out of any prison camp, New York City wasn't burned and the Northern border wasn't set into a constant state of panic. While the aftermath of various failed operations did create periods of fear and alarm, if was never significant or long lasting enough to substantially disrupt the Northern war effort.

In hindsight, it is easy to see what went wrong.

Thompson wasn't a capable manager of clandestine operations. None of his prior experiences as a planter, politician and quasi-soldier equipped him to lead such a massive and complicated endeavor.

He (or the Confederacy at large) never gained operational control of the SOL (or other dissident groups). While working together, often in a hand-in-glove mode, the Confederates couldn't direct the critical movement, thus when most needed, the SOL wasn't there. The Confederates also failed to really understand the true SOL strength and instead accepted what they were told by organization leaders.

Thompson too easily believed what his agents told him. The chances of success for any of his major clandestine operations were very limited, but his operatives believed in them, so he did too. He didn't require a true mission analysis. For example Beall's attack on Johnson Island was doomed from the beginning when he was forced to operate with a group of men who didn't know each other, never trained together or rehearsed the operation in a meaningful way. Neither was there a "Plan B," an alternative action if the primary failed. Further, everything depended on Cole being able to somehow "disable" the *Michigan* crew. This was at best a very tall order for a single, unproven agent. James Bond he wasn't.

His organization was riddled with Federal agents and he had no effective method to "vet" prospective agents or root "turned" men out. He had no counter espionage capability. It seemed the Union was always inside his decision loop.

What he did accomplish was to create a degree of confusion in the Northern rear area, a climate of uncertainty and for short periods, even hysteria. In spite of the fact none of his plans actually worked, they did provoke a Union reaction, either militarily or politically. The flow of reinforcements forward to the Union was disrupted. Prison camps were forced to ratchet up security. Additional force structure was employed to protect the rear. Port cities became more apprehensive and demanded military protection. In this regard he did effectively attack the soft underbelly of the Union, but without the needed impact. On a scale of one to ten he reached a three - maybe.

When the war ended Thompson did not exactly go quietly into the night. He and his wife took off for Europe and were received by the Prince of Wales and Queen Victoria. The Thompsons remained on the continent for a year living, some claimed, on the cash he had grabbed from his secret funds he managed in Canada. When you are running out the door always grab the cash box.

Controversy swirled over how much of the unspent secret service money he took with him. London newspapers openly speculated about funds Confederate secret agents spirited away when the South collapsed. A couple of the agents who operated in Canada claimed Thompson made off with $300,000. During the trial of the Lincoln conspirators following the assassination, witnesses gave evidence the actual amount was nearly $650,000! Any money Thompson "eloped" with was important since Confederate ex-Secretary of State Benjamin was trying to use it to pay off British creditors. When Benjamin and Thompson finally met in London, Thompson claimed the amount he had was far less and he was owed it anyway to pay for his losses during the war as well as expenses. After much haggling, he paid Benjamin roughly $60,000, refusing to go any higher.

John Yates Beall

John Y. Beall was made to order for the role of agent and provocateur. Virginia born in 1835, he studied law at the University of Virginia. Hearing the bugle call to arms when the war began he joined up with the 2nd Virginia Infantry, soon to be known as part of the famous "Stonewall Brigade" after its commander Colonel Thomas J. ("Stonewall") Jackson. Beall was severely wounded during the Shenandoah campaign of 1862. Since Confederate doctors thought he would never recover enough to allow hard campaigning again, he was given a medical discharge.

He next surfaced in Chesapeake Bay leading two small sailing vessels, the *Raven* and

Beall received the punishment due all traitors, execution although instead of the dignity of a firing squad, he was hung.

the *Swan*, raiding against Union supply ships. The coasts of Virginia and Maryland are rift with rivers and bays and during the war largely controlled by the Northern Navy. Doubtless he found rich pickings in what was a key area of the Union supply network. The raiders also cut a Union telegraph cable, blew up a lighthouse, and captured several supply ships. One of the captures was bound for Port Royal, South Carolina, and rather than destroy it, Beall put a prize crew aboard and managed to slip her through the Union Navy blockade to safety. He later wrote, "I do not know that we ever accomplished any great things but we deviled the life out of the Gun boats of the Chesapeake trying to catch us."

His imitation of Errol Flynn as a pirate ended in November 1863 when he and his crew were captured and thrown in prison at Fort McHenry for several months. He was formally exchanged in May 1864 and returned to Richmond. Prisoner exchanges were common early in the war but as the conflict dragged on became increasingly rare. Part of the exchange involved signing a formal parole agreement that he would not fight for the South again. Why he chose to break his word isn't known. Perhaps it was a belief that the greater good was serving the South rather than his own honor. Or perhaps he thought he was too smart to ever be caught again.

Not content to while away his time in Virginia when there was fighting to do, he worked his way to Canada and met briefly with Confederate agents concerning various covert opportunities. Given his intelligence, solid war record and clear ambition to help the South any way he could, it is likely they were supportive and welcoming of his energy.

Regardless of the reason, he became an integral part of the failed plot to seize the *USS Michigan* and free the prisoners on Johnson Island. His freedom ended on September 16,1864 when Beall and two other confederates were arrested near the suspension bridge in Buffalo while trying to reach safety in Canada. Earlier they tried to derail a train eastbound from Sandusky intending to steal the money from the express car.

After his apprehension at Buffalo, he was taken by train to New York City and temporarily held in a police jail. Desperate to escape he reputedly tried without success to bribe a police officer with $3,000 in gold. The inducement wasn't accepted and he was quickly transferred to old Fort Lafayette, a Federal prison on a desolate hunk of rock gratuitously called an island, at the mouth of Upper New York Bay.

The Union, fed up certainly with his activity, threw the book at Beall, charging him with six specifications of violating the Laws of War and three specifications of acting as a spy. It was especially charged that he held a commission from the insurgent authorities in Richmond, was in disguise, procuring information with the intention of using it to inflict injury on unarmed civilians in the U.S., that he was conducting guerrilla war against the U.S.

Federal authorities were particularly incised he was trying to throw a train off its tracks late at night when engineers and conductors were less likely to see the obstruction, thus potentially endangering the lives of hundreds of innocent men, women

Federal authorities were especially angered that Beall's plan to destroy the train put innocent women and children at horrible risk.

and children passengers. Such despicable actions were against the accepted spirit of honorable warfare.

His court martial was convened on February 10, 1865. Beall claimed his actions were lawful and under the orders of President Jefferson Davis and authorized agents of the Confederate government. His arguments didn't sway the court and sentence was passed. The Federals held that even if Jeff Davis was the head of an independent government recognized by other nations, he didn't have the authority to sanction actions civilized states have long condemned.

Understanding the seriousness of the charges and the inevitable penalty, on February 21, Beall wrote a frantic letter to the Confederate commissioner in charge of prisoner exchange stating, "I acted under orders," and further claiming he should be treated as a prisoner of war and not a spy.

The court ignored his defense, found him guilty, and sentenced him to death by hanging.

Lincoln received numerous pleas from U.S. senators and representatives, governors and private citizens to release Beall from the death sentence. He ignored them all. The only proper treatment for a spy is death.

In the stilted and formal language of the court, "The Proceedings, finding and sentence are approved and the accused, John Y. Beall, will be hanged by the neck until he is dead on Governor's Island, on Friday the 24th day of February 1865." The original execution date was February 18 but President Lincoln kindly granted the additional six days to allow a last visit between Beall and his mother. Then it was off to the gallows and a date with eternity. The risks of a spy are hard, indeed!

By the time the Confederate Commissioner received Beall's desperate plea, the spy was three days cold and in his grave. For once justice was sure and swift.

Even on the windswept gallows, Beall wailed his innocence. "I protest against the execution of the sentence. It is absolute murder, brutal murder. I die in the defense and service of my country."

Death for spies was common during the Civil War. For example, James J. Andrews, a secret agent for the Union, led a daring raid on the Western and Atlantic Railroad that became famous as the Great Locomotive Chase. The raid failed and Andrews and seven followers were hung by the rebels.

In April 1862 Andrews and 23 Union Army volunteers dressed in civilian clothes, seized a locomotive known as The General at Big Shanty, near Kennesaw, Georgia, and rocketed north, destroying tracks and telegraph wires as they rolled up the line to cut off pursuit as well as destroy the military use of the road. After running 87-miles the General lost power just north of Ringgold, Georgia. Andrews and his raiders attempted to evade through the woods. Andrews was captured and identified as the leader.

After a quick trial, the Confederates sentenced him to hang as a spy. Andrews escaped from jail but was quickly caught and taken to Atlanta just ahead of the rapidly advancing Union Army. On June 7 he was hung but the scaffold was so short his feet danced on the ground so he likely slowly strangled to death.

George St. Leger Grenfell[1]

As a British soldier of fortune, George St. Leger Grenfell claimed to have fought for the French in Algeria, in Morocco against the Barbary pirates, under Garibaldi in South America, in the Crimean War, and in the Sepoy Mutiny. Born in London, England, he came to America in 1862 and accepting a commission in the Confederate Army served with cavalryman John Hunt Morgan, General Braxton Bragg, and General J.E.B. Stuart. Always an adventurer he resigned from the Confederate Army in 1864 and, it is thought, joined the plot to take over Chicago as well as other Midwest cities and the

Grenfell was sentenced to life at Fort Jefferson but managed to escape in a small boat. He likely died at sea.

governments of Ohio, Indiana, and Illinois and establish a Northwestern Confederacy. Grenfell and 150 other plotters were arrested when the plan to take over was discovered. He was tried, convicted, and sentenced to hang, however, through the intervention of the British Minister in Washington, the sentence was commuted to life imprisonment at the isolated Fort Jefferson military prison 70 miles west of Key West, Florida, in the Dry Tortugas.

While most of the inmates at Fort Jefferson were Army privates imprisoned for desertion, there were four "state prisoners," including Dr. Samuel A. Mudd, Edmund Spangler, Samuel Arnold, and Michael O'Laughlen, all convicted at the Lincoln assassination conspiracy trial.

After Mudd attempted to escape a few days before Grenfell arrived prison officials took a strong hand to assure the impossibility of future attempts. All five men were confined together for the next three months in a ground level cell known as the "dungeon." Mudd later wrote about Grenfell to his brother-in-law:

"We are all at this moment in chains. Neither Colonel Grenfel (sic) nor myself has been taken out to work the past two or three days, but suffered to remain passively in our quarters. He is quite an intelligent man, tall, straight, and about sixty-one or two years of age. He speaks fluently several languages, and often adds mirth by his witty sarcasm and jest. He has been badly wounded and is now suffering with dropsy, and is allowed no medical treatment whatever, but loaded down with chains, and fed upon the most loathsome food, which treatment in a short time must bring him to an untimely grave. You will confer an act of kindness and mercy by acquainting the English Minister at Washington, Sir F.A. Bruce, of these facts."

Although struck down with yellow fever in September 1867, Grenfell survived under Mudd's personal care. Seeing no hope of release, Grenfell managed to escape the prison in March 1868. After bribing a guard, he and three other prisoners stole a small boat and made off into the storm lashed night. Although a government steamer searched for them the following day, they weren't found. It was assumed all had been lost at sea. However, on June 5, 1868, an announcement, originally published in the Mobile, Alabama, *Advertiser*, appeared in the *New York Times*.

"St. Leger Grenfell - The public was greatly gratified not long since to learn that this gallant English soldier had escaped his prison at the Dry Tortugas, and in his love of liberty at the risk of life, he had trusted himself to the mercies of a frail boat in an attempt to cross the Florida Straits to Cuba. We have the pleasure of stating that his voyage was made in safety, and that a letter has been received from him in Havana, sending his thanks and acknowledgements for kind treatment to some of the army officers at Tortugas, and stating that he was just about to sail for Old England. We do not doubt that every gentleman officer belonging to the garrison of his prison guard rejoices at his escape."

Regardless of the enthusiastic nature of the notice, most historians consider it a hoax since he was never heard from again.

Clement L. Vallandigham

Vallandigham was certainly one of the strange figures in the war. Born in Lisbon, Ohio he graduated from Jefferson College in Canonsburg, Pennsylvania, and returned to his home state to practice law. After a stint in the Ohio legislature and as a newspaper editor, he ran for congress as a Democrat in 1856 and was narrowly defeated. However, not one to let a vote get in his way, he appealed the election to the House and was seated on party lines on the next to last day of the term. He was reelected by very small margins in 1858 and 1860.

On the outbreak of the Civil War, his anti-Union politics angered his district electorate and he was defeated for reelection in 1862. He was a pro-states righter and very much against the end of slavery which he believed would lead to allowing blacks to vote. He also supported the South's efforts to secede and maintained the North had no legal right to

Since Vallandigham supported the Southern cause so vehemently, Lincoln had him forcibly delivered to Confederate lines.

militarily prevent it. Put a little differently, he was pure Confederate on the wrong side of the border! He was also the acknowledged leader of the Copperheads and later SOL.

To help control anti-Union activities in his military department, General Ambrose Burnside issued General Order Number 38, which sternly warned, "the "habit of declaring sympathies for the enemy" would not be tolerated in the Military Department of Ohio. The order also stipulated the death penalty for those convicted of "aiding persons found concealed within our lines belonging to the service of the enemy..." and crimes similar. Ever the contrarian, Vallandigham gave a major speech on May 1, 1863 charging the war was being fought not to save the Union but rather to free blacks and by sacrificing the liberty of all Americans to, "King Lincoln." He also damned, "King Lincoln," calling for his immediate removal from the presidency. Perhaps the action that broke Burnside's patience was when Vallandigham spit on a copy of his

official order! Clearly goaded by such calculated disrespect, Burnside ordered his arrest on May 5.

The actual arrest was made at midnight. When he refused to open his house door to the arresting soldiers they simply battered it down with an axe, followed by a second door before finally smashing the door to his wife's bedroom where he was hiding. (What was he going to do? Refuse to come out until the soldiers went away?). One of the soldiers later wrote, "...although up and dressed, he had to be taken from his wife's bedroom amidst a perfect torrent of tears and heart-rendering sobs." The troops hustled him off to the Dayton Military Prison.

After failing as commander of the Army of the Potomac at Fredericksburg, Ambrose Burnside was given command of the Military District of Ohio.

Vallandigham's supporters reacted to the arrest with a vengeance. It took a formation of troops with fixed bayonets to keep the rabble from breaking into the prison to free their "hero." Unable to break him out, the mob instead burned public buildings, looted shops, smashed into private homes, burned out the local newspaper office and fired their guns like a terrorist birthday party, the resulting stray rounds reportedly wounding innocent residents. Federal troops were needed to restore order.

Unlike today when justice is neither swift or necessarily just, Vallandigham was tried by military court May 6-7, and convicted of, "uttering disloyal sentiments" and attempting to hinder the prosecution of the war and sentenced to two years' detention in a military prison. The action was later upheld by a Federal judge as a valid exercise of the President's war powers.

Lincoln looked at Vallandingham as a "wily agitator" and was very wary of making him a martyr to the Copperheads. Thinking the matter through, Lincoln likely reasoned if Vallandingham was so much a Confederate, he might as well be with them. He thus on May 19 ordered him delivered through the military lines in Tennessee to the Confederacy. While Lincoln changed the sentence, his action fully supported the military court's actions.

Vallandingham was livid! In prison he was a sufferer for the Cause, a true "Holy Martyr." Safe behind the Confederate lines he was just another Southern supporter.

Vallandigham was reportedly arrested hiding in his wife's bedroom.

Lincoln's action was totally unexpected and the South was politically unprepared to deal with the situation. The actual delivery went like this: A private from the 51st Alabama was on picket duty five miles from Murfreesboro, Tennessee, when a single mounted Federal officer approached under a white flag and asked to speak with the commanding officer. When the commander arrived he saw a vehicle coming down the road with a second white flag. Drawn by a single horse, it contained a Federal lieutenant and a very upset Vallandingham.

Supposedly the lieutenant told the 51st commander, "Here is Vallandingham, sentenced to banishment." Vallandingham said, "I protest against this outrage - solemnly protest." To which the good lieutenant said, "Yes, but hurry up. I'll take your trunk off. Jump down now - good day." And with that short exchange the flustered politician was left standing in the dust as the wagon sped off.

Vallandigham didn't enjoy Southern hospitality for long. He was a "fifth-wheel," an unwanted guest. Making his way to the coast he took a blockade-runner to Bermuda and then to Canada, eventually reaching Windsor where his influence over the SOL was strong. He was lionized by visiting members of the SOL as well as Rebels hiding in Canada and leading Canadian businessmen and politicians. When he arrived in Montreal he was honored by a large banquet and traveled to Niagara Falls in a special coach provided by the Grand Trunk Railway. Such reception helped solidify the North's belief in Canadian support for the South.

Ohio Democrats even nominated Vallandigham for governor in absentia. He managed his campaign from a hotel in Windsor, Ontario, where he received a steady stream of visitors and supporters. His platform included withdrawing Ohio as well as any other Northern state desiring from the Union if Lincoln refused to reconcile with the Confederacy. This was Thompson's "Northwest Confederacy" by another means.

He lost the 1863 Ohio gubernatorial election in a thunderous landslide to pro-Union War Democrat John Brough. Growing restless with his Canadian exile, he returned to Ohio and openly attended the 1864 Democratic National Convention in Chicago, daring Lincoln to arrest him. It is (in my opinion) certainly likely he was involved in the Thompson plot to use the convention as springboard to a rising. He wrote the, "peace plank" of the platform declaring the war a failure and demanding an immediate end of hostilities. Regardless of his machinations he couldn't stop the nomination of General George B. McClellan. In an effort at party unity, Vallandigham joined the ticket as Secretary of War, but added little public value. Clearly given the crumbling of the South his value was quickly fading and Lincoln felt it best to let him just "fade away" into obscurity.

After the war he returned to Ohio and failed in bids for a house and senate seat, eventually resuming his law practice.

Vallandigham contributed to American literature, though in a backhanded way. His statement that, "he did not want to belong to the United States" prompted Edward Everett Hale to write "The Man Without a Country," a short story, that appeared in *The Atlantic Monthly* in December 1863 and was widely republished.

He died in Lebanon, Ohio, in 1871 at age 50. While representing a client accused of killing another man in a bar room brawl, Vallandingham managed to shoot himself demonstrating how the pistol could have accidentally discharged. While he lay dying he claimed he thought the gun was unloaded! At least his client was acquitted, perhaps the jury thinking the man's lawyer had certainly proved his point.

The Indiana SOL Trial

On October 21, 1864 the Federal Government put five of the leaders of the Indiana SOL on trial by Military Commission for treason and other related crimes. This was not directly related to the attempted insurrection in Chicago although there were connections. Some were condemned to the gallows although when the war ended and they were still languishing in prison, all were set free.

One of the conspirators was Harrison H. Dodd, on trial for treason and conspiracy. Since a considerable amount of arms and ammunition was discovered hidden in his storeroom he was deeply implicated in the rising. Rather than be locked up in a very confining and closely watched military prison, Dodd petitioned the commander of the military district to be allowed to occupy a room in the Post Office building. Since it was still an age of some chivalry, the district commander agreed on condition Dodd gave his word he would not try to escape. Dodd willingly did so, but it proved an empty pledge.

During the early morning hours he escaped out his window, shinnying his way to the ground three stories below on a length of rope. It seems one of his friends smuggled him a small ball of twine and when the friend (or others) showed up beneath the window with a heavy rope, he lowered the twine and used it to haul the rope to the cell where he secured it to an iron bar jammed between his bed and iron window shutter. The partner also snuffed out the streetlights outside his window, hiding the break out from clear view. Given Dodd's sacred pledge, the post commander didn't even station a guard beneath his window. Dodd safely reached Hamilton, Ontario and later relocated to Windsor, Ontario. The Union didn't bother pursuing him. He returned to the U.S. in 1867 settling in Fond du Lac, Wisconsin.

One of the conspirators turned state's witness at the trial and gave numerous details in exchange for having the charges against him dropped. He related that in Indiana there were nine SOL companies of infantry, one of lancers and an artillery company, all organized and ready to act. He also explained the ciphers used by the group for secret communications. The trial also revealed all of the SOL's secret signs and rituals.

As in Chicago, to prevent damage to their property by rebel forces, SOL members in Indiana were to display a white flag with a red ribbon along the top and bottom. It was planned Confederate General Price would come "a busting" through the Cumberland Gap on or about August 16, 1864 and key off the local rebellion. When Price didn't come, the conspirators were left hanging all alone.

Another witness from the SOL said they were to kidnap Governor Oliver Hazard Perry Morton of Indiana and either ransom him or, "take care of him." It was well understood the "take care of " meant kill him. There was even talk of assassination. Morton was a particular enemy of the SOL. A stalwart ally of President Lincoln during the war, he suppressed the Democrat controlled Indiana General Assembly. Enemies charged he also exceeded his constitutional authority by calling out the militia without approval and during the period of legislative suppression, privately financed state government through unapproved federal and private loans. He was also criticized for arresting and detaining political enemies and suspected southern sympathizers. Clearly the SOL wanted him gone, either looking at the grass from the wrong side or in harmless exile in the North.

The same witness also related being told that Confederate Vice President Stephens had gone to Nassau to arrange for a shipment of arms and ammunition to the South but since the Union blockade was too tight, they shipped it to Canada for Thompson to smuggle to the northern SOL.

When the trial was finished the first week of December 1864, the military court found three of the Indiana conspirators guilty of all charges and sentenced them to be "hanged at such time and place as the Commanding General of the district should designate." Although the execution date was set for May 19, 1865 with the end of the war, criminal proceedings were dropped and all sentences annulled. The conspirators walked free.[2]

John Wilson Murray became a famous Canadian detective following the war.

John Wilson Murray

John Wilson Murray, the gunner's mate from the *Michigan* who followed Cole went on to a long and colorful career as a Canadian detective. Born in Edinburgh in 1840, he relocated to Canada following the Civil War and became a detective for the Canadian Southern Railway. He soon drew the attention of the authorities and was named the provincial detective of Ontario in 1875. He kept the job for 31 years and was credited with solving hundreds of crimes.

He wasn't the typical "gumshoe" sneaking around hotel lobbies and cheap saloons but rather had a reputation of reconstructing crimes and painstakingly cross-checking information and statements to find the inconsistencies. Known as the "Great Canadian Detective," he pioneered scientific crime investigation including the using information from autopsies. No detail escaped his methods.[3]

Bennett Young

After the St. Albans raid charges were finally dropped, Young remained in Toronto studying law at the University of Toronto. Eventually, he returned to Kentucky becoming a lawyer and later judge.

Thomas Hines

Confederate agent extraordinaire Hines also remained in Canada until early 1866 when he returned to Kentucky becoming a lawyer and Chief Justice of the Court of Appeals.

The End of Records

Telling the full story of Rebel actions and plans in the Great Lakes area is very difficult. By the very nature of the activity, the plans were held secret from friend and foe. Many times written records were not kept for very good reason. An unexpected raid by the Union could destroy not only the mission at hand but the entire secret network! Instructions, etc., were then, as now, best kept verbal. For the researcher it means a dearth of hard facts. Although operational security by the Confederate operators was often transparent, it doesn't mean they left behind a huge paper trail for historians.

The entire problem is compounded since in April 1865, Secretary of State Judah P. Benjamin reputedly burned the bulk of the official papers of the Confederate Secret Service just before the government evacuated Richmond, making it impossible to fully document such activities with any certainty. Benjamin's concern was the records would form the basis for war crimes trials since many of the documented actions were beyond the pale of contemporary laws of war. Considering the vengeful mood of the Northern Congress, his thinking was valid. While transcripts of testimony for the various trials are generally available, they too are of questionable accuracy. After all, those testifying were presenting their own observations and positions rather than necessarily the truth.

Supposedly CSA Secretary of State Judah Benjamin destroyed many of the various secret service records to avoid uncomfortable questions following the war.

The perceived lack of energetic policing of the Confederates operating from Canada by the British was especially galling to the U.S. Congress and it threatened to withdraw from the Canadian American Reciprocity Treaty, (aka the Elgin-Marcy Treaty). This agreement between British North America and the United States covered raw materials and was in effect from 1854 to 1866. It was an important step toward free trade between both countries but was opposed by protectionist elements in the U. S. When British support for Confederates continued, at least in the eyes Congress, the treaty was ended in 1866.

What was seen as blatant Confederate support following the St. Albans attack caused the U.S. to threaten withdrawal from the Rush-Bagot Agreement of 1817 limiting naval forces on the Great Lakes. Only belated British/Canadian crackdown on Confederate activity saved the treaty.

References

William C. Davis, *Breckinridge, Statesman, Soldier, Symbol*, (Baton Rouge: Louisiana State University Press, 1974) pp. 560-562.

Confederacy's Canadian Mission: Spies Across the Border - http://www.historynet.com/confederacys-canadian-mission-spies-across-the-border.htm.

Frank L. Klement, Dark Lanterns, *Secret Political Societies, Conspiracies and Treason Trials in the Civil War*, (Baton Rouge: Louisiana State University Press, 1984), 222-223.

John Wilson Murray, - http://thecanadianencyclopedia.com/index.cfm?PgNm=TCE&Params=A1ARTA0005539.

John Wilson Murray, *Memoirs of a Great Canadian Detective, Incidents in the Life of John Wilson Murray*, (Toronto: Collins, 1977), x-xi, 11-19.

The Ohio Historical Society - http://search.ohiohistory.org/texis/search/context.html?query=capt&pr=public&prox=page&rorder=500&rprox=500&rdfreq=500&rwfreq=500&rlead=500&sufs=0&order=dd&cq=&cmd=context&id=4aaac2683f.

The Other Side of the Coin - http://www.scv674.org/SH-11.htm.

Benn Pitman, editor, *Trials for Treason - Indianapolis - Disclosing the Plans for the Northwest Confederacy*, (Cincinnati: Moore Wilstrach and Baldwin, 1865), 17-36, 45-52, 245-322.

Clement L. Vallandingham - http://en.wikipedia.org/wiki/Clement_Vallandigham.

Footnotes

[1] Alternatively spelled "Grenfel" in many sources.

[2] Benn Pitman, editor, *Trials for Treason - Indianapolis - Disclosing the Plans for the Northwest Confederacy*, (Cincinnati: Moore Wilstrach and Baldwin, 1865), 17-36, 45-52, 245-322.

[3] John Wilson Murray, *Memoirs of a Great Canadian Detective, Incidents in the Life of John Wilson Murray*, (Toronto: Collins, 1977), x-xi, 11-19.

CHAPTER EIGHT
COURTENAY
TORPEDO

One of the most insidious devices built during the war was the infamous "Courtenay Torpedo" also known as a "coal torpedo." During the Civil War the term torpedo meant any explosive device such as land mines, water mines, booby traps, etc., not the torpedo as thought of today. Period newspapers called them "infernal machines" while others used the term "coal shells."

A Courtenay torpedo was a hollow iron casting in the shape of a large lump of coal filled with explosives and covered with coal dust such that it looked identical to an actual piece of coal. All a Confederate agent had to do was drop it in a coal pile on a fuel dock or if intending a specific target, introduce it into the ship's coal bunker. In either case he was certain it would eventually be shoveled into a boiler firebox resulting in a powerful explosion probable at least to damage the boiler and more likely to kill the black gang (as the engineer room crew on coal burning steamers were called resulting from being covered in coal dust) and burn and destroy the boat. Given the huge amounts of coal used by the old steamers inspecting each lump was virtually impossible.

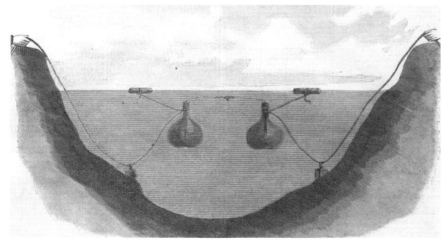

During the Civil War the term "torpedo" generally was synonymous with both land and water "mines." In this case the torpedoes are underwater and manually detonated by soldiers ashore.

The torpedo was invented by 41-year old Captain Thomas E. Courtenay later associated with the Confederate Secret Service (Torpedo Bureau). Prior to the war he ran a shipping business in St. Louis catering to southern cotton plantations.

The infernal devices were manufactured at the 7th Avenue Artillery shop opposite the Tredegar Iron Works in Richmond. Apparently the first batch was made in January 1864. In manufacturing they were not dissimilar to normal artillery shells, a molded iron case filled with explosive, thus the symbiotic relationship between the iron works and artillery shop. The sides of the shell were about

The Courtenay torpedo was a deadly method of sabotage.

3/8 inch thick and the space inside typically held 3-4 ounces of gunpowder. A threaded plug closed the fill hole. The entire shell was then dipped in molted beeswax or tar and rolled in coal dust to achieve the desired deceptive coal lump look. The finished "infernal devices" were about 4 by 4 by 3 inches in diameter and weighed between 3-4 pounds. They not only looked like coal but even smelled like it!

While the bombs were not very large their job wasn't to sink the ship itself but to start a series of secondary events that would destroy her. For example a boiler explosion of sufficient force to destroy the ship or cause secondary fires perhaps even igniting dangerous cargos of ammunition or other flammables.

During this period of history boiler explosions were relatively common so tracing the blast to a torpedo was virtually impossible. It would be assumed the ship sank from "normal" causes, not a secretly introduced explosive device.

Instead of mass producing the torpedoes and distributing them to agents throughout the Union rear area, the South instead authorized Courtenay to form a special company of 25 men to penetrate Federal lines and place them in the coal piles used to fuel Union steam ships. A key target were the Navy warships blockading the southern ports. He was also directed to plant them against Union shipping in Southern waters. By limiting their distribution only to Courtenay's unit, the impact they could have had against the North was also limited.

Apparently there were also plans to use the torpedoes against Union locomotives. The engines of course, were coal fired with massive boilers and therefore lucrative targets. Whether they were ever so employed is unknown but considering the huge

Captain Thomas E. Courtenay

reliance of the North on railroad transportation the impact in terms of actual destruction of equipment and psychological damage would have been significant.

The secret of the torpedo didn't last for long. On March 19, 1864, a vigilant Union gunboat captured a Confederate messenger trying to cross the Mississippi River. After a quick search, the Federals found a letter from Courtenay fully describing the device. Recognizing the danger, the letter was quickly sent to Admiral David Porter who in turn published General Order 184, which in part stated:

"The enemy has adopted new inventions to destroy human life and vessels in the shape of torpedoes, and an article resembling coal, which is to be placed in our coal piles for the purpose of blowing the vessels up, or injuring them. Officers will have to be careful in overlooking coal barges. Guards will be placed over them at all times, and anyone found attempting to place any of these things amongst the coal will be shot on the spot."

Considering the mass destruction of Confederate Secret Service records just before the fall of Richmond in April 1865 it is virtually impossible to know the number of devices produced or the effectiveness of them in terms of damage to the Union.

However, Admiral Porter believed the torpedo destroyed the *Greyhound* on November 27, 1864. She was a private steamboat used by General Benjamin F. Butler

The destruction of the Sultana *and death of 1,800-2,400 wounded Union soldiers has recently been attributed to a Courtenay torpedo.*

as his headquarters on the James River in Virginia. Admiral Porter was aboard when the torpedo blew up thus could speak first hand to the deadly results. Just the day before a torpedo with its fuse burning was found on the steamer *City Of New York* minutes prior to casting off from her dock.

The torpedo was also blamed for the boiler explosion on the Navy gunboat *USS Chenango* killing 33 men. The gunboat was bound out from New York Harbor for Fort Monroe, Virginia, on April 15, 1864 when the blast rocked her. The boilers were brand new and a very reliable design so a coal torpedo was thought the most likely culprit.

An ex-Confederate agent made a deathbed confession that he slipped a torpedo into the steamboat *Sultana* killing approximately1,800 of 2,400 passengers and crew when her boiler exploded and the steamer burned in the Mississippi on April 27, 1865. Most of the men aboard were freed Union prisoners of war, many ill and wounded. Like most of torpedo claims, it can't be verified. By April 27, however the war was over and the loss of life criminal.

The *Sultana* was certainly not the only steamer lost due to the torpedo. Some estimates claim at least sixty Union steamboats were destroyed during the war by boiler explosions. Since the torpedo left no physical evidence, whether it caused the destruction or not is unknown. Again, boiler explosions were relatively common. Perhaps the genius of the torpedo was being untraceable. In effect the Union was losing ships without being aware the torpedo was the cause.

A variation of the coal torpedo also used against river steamboats was a hollowed out piece of wood filled with gunpowder and like the coal torpedo could easily be concealed in fuel piles of cordwood stacked along riverbanks for refueling. Like the infamous coal torpedoes, the explosive ones were visually identical to regular cordwood so it was nearly assured they would find their way into the firebox. The explosive result was just as deadly as their iron brethren.

One of the Confederate saboteurs who successfully burned a number of steamboats on the Mississippi eventually ended up in the St. Lawrence Hall Hotel in Montreal, the local headquarters for Confederates plotters. Clearly there was a link between the Lakes and other areas. To provide proper incentive for the boat burners, the Confederate government agreed to pay them 10% of the value of the vessels lost as reported in Northern newspapers.[1]

Whether the infamous torpedo was ever used on the Great Lakes is also unknown for certain. But in the Spring of 1865 with the war all but over, when Canadian authorities raided a house in Toronto rented by Jacob Thompson, they reportedly found torpedoes and other incendiary devices hidden under the floorboards. Others were discovered in his office. Did Thompson have them for use as paperweights or did he actually plan to use them? Or were they what was leftover from those already issued to Confederate agents operating in the Great Lakes?

Understanding the huge number of steam driven engines and, therefore, coal fired boilers in the industrial areas of the Great Lakes provides stark recognition of the thousands of potential targets the torpedoes could have been used against. Admiral Porter's order not withstanding, every coal pile couldn't be guarded and it was too easy for a Southern sympathizer to drop a torpedo on the pile when no one was watching. At some point the torpedo would be shoveled into the firebox and destruction would follow.

There is no irrefutable evidence Courtenay torpedoes were ever used on the Great Lakes but there is another intriguing possibility. Given the torpedoes found in Thompson's office and home, why would he have had them other than as part of shipment intended for use on the Lakes? It is reasonable to assume others were already distributed to field saboteurs who would have disposed of any still in their procession at the end of the war rather than be caught with them since they could be considered in violation of the rules of war. The unused torpedoes just disappeared.

Examining the list of Great Lakes ships lost during the war by fire related incidents, explosions or sudden conflagrations, provides some examples that could have been the victims of the torpedo. Remember they were very simple to use; just drop them on a pile of coal and eventually something would be blown up. I do not consider it complete or certainly 100 percent accurate but it is intriguing.

Possible Victims

Propeller *Kenosha* (October 26, 1864), burned at her Sarnia dock supposedly from a lantern fire, after burning through hawsers drifted into river imperiling other boats and docks before sinking downstream.

Sidewheeler *Pontiac* (May 14, 1864), exploded and burned near Grand Haven with the loss of three lives and five more injured.

Tug *Phoenix* (1863), burned and sank on Lake Ontario.

Sidewheeler *Zimmerman* (August 21, 1863), burned alongside her dock at Niagara on the Lake.

Sidewheeler *Nile* (May 21, 1864), destroyed by boiler explosion alongside her dock at Detroit killing eight crewmen and injuring 14 others.

For unclear reasons Courtenay went to England in 1864 in an effort to market the torpedo to various foreign governments. Apparently none took the bait, especially as he wouldn't tell them "secret" of manufacture. After he returned to the U.S. in 1867 the man he was working with in Europe who apparently knew the secret, may have made his own deals since in 1873 a newspaper reported some notorious ship owners were using the device to destroy their own ships for the insurance money. Throw a couple lumps of "coal" into the bunker, make sure the ship is heavily insured, wave goodbye as she sails out of port and just wait for the insurance check. Not a bad racket.

The concept of the Courtenay torpedo, concealed explosive in an everyday object, continued in history. The Fenian Brotherhood of Irish criminals considered using such coal torpedoes for terror attacks against New York City hotels and British steamers in the 1860-70 period. During World War II both the U.S. Office of Strategic Services (O.S.S.)and British Special Operations Executive (S.O.E.) used them against the Axis. German saboteurs coming ashore from U-Boats on Long Island in 1943 also carried plastic explosive shaped like coal.

Other Opportunities

Considering the huge number of potential targets and the ease of use, it is amazing Confederate saboteurs operating from Canada or elsewhere didn't make far more use this devastating effective weapon of terror.

Other Infernal Devices

The South also used other infernal devices. For example on August 9, 1864, a Confederate arranged to place a wood box labeled "candles" in an ammunition barge loaded with several thousand artillery shells at the Union supply depot at City Point, Virginia. The box was really a time bomb using a clock and spring released plunger designed to strike a percussion cap setting off a large 12-pound charge of black powder. The resulting explosion of the ammunition barge killed at least 43 people and wounded another 126. Damage was estimated at over $4 million.[2]

General Grant was in his tent at City Point when the detonation occurred and a veritable hailstorm of bullets, shells and hunks of wood came though his canvas roof. Outside the tent an aide was struck dead by a shell fragment and several horses killed. The loss of Grant wouldn't have changed the outcome of the war, but it is reasonable to say it would have lasted longer.

The device at the top uses a clockworks set to a predetermined time, then firing the explosive.

Greek Fire and Burning Transports

Following the failure in Chicago to spark a "rising" some of Hines's cohorts moved to the St. Louis area with the mission of burning the many Federal transports docked in the river. After a careful recon of specifically what steamers were where, the men divided up bottles of Greek Fire and went after their individual targets. Union security was nonexistent and the men were allowed to wander where they choose, even aboard the steamers. With remarkable casualness the rebels threw their bottles at whatever spot on the steamers that seemed most likely to burn easily. Some bottles worked and flames spouted quickly. Others did nothing, total duds. In the end only five or ten steamers of the 75 or so in port were burned, some suffering major damage while others only minor scorching.

Had the Greek Fire worked as advertised, huge harm could have been done to the fleet, impacting the flood of supplies to the Union armies. By the same logic, had the rebels taken their Greek Fire to a crowded ore port with wooden docks like Marquette, or transshipment port like Buffalo, or crowded waterfront like Chicago and used it in the same manner, results could also have been significant. In this case it wasn't a failure of security that caused the plan to fail, but rather a failure of technology and perhaps targeting.

A second rebel arson team had more luck in Mattoon, Illinois, burning several Federal warehouses. Loose talk in local saloons apparently led the Federals to arrest most of the warehouse burners as well as the steamboat fire bombers. The Confederates never quite figured out this thing call operational security.

The explosion at City Point in 1864 was caused by a Confederate "infernal machine" introduced to an ammunition barge.

References

Civil War Torpedoes, Examination of the Civil War's Infernal Machines http://www.infernal-machines.com/_sgg/m1m3_1.htm.

The Courtenay Coal Torpedo - http://us-civil-war.suite101.com/article.cfm/the_courtenay_coal_torpedo.

The Courtenay Coal Torpedo - http://192.220.96.192/coal.htm.

James D. Ladd, *Keith Melton and Captain Peter Mason, Clandestine Warfare,* (New York: Blandford Press, 1987), 14.

Ann Larabee, *The Dynamite Fiend,* (New York: Palgrave MacMillian, 2005).

Military History Online - City Point Explosion - http://www.militaryhistoryonline.com/civil-war/articles/citypoint.aspx.

New York Times, May 18, 1865.

The Official Records of the Union and Confederate Navies in the War of the Rebellion, Washington, DC, 1888. Series I, Vol. 22 part 2, pg. 970. Available online at Cornell University Library's Making of America collection, link verified October 31, 2006.

The Official Records of the Union and Confederate Navies in the War of the Rebellion, Washington, DC, 1897. Series I, Vol. 26, pp. 184-187. Available online at Cornell University Library's Making of America collection, link verified October 31, 2006.

The Official Records of the Union and Confederate Navies in the War of the Rebellion, Washington, DC, 1897. Series I, Vol. 5, pg. 395. Available online at Cornell University Library's Making of America collection, link verified October 31, 2006.

Milton F. Perry, *Infernal Machines, the Story of Confederate Submarine and Mine Warfare,* (Baton Rouge: Louisiana State University Press, 1965), 133-138; 194.

G.E. and Deb Rule, "The Sultana: A case for sabotage," in *North and South Magazine*, Vol. 5, issue 1, December 2001.

Felix G. Stidger, *Treason History of the Sons of Liberty,* (Chicago: Felix G. Stidger, 1903), 49-50.

Joseph M. Thatcher, "The Courtenay Coal Torpedo," Military Collector and Historian, Vol. XI, Spring 1959.

The "USS Chenango" Boiler Explosion, April 15, 1864 - http://www.tfoenander.com/uss-chenango.htm.

Footnotes

[1] Felix G. Stidger, *Treason History of the Sons of Liberty,* (Chicago: Felix G. Stidger, 1903), 49-50.

[2] Military History Online - City Point Explosion - http://www.militaryhistoryonline.com/civil-war/articles/citypoint.aspx.

CHAPTER NINE

THE SHADOW WAR–
UNION AND
CONFEDERATE SECRET
OPERATIONS

By any rational evaluation the Confederate "Secret Service" was an organizational mess. A detailed analysis of how it or more properly it functioned is beyond the scope of this book but certainly a cursory look is valuable in understanding what was happening during the war as well as the Great Lakes area.

There was no "Secret Service" as an over arching agency or group of agencies under a coordinating authority. Rather, it evolved over time from disparate agencies, groups and field armies. There was no central clearing house of information gained or directorate of operations unless Jefferson Davis is defaulted to the job by virtue of

Some intelligence work involved purloining secret documents.

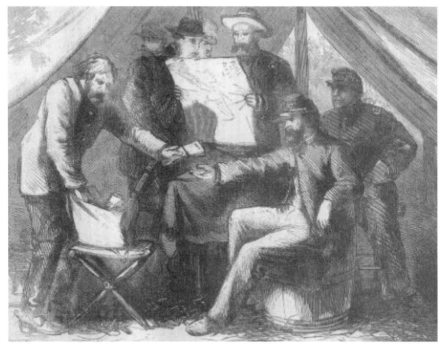

Turning secret material over to the enemy.

being the President of the Confederacy. No group of intelligence specialists analyzed the information obtained from the various sources.

Ten different Confederate agencies ran secret operations of varying sorts and objectives. They included the State Department, War Department, War Department Signal Bureau and Signal Corp, Provost Marshal of Richmond, War Department Torpedo Bureau, Navy Submarine Battery Service, War Department Strategy Bureau, The Greenhow Group, Cavalry Scouts and the conglomerate of operations in Canada. Added to this list are such guerrilla bands operating near or behind enemy lines and such secret operations staged by various field armies.

The activities of various spies and intelligence agents both North and South involved the Great Lakes area, either directly or indirectly. Understanding their movements and missions helps to place the role of the Great Lakes in proper context.

Sarah Slater

The Confederates used a variety of couriers to communicate between the Canadian mission and Richmond. One was known as Sarah Slater although it is uncertain if that was her real name or a "nom-de-guerre." Everyone, however, agreed she was smart, beautiful and sophisticated. Brains and beauty could be a deadly combination, especially in the chameleon world of espionage.

Sarah first came to light following the Lincoln assassination when during interrogation of the conspirators the actions of a mysterious French speaking woman were revealed. Most of the men who knew of her just called her the "French woman." Beyond that simple knowledge she was a cipher, a will of the wisp, an unknown player is the most deadly game of political murder. Conspirators claimed she also carried the name Kate Thompson and Kate Brown and she met often in Washington with John Wilkes Booth whenever both were in town.

Supposedly she was born as Sarah Antoinette (Nettie) Gilbert in Connecticut of French parents and moved to North Carolina just before the war. There she married one Rowan Slater in 1861. He promptly joined a North Carolina unit and marched off to war. She never saw him again. Whether he was killed in action, died in a prison camp or just ran off is unknown.

She surfaced again in January 1865 traveling north to visit her mother in New York. This required a pass but such documents were not uncommon or difficult to obtain for an obviously innocent young woman, especially one who knew how to bat her eyes at both Confederate and Yankee officers. Somehow she attracted the attention of Confederate authorities who clearly realized her potential as a courier and provided her the appropriate travel credentials without delay.

Her first assignment was delivering critical documents to Canada for the defense of the Confederates who attacked St. Albans, Vermont. The journey was arduous. A local guide led her down the bed of the Richmond, Fredericksburg and Potomac Railroad to Milford Station, Bowling Green to Port Royal crossing the Rappahannock

Depending on the location and situation, passes to move freely through enemy lines were possible to obtain.

River by ferry into Maryland and Union territory, then to Bryantown, Washington, and by train to New York and the European Hotel where she took on the disguise of a French woman. After a brief rest, it was back on the train to Montreal and then finally the St. Lawrence House in Toronto. The St. Lawrence was the unofficial headquarters of the Confederate mission in Canada.

It was a successful mission. No one suspected she was a Southern spy. She also triumphantly returned to the Confederacy with a packet of documents passing through Northern lines by guile and subterfuge. She apparently did another mission in March 1865 also completing it successfully.

Her last assignment is shrouded in mystery. She left Richmond on April 1, 1865. By this point it was clear to everyone the war was over. Lee would surrender within days and the "rats" were fleeing the sinking ship by any means possible, especially if they could be connected to any activity the North could construe a violation of the rules of war. And many of the secret missions could be considered that, so it was time to evade and escape. Richmond knew Thompson in Canada still had great deal of unspent money and Secretary of State Benjamin was anxious to have as much as possible transferred to Europe. There it could be used to pay off debts the South owned to various shipping companies and suppliers. More creatively it could also be used to support the fleeing Confederate leaders if they were able to reach Europe. Having personal access to a pot of essentially unaccounted for money is a good thing! Apparently, Slater's mission was to deliver special instructions to Thompson regarding how and where to transfer the money. It was a simple job for the accomplished "French woman."

She was said to have stopped in Washington on the way North taking the opportunity to meet again with the engaging actor John Wilkes Booth and on the 4th, boarded the train for New York. And then she disappeared! Poof, she was gone!

According to later testimony during the Lincoln assassination investigation she was acquainted with the Surratts, mother and son, and at least once stayed at their Washington house. Considering the mother was hung for her role in the Lincoln assassination plot, this was damning evidence of the "French woman's" involvement, at least circumstantially.

There is considerable speculation what happened to her. Did she somehow manage to acquire the money herself? Did she reach Toronto and make a private deal with Thompson? Did she just "disappear" after Lincoln's assassination with the realization she could be implicated based on her meetings with Booth?

The Moon Sisters

As anyone in media knows well, sex sells - everything, always! And sex was a staple in the armory of every female spy in the Civil War just as it is today, at least in imagination.

One of the more fascinating cases is that of the Moon sisters, Lottie and Ginnie, the only known spy sister act during the war. Their given names were Charlotte and Virginia but it was as Lottie and Ginnie they were best known.

Born in Virginia to a doctor and his wife, the family moved to Oxford, Ohio, in the 1830s. Oxford was in the extreme southwestern part of the state, just north of Cincinnati and a couple of miles from the Indiana line. Both girls were small and dark featured but Ginnie's blue eyes set her off as perhaps the best looking of the pair. The third Moon sister, Mary, was said to be rather plain and certainly didn't have the same adventurous spirit of her sisters, content to stay home. In addition there were two brothers in the family.

Before the war, Lottie was engaged to a young army officer named Ambrose Burnside, who would later command the Army of the Potomac during the disastrous Fredericksburg campaign. According to legend she left him waiting at the church after changing her mind about the match. She finally married a fellow named Jim Clark, who later became a judge and one of the leaders of the Copperheads in Indiana.

When her father died, Mother Moon deciding young Ginnie perhaps needed some more structured education and guidance, enrolled her in the Oxford Female College and decamped to Memphis. After a teacher criticized her for being too pro Southern, Ginnie fled school and moved in with Lottie and Jim. At the time, Lottie was 31 and Ginnie 15. Both brothers were already in the Confederate Army.

As key supporter and later leader of the Indiana Copperheads (aka Knights of the Golden Circle, Sons of Liberty, et. al.) various couriers often came to the Clark house with secret messages. Wanting to do her part, Lottie volunteered to act as a courier too, sometimes taking the role of an old woman. On one occasion she went to Lexington, Kentucky, by boat to deliver her messages to Confederate General Kirby Smith then switched gears and acting the role of a poor and lost woman ("Oh woe is me," etc.) convinced a gallant Union officer to help her return to Oxford by train. Lottie grew up performing amateur theatrics so acting was a skill that just came naturally. Based on this early success, Lottie carried secret messages to other leaders, including to Thompson in Toronto.

Meanwhile, Ginnie moved to Memphis to be with her mother. As the violence of the war drew tighter around the city, she helped her mother wrapping bandages and comforting wounded Confederate soldiers. When the Union captured the city in June, 1862, she started her career as a spy, couriering supplies and messages through the Federal lines. Her cover story was she was supposedly seeing her beau living in an outlying village.

Union officers were not completely fooled by her justification. They knew she was acting as spy and in 1863 when she and her mother were taking messages to Jim Clark in Oxford, they set-up a trap of sorts. As the tale goes, a Union officer waited until the pair were in their cabin in a riverboat to return to Memphis, when he forced his way into their cabin with orders to search them.

In her memoir published long after the war, Ginnie explained. "There was a slit in my skirt and in my petticoat I had a Colt revolver. I put my hand in and took it out, backed to the door and leveled it at him across the washstand. If you make a move to touch me, I'll kill you, so help me God!" The cabin was likely small and very confining

A fashionable dressed woman had many locations to conceal secret documents or small high value contraband.

so the officer must have been standing very close to her. As a youngster, Lottie learned to shoot a pistol so she was capable of hitting her mark; whether she had the stomach to plug a human target is the question.

She must have lacked the killer instinct or was distracted by a sound or other movement because the Union officer quickly disarmed her but she managed to pull the secret message from her bosom (no man would ever look there!) then "dipped it in the water pitcher and in three lumps swallowed it."[1]

Both women were arrested and trundled off to the Provost Marshal's office where their luggage was thoroughly searched. Ripping open a quilt taken from a trunk, the men found 40 pounds of morphine and 7 pounds of opium as well as a quantity of quinine, all very important drugs and in critically short supply in the South. Quinine was made from the bark of the cinchona tree and was the first effective treatment for malaria making it very valuable medically and financially, selling in the South for $400-$600 an ounce, a very lucrative product for smugglers like Lottie.[2]

Likely thinking what else could these women be hiding, a Union officer noticed Ginnie was wearing quilted skirts around her fashionable hoops. He summoned a housekeeper (necessary by decorum, of course) to search her skirts. More drugs came tumbling out of the pleats as well as from her large bustle. She was a veritable walking pharmacy!

Instead of being hauled off to the local jail as male spies would have been, Ginnie and her mother were taken to a hotel and locked in their room. Ginnie knew she had a good "hole card," however, and asked to see Union General Ambrose Burnside, the same man her sister left at the alter years before. Burnside was the new Commander of the Department of the Ohio with his headquarters in Cincinnati. After being tested and found wanting at Fredericksburg, he doubtlessly wanted to make amends in his new assignment. His policy was clear that Southern sympathizers would not be tolerated. Arrests would be made and traitors prosecuted with the death penalty on the table.

Burnside arrived the next morning and was very apologetic saying if she had only asked for a pass to go south he certainly would have given her one and no one would have dared stop her. How the general rationalized the large amount of contraband found on her is unknown but as his staff saw which way the wind was blowing and while she was essentially under house arrest was given wide latitude to roam the city. Always happy to find a new "lady" to entertain, she was invited to numerous soiree's in town by Union officers, many doubtless geographic bachelors looking for pretty face and Ginnie certainly had one, and a figure to match somewhere under the heaps of hoops and bustle every fashionable woman felt obligated to wear.

Meanwhile Lottie, having heard of the trouble her little sister and mother were in, disguised herself and came to Burnside's headquarters to plead with him to release them. After revealing herself to him and reminding him of old times spent together, she doubtlessly thought she could cajole him into releasing Ginnie and her mother. Burnside had none of her line, placing her under house arrest, too! Given that she left him at the alter, what did she expect?

Burnside kept the women under house arrest for weeks until finally ordering them to depart Union territory and never return. Regardless of the general's instructions both women apparently continued to act as spies and made trips to Toronto on behalf of Copperhead issues.

After the war ended Ginnie returned to Memphis but Lottie headed back home where she became a journalist and did a bit of traveling herself becoming a novelist and pioneer woman newspaper correspondent, working the European capitals during the Franco-Prussian war. Ginnic itched her travel bug, too, and traveled around the country. Stopping for a while in Hollywood, she had bit parts in two movies, "The Spanish Dancer" and "Robin Hood" in the 1920s. She later lived in Greenwich Village in New York, passing at age 81, a Confederate to the end.

Mrs. E. H. Baker - Union Secret Agent

The Union also used female spies. Southern belles were not the only ones capable of using their charms to wheedle information from gullible males. Mrs. E. H. Baker is a case in point.

A previous resident of Richmond, she was working in Chicago as an agent for the Pinkerton Detective agency when the war broke out. The agency considered her very, very, good; perhaps the best female agent they had. While female detectives were unusual at this time, they were not unheard of. After all, there are things a female detective can do a male never could. Early in the war Allen Pinkerton was working as the intelligence chief for Major General George McClellan, Commander of the Army of the Potomac, the principal Union field army.[3] Neither man was very good at the job. Pinkerton was a great detective, successful at running bank and train robbers to ground but evaluating multiple sources of military intelligence and translating it to usable information for a field commander was a skill he didn't have. Little Mac, by contrast, was a great trainer of men and units and a terrific organizer but lacked the backbone to "fight" the army he created. Between Allan and Mac they inflated the strength of whatever army Mac faced to the point he obviously couldn't attack a force twice his size, could he? That the force was in reality only half his size made little difference. Lincoln finally yanked Mac out of the saddle and put a new man in his place, going through generals like clean socks until he finally found Sam Grant who did what all the others didn't - Fight and Win! But this is another story.

In his defense, Pinkerton also planted a number of, "deep cover" agents in Richmond to provide strategic intelligence. When McClellan was fired as Army commander by Lincoln on November 7, 1862, Pinkerton resigned.

It seems Mrs. Baker performed only a single mission for the North but it was one of vital importance. In November, 1861, Pinkerton sent her from Chicago into the deep South to learn what she could about the rumors of undersea boats and a super ironclad said to be building.

One of the keys to being a good detective or spy, too, was blending in to your surroundings. Not running around with a fake beard and mysterious foreign accent but being so normal, so ordinary, so average, you are just overlooked. And that was what Mrs. Baker became. She had friends in Richmond from before the war and they had continued to keep up a close correspondence regardless of the present "unpleasantness." She wrote and asked one of her old friends if it were ok if she visited and the reply was a warm "of course." After securing a pass to enter Confederate lines, which wasn't an extraordinarily difficult thing to do for a "boring" woman going to visit

Allen Pinkerton, his Detective Agency dispatched Mrs. Baker to Richmond to spy for the Union.

old friends, she carefully prepared for her trip. Prior to entering Southern territory she stopped in Washington where Navy officers briefed her on what to look for; what details of vessel construction would be most important to them. Although an experienced agent, her field of expertise was certainly not naval architecture.

The family she stayed with in Richmond was the Atwaters, who had a son serving as a captain in the Confederate Army and stationed in the city. The Atwater family reintroduced Mrs. Baker into Richmond society, an easy affair based on her previous residence there. Soon she was swept into various special social events and activities, mixing with the leadership of the city and picking up interesting pieces of information useful to the North. One of the more unusual activities was touring the massive fortifications around Richmond (Southern security was very lax). She also asked Captain Atwater if she could see the famous Tredegar Iron Works. She had heard so much about it in the North. Her Navy briefers in Washington told her this was where some of the secret submarines were being built so getting a good look at it was very important. Captain Atwater, ever ready to please an old family friend said of course.

In conversation with Captain Atwater she learned he was a secret Union man, believing the South was dead wrong in the conflict. Mrs. Baker thought long and hard about whether she should reveal her mission to him or not but in the end she felt she had no real choice. She needed his help to complete her mission so she compromised. While she didn't tell him about her real mission, she did let him know her political views agreed with his. Whether Captain Atwater thought there was more to her than she was revealing is unknown.

When the agreed day came to tour the Tredegar works, however, the captain was involved in the sea trials for one of the new submarines. He asked if instead she wanted to go with him for the day? Bring a picnic basket and it would be fun. She agreed with the change in plans.

Mrs. Baker soon learned more about the new Confederate secret weapon than anyone in the North ever suspected. It wasn't a true submarine, able to dive below the surface, run underwater and deliver it's attack but rather a semi-submersible always linked to the surface with an air hose.

The end of September 1861 Mrs. Baker watched the strange craft in operation in the James River near Richmond. The air for the two or three man crew was supplied through a hose attached to a dark green flotation collar, a color intended to camouflage it from sharp-eyed Northern lookouts. Propulsion was by a propeller the crew worked with a hand crank. The air hose was a strength and weakness. It allowed the crew to stay submerged for extended periods but also marked their location on the surface.

She watched carefully as the green float slowly approached an anchored target barge. Close by the barge a diver exited the craft and attached an explosive charge to the wood hull of the "enemy." A long hose trailing from the submarine provided air for the diver. The job finished, the diver crawled back into the submarine and the craft backed away from the target as shown by the moving green collar floating on the surface and dropping a electric firing cable as she retreated. Anxious minutes passed

Without Mrs. Baker's detective work, the Union fleet would have been surprised by the Confederate "submarines."

before the silence was shattered by the explosion and the old barge slid to the bottom, destroyed by the South's latest secret weapon. The strange craft worked exactly as Captain Atwater said it would. He later told her it was only a small working model of a much larger one intended for operational employment.

Captain Atwater further explained the bigger semi-submersible would be used to break the Union blockade and allow Southern shipping to escape the port. And without an effective Northern counter, the South could keep the port open! The Union ships would just be so many helpless targets.

The day following the test Baker toured the iron works and took a close look at the full size craft under construction. Entering the iron works was only possible through the escort of Captain Atwater. The factory was closely guarded against spies but as a special friend of Captain Atwater this harmless woman was certainly not a spy! One of the engineers proudly told her a couple of the craft would be at the mouth of the James River in two months. She also looked over a new submarine torpedo (underwater mine), submarine ram (a long pole placed at the bow of a ship with an explosive device on the end) and some preliminary design work for the *CSS Virginia*.

Mrs. Baker was careful not to trust her memory for her observations. Each evening after she retired to her room she made detailed notes and sketches on very thin paper later sewing them into her voluminous bonnet.

Eventually she told her Richmond friends all the war activities disturbed her so much she had to return home. Could Captain Atwater secure a pass through the

The Tredegar Iron Works was the major iron foundry in the CSA.

Confederate lines for her? Of course he could and did. When she reached Fredericksburg, Maryland, she met Allan Pinkerton who recovered her drawings and notes, sending them immediately to the Navy Department.

Mrs. Baker's very precise account of the new weapon and results caused the Federals at Hampton Roads to consider how to defend anchored ships against this new type of menace. What they did was literally invent the submarine or anti-torpedo net. A number of spars projected outward from every ship from which heavy nets or chain was suspended to a depth of around 14 feet or so. In theory any vessel trying to ram the ship with a spar torpedo or diver set torpedoes (explosives) from a semi-submersible would be kept away by the nets. The same concept would be employed through World War II. Considering the tremendous disparity in relative fleet size between the Federal Navy and the Confederate Navy, the North was aware that cheap devices like torpedoes (mines/torpedoes), rams and semi submersibles or even submarines would be used to attrite them.

The Federal nets were timely. On October 9, 1861, a Confederate semi submersible attempted an attack on the *USS Minnesota* off Sewall's Point. It was trapped in the anti-submarine net and barely escaped capture or destruction. In one of those unique incidents to the Civil War, on October 12, a *New York Herald* reporter claimed interviewing a man who came through the Union lines under a white flag telling him details of the attack plan which while different than the attack Mrs. Baker witnessed, contains the essentials: "On arriving at the place desired, a grapple catches the cable of a vessel, and the machine is veered away until it is supposed to be near one of the magazines, the water ballast is pumped out, and the machine floats up under the ship's bottom. By means of an India-rubber sucking-plate this machine is attached to the bottom of the ship, while a man-hole plat is opened and the torpedo screwed into the vessel. It is fired by means of a time fuse."

Mrs. Baker's intelligence was "actionable" in that when she reported the submersibles would be in the James River, the Union Navy started dragging the river mouth with grapples. One of the patrols managed to hook a set of air hoses from float submarine. As the story goes, the Confederates were in the act of attaching the torpedo to a Union craft when the grapples ripped off the hoses drowning the crew trapped below! With the element of surprise gone, the Confederates stopped using the semi-submersibles.

What makes this story so remarkable was the excellent job done by Mrs. Baker, the female Pinkerton agent from Chicago, who so calmly went into the deep South and came back with sufficient information to neutralize perhaps the South's most valuable secret weapons!

Richard Montgomery - Doubled Courier

The most reliable method of transmitting information between Jacob Thompson's Canada operation and Richmond was by courier. But most reliable doesn't imply certain. Many things could and did go wrong. The courier could be intercepted by Union agents while traveling anywhere along his route. He could be "nabbed" crossing through Union lines coming or going. If traveling by sea, shipwreck was possible or drowning coming ashore via small boat. And if the courier was "doubled" working for the Union, the game was lost.

Richard Montgomery (working under the aliases James Thompson and George Peterson) was a doubled courier. Every message he carried to or from Richmond for the Canadian mission went to Washington for copying and decrypting! And just as important for Montgomery, he was never caught or apparently even suspected of playing the most deadly game.

His "handler" in the North appears to have been Charles Dana, the Assistant Secretary of War. According to Dana, Montgomery was not recruited as a double agent, rather he literally walked in the door. As Dana recalled in his *Recollection of the Civil War* during the winter of 1863-64, "...a slender and prepossessing young fellow between 22 and 26" volunteered at the War Department to spy for the Union. Dana remembered him as. "...well dressed and intelligent and professed to be animated by motives purely patriotic." Since Lee's army was not too distant at Gordonsville and the Army of the Potomac nearby at Culpeper Courthouse, to test the young spy, he was given a horse, a pass through the Federal lines and instructions to see what he could find out.

Several weeks later he was back with first hand information of the Lee's army plus most remarkably a letter from Jefferson Davis, he was to deliver to Clement Clay in Canada! Dana and his staff carefully examined the envelope determining the handwriting indeed was Jefferson Davis'. Clearly this young fellow had the remarkable ability to ingratiate himself into the highest circles of Southern society. According to Montgomery all it contained was a letter recommending him to Clay for further service and attesting that he was an ardent Confederate true to the cause. Not wanting to tamper with letter and possibly reveal to Clay it had been opened, Dana took the spy's word for the contents. Since Montgomery's information on Lee's army agreed with what the Union already knew from other sources, Dana decided to allow him to continue to St. Catherines (Clay's current location) and see what developed.

Montgomery was soon back in Dana's office with dispatches from the Canada mission bound for Richmond. Initially this presented a problem since the paper (including the envelopes) was British and the envelopes were sealed with Clay's personal seal embossed in wax. Opening the letters meant breaking the seal and thus revealing to Jefferson the contents were tampered with. It took searching but Dana was able to obtain a supply of similar paper and even had a duplicate made of Clay's seal. This allowed the envelopes to be opened, messages read and copied, resealed and addressing carefully forged.

Montgomery wasn't just a letter carrier ignorant of what the contents and value were of his dispatches. Once he appeared at the War Department stating he had a message of, "extraordinary consequence." It was the outline of the scheme to burn New York City! Mention was also made of a similar scheme for Chicago! As normal, after the message was copied and resealed, Montgomery was sent on his way.

This message presented a problem for the North. If they acted on it openly, warning the civil authorities of the imminent danger, they compromised Montgomery losing the stream of information he was feeding them, not to mention the South would surely execute him as a spy. If they didn't warn New York potentially the loss of life and damage could be horrific. Instead of either course of action, the Secretary of War compromised, sending a confidential officer to warn Major General Dix, Commander of the Department of the East and John A. Kennedy, the Superintendent of Police. Neither man could believe the Confederates would do such a dastardly deed.

Regardless of their personal beliefs both men arranged quietly for extra guards and police. It effect they increased vigilance but not in a fashion to attract attention. Partially as a result the Confederate terror effort failed. And just as important, Montgomery was not suspected as the "leak." The Chicago effort apparently never got to the point of execution.

Sometime after the October 19, 1864 attack on St. Albans, Vermont Montgomery arrived with another critical dispatch. This time a major military expedition from Canada was to be launched against Burlington, Vermont! The dispatch was considered so important instead of being handled in normal fashion, it was, "...placed between two thicknesses of the pair of re-enforced cavalry trousers in which the messenger wore, and sewed up so that when he was mounted it was held between his thigh and the saddle."

Once the dispatch was very carefully removed it was immediately sent to the Secretary of War who was restricted to his home with a heavy cold. He considered it so serious he asked President Lincoln to immediately come over and see it. To both men it was a bombshell since it established beyond a legal doubt that the Confederates were using "neutral" Canada to launch attacks against the Union! It needed to be immediately sent to the Secretary of State to present to the British crown to force them to stop such overt Confederate support and it had to be the original document. A copy would not suffice. But if they kept the original, Montgomery's cover was "blown."

To solve the dilemma the message was sewed up again in the trousers and Montgomery was told to be at a certain tavern just outside Alexandria, Virginia, at 9:00 p.m. and to water his horse there. The tavern was a normal stop on his trips north and south so no suspicion would be aroused. Dana arranged for Major General Christopher Augur, Commander of the Military District of Washington to carefully instruct Colonel Henry Wells, Provost Marshal of the Potomac defenses and stationed at Alexandria, to be at the tavern and arrest "a Confederate dispatch bearer." Wells was given his description and warned not to harm him but to bring him immediately to the War Department under guard. General Augur was also told to be at the War Department when Montgomery arrived. Clearly, neither officer was aware of Montgomery's true role and were deliberately "kept in the dark".

Wells reported the prisoner offered no resistance when arrested but was, "...very violent and outrageous in his language and that he boasted fiercely of his devotion to the Confederacy and detestation of the Union." Once at the War Department he was interrogated and searched. Piece by piece every article of clothing was closely examined. Boots and clothing was sliced open searching for hidden messages. Sometimes dispatches were written on silk, which would not rustle and was nearly impossible to "feel" through layers of cloth. Even buttons were closely examined. It was possible to "compress" a message into the shape of a button and sew it to a shirt or coat. The Northern men were experienced and knew it was necessary to be most thorough. Finally the vital dispatch was found.

All the while Montgomery protested his innocence and love of the South. Dana later related he was "an incomparable actor." Once all the evidence was gathered, Montgomery was sent over to the Old Capitol Prison.

Most important, the dispatch was now in the eyes of the Confederacy just intercepted by bad luck. Montgomery was still a trusted courier. Whatever question Confederate agents may ask of witnesses to the capture, read in the Northern newspapers or leaked from clerks in the Federal government, he clearly did no wrong.

A day or two afterward the warden of the Old Capitol Prison was secretly directed to give the dispatch bearer an opportunity of escaping. Montgomery took it and was gone in a flash. Several days later he met with Dana who asked, "Did they shoot at you," Montgomery replied, "They did and didn't hit me but I didn't think that would answer the purpose. So I shot myself through the arm." Montgomery was careful though to miss the bone. After Montgomery fled, Dana immediately advertised a reward of $2,000 for his capture in papers in New York, Pittsburgh and Chicago. No one ever claimed it.

Montgomery returned to Canada and within two weeks was back in Washington with a new batch of dispatches. It is reasonable to conclude much of the Confederate failure in Canada could be traced to the courage of Richard Montgomery and the skill of Charles Dana as a "handler."

Montgomery was later called to testify in the summer of 1865 at the Lincoln assassination trial relating to messages carried between Toronto and Richmond and his observation of John Wilkes Booth in Canada before the murder. There is no evidence any of the messages he carried directly pertained to heinous crime.

As you expect from a good secret courier, Montgomery was very careful in his movements. During the Lincoln assassination trial he testified, "At any hotel I was stopping I never registered as Thompson (his principal alias) in the book."

Following the war a good position was found for him in the War Department office but he didn't stay long. He soon faded into obscurity just like a good spy should.

References

Thomas Boaz, *England Arms the Confederacy,* (White Mane Publishing: Shippensburg, Pennsylvania, 1996), 62.

Gabor S. Boritt, *War Comes Again, Comparative Vistas on the Civil War and World War II,* (Oxford University Press: New York, 1995) 54.

Conspiracy in Canada, Central Intelligence Agency - https://www.cia.gov/library/publications/additional-publications/civil-war/p37.htm.

Tom Chaffin, *The* H.L. Huntley, *Secret Hope of the Confederacy,* (Hill and Wang: New York, 2008), 61.

Roy Z. Chamlee, Jr., *Lincoln's Assassination, A Complete Account of their Capture, Trial and Punishment,* (Jefferson, North Carolina: McFarland and Company, 1990), 259.

Civil War Women Blog - Lottie and Ginnie Moon - http://www.civilwarwomenblog.com/2006/07/lottie-and-ginnie-moon-confederate.html.

Bernard A. Cook, ed., *Women at War, an Historical Encyclopedia From Antiquity to the Present,* (ABC-CLIO: Santa Barbara, California, 2006), 49.

Charles A. Dana, *Recollections of the Civil War,* (New York: Collier Books, 1963), 209-216.

Larry G. Eggleston, *Women in the Civil War, Extraordinary Stories of Soldiers, Spies, Nurses, Doctors, Crusaders and Others,* (McFarland and Company: Jefferson, North Carolina 2003), 110-111.

Donald E. Markle, *Spies and Spymasters of the Civil War,* (New York: Hippocrene Books, 1988), 171-172, 218-219.

Allan Pinkerton, "The Spy of the Rebellion Being a True History of the Spy System of the United States Army During the Late Rebellion Revealing Many Secrets of the War Hitherto Not Made Public," (G.W. Carlton and Company: New York, 1883), 395-403.

Public Affairs, *Central Intelligence Agency, Intelligence in the Civil War,* (Public Affairs, Central Intelligence Agency: Washington, DC), 43-45.

Donald E. Markle, *Spies and Spymasters of the Civil War,* (New York: Hippocrene Books, 1988), 164-166.

Ginnie and Lottie Moon - http://www.scvcamp469-nbf.com/ginnielottiemoon.htm.

Moon Family Line, Stories and Histories - http://www.suite101.com/external_link.cfm?elink=http://philsgenes.org/Moons/S%20and%20H/SisterAct.html.

Meriwether Stuart, "Of Spies and Borrowed Names: The Identity of Union Operatives in Richmond Known as "The Phillipses" Discovered," *The Virginia Magazine of History and Biography,* Virginia Historical Society, Vol. 89, No. 3 (Jul., 1981), 308-309.

Elizabeth Steger Trindal, *Mary Surratt, An American Tragedy,* (Grendal, Louisiana: Pelican Publishing, 1996), 96-98.

Meriwether Stuart, "Operations Sanders: Wherein Old Friends and Ardent Pro-Southerners Prove to be Union Secret Agents," *The Virginia Magazine of History and Biography,* Vol. 81, No. 2, (April 1973), 157-199.

Submarines in the Civil War - http://www.navyandmarine.org/ondeck/1862submarines.htm.

Footnotes

[1]Civil War Women Blog - Lottie and Ginnie Moon - http://www.civilwarwomenblog.com/2006/07/lottie-and-ginnie-moon-confederate.html.

[2] Thomas Boaz, *England Arms the Confederacy*, (White Mane Publishing: Shippensburg, Pennsylvania, 1996), 62.

[3] Born in Scotland, Pinkerton immigrated to the U.S in 1844 and later joining the Chicago Police Department. He founded the Pinkerton National Detective Agency in 1850. His detectives specialized in tracking down train robbers, a task that brought him into contact with George McClellan president of the Illinois Central Railroad and its attorney Abraham Lincoln.

CHAPTER TEN
THE LADY ELGIN, A PRECURSOR OF WAR

The *Lady Elgin* is mostly remembered as a horrific shipwreck. When she sank off Winnetka, Illinois, on Lake Michigan on September 8, 1860, roughly 350 people lost their lives making her the second deadliest shipwreck on the Great Lakes to the *Eastland* rolling in the Chicago River in 1915 taking 845 or so with her. But the *Lady Elgin* is really a Civil War story, too, her ultimate loss linked tightly with the building storm that would soon burst across the nation.

The 252-foot long *Lady Elgin* was a double-decked wooden sidewheel steamer built in Buffalo in 1851 by Bidwell, Banta and Company at a cost of $96,000. She was named for the wife of Lord Elgin, the Governor General of Canada's. He held the post from 1847-1854. Reputedly her engines were taken from the steamer *Cleopatra*, a slaver captured by the U.S. Navy. Some folks claimed using such "tainted" engines cursed the new ship but fact or fiction, it is a good tale. She had a capacity of 200 cabin

The Lady Elgin *was an elegant and popular steamboat.*

passengers, 100 deck passengers, 45 crew and 800 tons of freight. Initially owned by Aaron D. Patchin and Gillman D. Appleby of Buffalo, she was used to carry passengers and freight along the northern shores of the lakes but when the ports were soon linked by rail, she quickly became redundant and was shifted to general work including excursions. She was purchased in 1855 by Chicago's Lake Superior Line. Her final owner was Gordon S. Hubbard & Company of Chicago.

The interior appointments in the *Lady Elgin* were excellent and as an added bonus she was fast too! Some travelers also thought her beautiful with her tall black stacks and graceful wooden arches adding a certain charm. She was a perfect boat for excursion trips on Lake Michigan.

Her last cruise left Milwaukee in the early morning of Friday September 7. Aboard were 400-500 passengers including members of several Milwaukee private militia companies including members of the Union Guards, Black Watch Jagers, Green Jagers and Milwaukee Light Guards. Various city organizations including the city band, fire and police department delegations, city officials and assorted friends and supporters also joined the military men. The *Lady Elgin* was supposed to depart Milwaukee at 7:00 p.m. but didn't arrive at her dock until well after 10:00 p.m. The long delay caused many of the folks waiting eagerly to just say, "Forget it." "I'm going home." It was a decision that likely saved their lives!

Why the steamer came to have such an unusual passenger list is fascinating and well illustrates the tensions leading up to the Civil War.

Milwaukee was a seething cauldron of politics in many ways mirroring the national concerns of slavery and states rights. Abolitionist fever ran so high there were rumors the state would secede from the United States if the Federal government didn't outlaw slavery. Governor Alexander Randall was a rabid abolitionist and fed the increasing anxiety. Things went so far that in March a member of the Wisconsin legislature introduced a bill directing the governor to declare war on the United States unless its demands for abolishing slavery were met. Supporters of secession sent agents to Milwaukee

Governor Randall's treasonous plans were no honor for Wisconsin.

to see whether the city's militia companies would support such a radical move. Since the militia was the governor's "army," their support was vital.

Anti-slavery feeling clearly ran high in Wisconsin, especially as epitomized by the Federal Fugitive Slave Act requiring government assistance to recover "runaways." In effect the Act turned every government official into a slave catcher! Wisconsin wasn't alone in its hostility to the law. Many citizens in other northern states felt the same and like Wisconsin, sometimes took strong action.

The issue came to a boiling point in Milwaukee on March 10, 1854 when a Missouri slave owner arrived in Racine demanding one Joshua Glover, an escaped slave, be apprehended and given to him under the Federal law. Local authorities complied but when the local citizens found out about the slave catcher in their midst and what he wanted, tempers boiled. Afraid to keep Glover in the local jail, authorities clandestinely took him to Milwaukee where the jail was stronger.

Folks in Milwaukee were no less angry than their Racine brethren. When the police refused to release Glover, they stormed the jail and broke him out, hustling him away to safety in Canada via the Underground Railroad. Police eventually arrested one of the instigators and prosecuted him but when the case reached the State Supreme court

Milwaukee's Irish Union Guards stood loyal to the Union.

the justices ruled the Federal Fugitive Slave Act unconstitutional in Wisconsin so he was released.

Given the uproar in the state about the Fugitive Slave Act, abolition in general and Randall's treasonous plans, the governor wanted to know what militia companies would support a secessionist movement. Thus the question was put to the state's militia companies.

The Union Guards, primarily from the Irish Third Ward and reputedly considered the best of the city's four companies, refused to join the movement. Originally named the Irish City Guard, it is claimed they changed their name in response to many Germans and Poles joining.

While against slavery, the Union Guards saw it as a proper issue for the national government, not Wisconsin to deal with. They would not commit treason against the Federal government. Governor Randall promptly removed the commander, one Captain Garrett Barry, and directed all state issued arms and equipment be turned over to the Milwaukee Light Guard, a city company willing to support the secessionist movement or at least tell Randall what he wanted to hear! There is some confusion whether he actually disbanded the company or not but without arms it was a toothless tiger and could be ignored. The fact all the militia units, including the German Black Jagers and Green Jagers and Light Guards were on the steamer clearly shows the general unity among them regardless of the governor's plans.

The Union Guards was organized in 1848 as the Milwaukee City Guards under Captain J. McManman. Primarily made up of young Irishmen, the company suffered from a lack of discipline and was reorganized in 1854 under Captain John Jennings as the Milwaukee Union Sarsfield Guards. Jennings was no more successful than McManman in building a disciplined unit and it reorganized a third time in 1856 as the Union Guards. It still suffered from a lack of discipline and two years later Barry took over command and went to work. He selected 50 men out of the old company and recruited another 20 to bring it up to 70 men strong. It didn't take him long to bring the unit to a high state of discipline and efficiency. Barry knew the business of soldiering and passed the hard lessons on to his men, some the "hard" way. Doubtless it was necessary to take a man behind the armory once in a while to "council" him a bit, the miscreant perhaps emerging with a bloody nose and black eye! This was the "Old Army" way to "knock" sense into a difficult recruit. There was a proper time for drinking and carousing and a proper time for soldiering and Barry made certain his men understood the difference! It wasn't long before he drilled them to precision in the manual of arms, cadence, route step, alignment, various marching and parade formations and maneuvers. The company soon gained the reputation of being the "best in the Northwest" and made sojourns to Buffalo, Detroit and Chicago to demonstrate their skill. Often called "Barry's Guards," membership was critical for any young Irishmen wanting to advance in politics or love. Women were always impressed with the sharply turned out guardsmen.

Garrett Barry was especially well suited to command the Union Guards and certainly no push over for Randall. After graduating from the U.S. Military Academy in

Captain Barry was an experience West Point officer.

1839, he served in the Florida War against the Seminole Indians; did a stint of garrison duty at Ft. McHenry; taught tactics at West Point instructing such soon to be famous officers as Generals Sherman, Grant, McDowell and Thomas. He continued his career with duty on the frontier at Fort Snelling, Minnesota; more garrison duty at Fort Crawford, Wisconsin, and Jefferson Barracks, Missouri, and fought in the Mexican-American War seeing combat during the bloody Battle of Monterrey. He resigned from the Army on March 31, 1847 to seek his own fortune. He was engaged as a merchant in Milwaukee until 1851 and superintended the construction of the Customs House from 1857-1860. In 1859 he was elected treasurer of Milwaukee County. He took command of the Union Guards in 1858.

The Union Guards were hopping mad! They felt the governor could take their equipment back but not disband the unit since they were after all, private. They would just buy their own equipment and would raise the money with a lake excursion to Chicago on the popular *Lady Elgin*. The members of the other militia companies as well as city organizations and private individuals were folks who supported the Union Guards and were happy to join them.

The steamer arrived in Chicago on Friday morning, mooring at her normal position between Clark and LaSalle Streets. The Union Guards paraded and later everyone went sightseeing in Chicago and had a rousing good time. In the evening, the holiday makers gathered for a banquet followed by appropriate speechmaking and dancing. By 11:30 p.m. the party was back aboard the steamer and continued as the steamer pushed north for Milwaukee through freshening northeast wind and waves. The exact passenger count is impossible to determine today but period newspapers estimated as many as 600 folks could have been aboard since additional passengers joined in Chicago.

The trip went well until about 2:00 a.m. when the steamer was buffeted by a powerful squall. The stormy weather made little difference to the boisterous passengers who continued to dance, laugh and imbibe. The *Lady Elgin* continued north for Milwaukee pushing her way through stormy seas.

The Lady Elgin *in Chicago.*

The schooner Augusta *rammed the* Lady Elgin.

About seven miles off Winnetka she was struck by the two-masted schooner *Augusta* bound from Port Huron to Chicago with a cargo of lumber. Considering the black night and blowing gale, the damage done to the steamer was initially difficult to determine but the *Lady Elgin* was mortally wounded. Once the schooner broke free the bigger vessel rolled slowly hard over to port then back to a level keel.

Water flooded into her at an unholy rate. The crew tried to plug the hole with mattresses, but to no avail! In a last desperate maneuver the captain headed the dying ship to shore. Maybe, just maybe, he could find bottom close enough to the beach for his passengers and crew to struggle to safety. It wasn't to be. The surging water flooded the boiler fires and she slowly lost headway.

Hammered by the gale and sinking ever deeper into the cold and heartless lake, the *Lady Elgin* died along with perhaps 350 of her passengers, many of them members of not only the Union Guards but other Milwaukee militia units angered by Randall's treasonous plans. Garrett Barry did not survive the wreck but is credited with heroically perishing while saving others. Of course in comparison to the bloodshed soon to engulf the nation, it was virtually nothing, but still part of the Civil War story on the lakes. See my book, *Wood on the Bottom* for the full story of the tragedy.

After the fatal blow, the Lady Elgin *sinking beneath the waves.*

References:

Association for Great Lakes Maritime History *Newsletter*, February 1989; May 1993.

Dana Thomas Bowen, *Shipwrecks of the Lakes,* (Cleveland; Freshwater Press, 1952), 38-46.

Dwight Boyer, *True Tales of the Great Lakes,* (Dodd, Mead and Company, New York, 1971), 177-208.

William George Bruce, editor, *History of Milwaukee City and County*, (Chicago: The S.J. Clarke Publishing Company, 1922), 198-199.

C. Patrick Labadie, "Letters" *Inland Seas*, Spring 1991.

Chicago Daily Press Tribune, September-October 1860.

Chips, November 13, 1889; January 21, October 14, 1991; December 7, 1992 September 20, 1993; October 4, 1993, April 1, June 24, 1996.

David J. Cooper, "Letters" *Inland Seas*, Winter 1991.

Institute for Great Lakes Research, Bowling Green State University

Mansfield, J.B., *History of the Great Lakes*, (Chicago, 1899), 689.

Charles M. Scanlan, *The* Lady Elgin *Disaster* (Milwaukee, 1928).

Detroit Free Press, September 12, 1860; August 29, 1878.

Milwaukee Public Museum, The *Lady Elgin* - http://www.mpm.edu/education/ladyelgin/explore/.

Milwaukee Sentinel, September 2, 1854; October 30, 1857 November 17, 27, 1858; August-October, December 13, 22, 1860.

New York Times, March 13, 1854.

Nor'Easter, Journal of the Lake Superior Marine Museum, September-October 1990; September-October 1991; July-August 1996.

Odd Wisconsin: Abolitionists stormed Milwaukee jail to free escaped slave - http://host.madison.com/wsj/news/local/article_edcc101e-aa36-11df-980c-001cc4c002e0.html.

A Rising Wind - http://damnedtheatre.com/projects/a-rising-wind/.

Runge Collection, Wisconsin Marine Historical Society.

Wisconsin Daily Patriot, March 10, September 10, 11, 13, 1860.

Wisconsin State Journal, September 8, 10, 11, 17, 1860.

Wreck of *Lady Elgin* - http://www.ship-wrecks.net/shipwreck/projects/elgin/.

Dr. John L. Mahar, "One Hundredth Anniversary of the *Lady Elgin*," *Inland Seas*, Spring 1960, 4-13.

June Skinner, Chicago Sketches, (Chicago: Loyola University Press 1995), 169-170.

Superiorland, October 15, 1994.

Thompson, Thos. S., *Thompson's Coast Pilot: for the Upper Lakes, on both shores from Chicago to Buffalo, Green Bay, Georgian Bay, and Lake Superior; Including the Rivers Detroit, St. Clair and Ste. Marie, with the Courses and Distances on Lake Ontario, and other information relative thereto*, (Detroit: Thos. S. Thompson, 5th ed., 1869), 119-121.

Footnotes:

[1]Parts of this story are taken from my book *Wood on the Bottom*, Avery Color Studios, 2008

"For all sad words of tongue and pen, The saddest are these, 'It might have been'."[1]

CONCLUSION

These simple words sum up the entire Confederate Great Lakes experience. Had they,

> planned better,
> recognized their opportunities earlier,
> committed resources sooner,
> put more qualified men in charge,
> practiced "operational security",
> and been luckier,

They could have achieved successes perhaps powerful enough to alter the course of the war. Instead they failed as did the "Cause."

I have tried to pull the many threads of the Confederate operations on and around the Great Lakes together and relate them to both the general political climate and impacting military operations. It is like unraveling spaghetti. Everything is connected and influenced by activities elsewhere. And just as the pasta is often hidden by the sauce, making those connections isn't always easy. It is at best confusing.

I encourage the reader to dig into the history of the Civil War not just as it affected the Great Lakes but across the length and breath of the country and the rest of the world. It is a fascinating topic with lessons that still resonate today.

[1]John Greenleaf Whittier, American writer, 1807-1892.

ABOUT THE AUTHOR

Frederick Stonehouse holds a Master of Arts Degree in History from Northern Michigan University, Marquette, Michigan, and has authored many books on Great Lakes maritime history. He is the 2006 recipient of the Association for Great Lakes Maritime History Award for Historic Interpretation and received the 2007 Marine Historical Society of Detroit Historian of the Year Award. *The Wreck Of The Edmund Fitzgerald; Steel On The Bottom, Great Lakes Shipwrecks; Wood On The Bottom, Great Lakes Shipwrecks; Great Lakes Crime, Murder, Mayhem, Booze And Broads; Great Lakes Crime II, More Murder, Mayhem, Booze And Broads; Great Lakes Lighthouse Tales; Women And The Lakes, Untold Great Lakes Maritime Tales; Women And The Lakes II, More Untold Great Lakes Maritime Tales; Lake Superior's Shipwreck Coast; Went Missing Redux, Unsolved Great Lakes Shipwrecks; Final Passage, True Shipwreck Adventures; My Summer At The Lighthouse, A Boy's Journal* and *Cooking Lighthouse Style, Favorite Recipes From Coast To Coast* are all published by Avery Color Studios, Inc.

He has also been a consultant for both the U.S. National Park Service and Parks Canada, and an "on air" expert for National Geographic and the History Channel as well as many regional media productions. He has taught Great Lakes

Maritime History at Northern Michigan University and is an active consultant for numerous Great Lakes oriented projects and programs. Check www.frederickstonehouse.com for more details.

His articles have been published in numerous publications including *Skin Diver, Wreck and Rescue Journal* and *Lake Superior Magazine*. He is a member of the Board of Directors of the Marquette Maritime Museum and a member of the Board of Directors of the United States Life Saving Service Heritage Association.

Stonehouse resides in Marquette, Michigan.